Protecting Abused and Neglected Children

Protecting Abused and Neglected Children

MICHAEL S. WALD,

J. M. CARLSMITH & P. H. LEIDERMAN

with Carole Smith & Rita deSales French

Stanford University Press
Stanford, California

48655

Stanford University Press
Stanford, California
© 1988 by the Board of Trustees of the
Leland Stanford Junior University
Printed in the United States of America

CIP data appear at the end of the book

To Evelyn, Fannie,
Johnetta, Kay,
and Ruth

Preface

——————

In 1975 THE BOYS' TOWN FOUNDATION of Omaha, Nebraska, gave Stanford University funds to establish a Boys' Town Center at Stanford, to conduct policy-oriented studies related to the problems of children and youth. One of the first activities of the center was the creation of a study group whose goal was to explore ways to assess the impact of various types of interventions being used by courts and child welfare agencies in their efforts to help abused and neglected children. The group was led by Michael S. Wald, a professor in the Stanford Law School. He was joined by J. Merrill Carlsmith, a psychology professor, and P. Herbert Leiderman, a professor of psychiatry. These three began meeting with a group of social workers and probation officers from a number of San Francisco Bay Area counties, in order to develop a research project that would be useful to agency personnel responsible for intervention decisions.

Shortly after the group began meeting, the state of California embarked on an experimental program in two California counties, providing special funds to county social service agencies to help abused and neglected children without moving them away from their own homes. One of the counties selected, San Mateo, adjoins Stanford University. The study group decided to focus their research on the impact of the experimental program by comparing the effects of removing abused and neglected children from their homes with the effects of maintaining them there. The legislation establishing this program was drafted by Michael Wald, along with Robert Mnookin, professor of law at Stanford. The research was designed to test whether the assumptions underlying the legislation (see Wald 1976) were valid.

Using funds provided by the Boys' Town Center at Stanford (now

the Center for the Study of Youth Development), a study was designed and a pilot study conducted in 1976–77. Carole Smith became
the study director and remained in charge until 1983. The study proper,
reported here, began in January 1978. It was funded by the National
Center on Child Abuse and Neglect in the United States Department
of Health and Human Services, by the Family and Children's Services
Branch of the California Department of Social Services, and by the
Center for the Study of Youth Development, at Stanford. Data collec-
tion ended in August 1982. Data analysis and the write-up of results
began in 1982—undertakings that were marred by the untimely death
of J. Merrill Carlsmith in 1984 after a protracted illness. Rita deSales
French joined this project in 1981 and played a major role in data
analysis.

From the inception of the project, the goal of the research was to
provide policy-relevant data to professionals in the child welfare system. As we conducted the research and began writing up the results, it
became clear that we had learned at least as much about issues relating
to conducting policy-oriented research and general child development
as we had about the impact of particular interventions. Thus, this
book is addressed to several audiences; in addition to public policy
makers, we believe the findings will be of interest to professionals
working with children, people interested in child development in general, and people who conduct and fund policy-oriented research.

In addition to the collaboration by the principal authors, this project has been a joint effort of many others without whom it could not
have been completed. A number of people spent many years working
on the study, and we are extraordinarily grateful to them. Most important, the final product reflects the outstanding work of Fannie Haugh-
ton, Johnetta Moore, Ruth Sabori, Evelyn Schreck, and Kay Wilson,
field researchers. For several years their lives were closely linked with
those of the study's families. Interviews often had to be conducted
in the evening or on weekends, in parking lots, bars, and psychiatric
facilities, as well as homes. Perhaps their most difficult task was to provide objective data as researchers while remaining caring individuals
who saw the families as more than just subjects of academic scrutiny.
They performed this difficult task extraordinarily well. Kay Wilson
also helped set up our data management system, and Evelyn Schreck
helped with every aspect of the project. Philip Ritter and Barbara
Aschenbrenner also participated in the research for several years. Their

work in managing the data, calculating the statistics, and helping with the interpretation of results was outstanding.

Our colleagues at the Center for the Study of Youth Development were also members of our research team. From the inception of the project they provided valuable advice, both at regular meetings of the center and in many hours of informal discussion. We particularly thank J. Lee Cronbach, Sanford M. Dornbusch, Eleanor E. Maccoby, John Meyer, and Lincoln Moses, who were our always available advisers for many years. They endured the task of reading and critiquing several drafts of the manuscript and share with us the pleasure of this final version of the project. Robert Sears and Albert Hastorf, directors of the center, provided much-needed encouragement at critical points early in the project's life.

Many other people were members of the research family for shorter periods. At the inception of the project, Grace Massey served as research associate, helping to create the research design and the research instruments. Joan Bazar and Gerald Davenport spent many hours administering psychological tests to the children in a specially equipped van, which they took to the children's homes. Their dedication, like that of the other field researchers, was critical to our obtaining complete and accurate data. Sabrina Lin, Lisa McPherson, and Laurey Selz, all research assistants, contributed to many aspects of the study. Charlayne Mattingly, Gail Garrett, and Elaine Katsaris were project secretaries for extended periods. Beyond her secretarial duties, Garrett helped with the enormous task of coding the data. Christine Hutchinson, Tom Prussing, and Geneva Haertel also conscientiously assisted in the coding of subjects' responses to the questionnaires. All these people's lives were made easier by Patricia Shallenberger, administrative assistant at the Center for the Study of Youth Development.

A number of colleagues, at Stanford and other institutions, carefully read and commented on earlier drafts of the manuscript. We are grateful to David Chambers, Robert Emde, Shirley Feldman, Robert McCall, Robert Mnookin, Arnold Sameroff, Alan Sroufe, Cecilia Sudia, and Elsa Ten Broeck for their time and insights. We also received helpful comments from the staffs of the participating counties and the California Department of Social Services. We are exceptionally grateful to Elizabeth Ann Scroggs, who cheerfully processed and reprocessed the words of innumerable drafts of this book. Michael J. Fraleigh provided invaluable assistance in producing the final manuscript.

The project would not have been possible without the enthusiastic cooperation of the child welfare staffs in Alameda, San Mateo, and Santa Clara counties. Throughout the research, workers in these three participating counties gave their time generously and facilitated our contact with the families.

The study received financial support from a number of sources. Primary funding came from the Stanford Center for the Study of Youth Development, which was supported by Father Flanagan's Boys' Home of Omaha, Nebraska. The staff of Boys' Town was especially supportive and helpful throughout the project. We also received grants from the National Center on Abuse and Neglect in the United States Department of Health and Human Services, the California State Department of Social Services, the Edna McConnell Clark Foundation, the Walter S. Johnson Foundation, and the William and Flora Hewlett Foundation. Norman Stone of San Francisco provided gift funds to P. Herbert Leiderman; support to Michael S. Wald from the Stanford Legal Research Fund was made possible by a bequest from Ira S. Lillick and by gifts from other friends of the Stanford Law School. We want also to express appreciation to Stanford University, which in myriad ways provided the environment and opportunity for multi-disciplinary public policy research.

Finally, we express our deep appreciation to the children and families who so willingly gave of their time and feelings at what must have been a very painful period in their lives. Though they knew we could not directly help them, they were sufficiently courageous to gamble with us on the possibility that more knowledge would ultimately help them and perhaps others in similar circumstances. The sadness of their situations will remain with us forever. We can only hope that our efforts to help will bear fruit, and that this study will provide ideas and information that will enable those who care about helping abused and neglected children and their families to improve their performance of this critical task.

M.S.W.
P.H.L.

Contents

───────

Tables

Foreword

─────────

WHENEVER I am asked to speak on the topic of research and its implications for child development policy, I recite the following story as an introduction.

On his way home from a party one Saturday night, George encounters his friend Bob on his hands and knees on the sidewalk, groping around on the ground at the base of a streetlight. Naturally, George stops to ask Bob what he is doing. "I lost my car keys," Bob replies, "and I am looking for them so that I can go home." "Let me help you," offers George, and he too proceeds to search on hands and knees. After a few minutes George gives up, saying, "Well, Bob, I don't think we're going to find them. Now where exactly did you drop them?" To George's great surprise, Bob responds, "Oh I dropped them over there" (pointing to a spot halfway across the darkened street). George is naturally shocked. "If you dropped them over there, why are you looking over here?" Bob responds, "The light is better over here."

I think of this story whenever the topic of research and policy comes up because the research needs doing "over there" in the dark. So many of the most important issues of policy that need researching are so very difficult to study in the times and places and with the people most relevant to those policy issues. The topics easy to research tend to be divorced from the perplexing and frustrating realities of the social environment that policy must address. The light is better over here, even though the keys are over there. Years ago Urie Bronfenbrenner criticized child development research on the grounds that it had so few answers to the policy questions people in positions of institutional authority were really asking, and instead had a plethora of answers to unasked policy questions. Michael Wald provided a powerful case study of this when he wrote his "lawyer's plea" for help in resolving a host of child development issues faced in courtrooms, as lawyers dealt with children and families (*Child Development*, 1976, *47*, 1–5). He's still asking, and this book reflects that arduous and often painful process.

Some years ago, Bronfenbrenner and I collaborated on an article entitled "Research on parent-child relations and public policy: Who needs whom?" Our point, and it is one that I think would find a home in this book, is that research needs policy to define the specific questions that need answering, just as much as policy needs the fruits of empirical research on children and families. Policy forces us to look for answers over there, in the dark.

This book reports the saga of Michael Wald and his colleagues as they sought an answer for a burning policy issue: Do abused and neglected children fare better when placed in foster care or when kept in the home? Many of us have a preconceived answer to this question. Some cite research critical of "foster care drift," the incidence of maltreatment among foster parents, and the primacy of the attachment relationship in child development. Conclusion: Home-based services are best. Others cite data on the chronicity of maltreatment and the recurrence of abuse by parents while in treatment, the reports of adult survivors of abuse who speak to the need for alternative, safe relationships, and the data on the developmentally destructive effects of chronic child maltreatment. Conclusion: Prompt placement in foster care.

Who's right? An ecological perspective on development (cf. Urie Bronfenbrenner's *The Ecology of Human Development* or my own *Children and Families in the Social Environment*) tells us to be skeptical whenever a question is put to us as "Does X cause Y"? The answer is usually neither "yes" nor "no." The best answer is "It depends." It depends upon the context in which "X" is operating. It depends upon the operational definition of "Y." What kind of foster care? What is the quality of the parent-child relationship in the abusive home? What kind of support and monitoring is available in home-based services? How well are the children functioning at the time of placement? Is foster care better than remaining at home? It depends. Wald and his colleagues have given us a good case study of the frustrations, the demands, the complexities, the vagaries, and the challenges of doing policy-relevant research, of getting down on your hands and knees and groping around in the dark looking for the keys we need if research is to do what research should do, namely, raise the quality of public debate. I applaud them.

James Garbarino
Erikson Institute

Protecting Abused and Neglected Children

One

Framing the Issues

———

John, five years old, came to the attention of child protective services along with his younger sisters, Sandi and Laura, when a next-door neighbor reported hearing a child screaming. When the police responded they found that John had bruises on his back and legs; there were large welts on Sandi's and Laura's bodies. Their mother said that the children had been disciplined by her boyfriend, whom she was no longer seeing. On several previous occasions the family had been referred to social service agencies because the children were found unattended, filthy, and malnourished.

Mrs. P. went to pick up her seven-year-old son, Sean, at school. He misbehaved, and she kicked him, hit his head, shoulders, and back, and tried to choke him. The school notified child protective services. Sean's mother told the protective services worker that Sean had emotional problems and a learning disability, and that he was defiant of her. She indicated that she frequently used physical discipline to control his behavior.

Liz, a seven-year-old, lived with her father and mother and two dogs in a van. The vehicle had been their home for six months. Liz was found locked inside the van while it was parked in a shopping center lot; she used a pan containing sand for a toilet. Her mother had a history of mental illness, her father a severe alcohol problem. Liz was not going to school. When the police found Liz, they took her to a county children's home.

Chris, eight years old, his mother, and his two younger siblings were evicted from the motel where they had been living because the mother had spent her AFDC grant on alcohol and could not pay the rent. She had a history of providing inadequate food and physical care for the children. When Chris described his situation to his teacher, she called the county protective services.

JOHN, SEAN, LIZ, AND CHRIS were considered to be abused or neglected by the agencies that responded to their plight. Identifying

such children is only the first step in preventing future abuse or neglect. After it is determined that a child has been mistreated, a social
service agency or court, in order to protect the child from future abuse
or neglect, must adopt one of two basic intervention strategies: the
child can be left in its home while attempts are made to change the
parents' behavior, or the child can be removed from the home and
placed with relatives or other nonrelated foster parents, or in a residential center that provides group care. Placement can be temporary, in
the hope that the child can later be reunited with the parents, or the
agency can request permanent termination of the parents' custodial
rights so that the child can be raised in another family.

Which of these options should be preferred for John, Liz, Sean,
Chris, and others like them? Until the mid-1970s, foster care placement
was seen as the surest way of preventing reabuse or continued neglect.[1]
However, during the 1970's foster care came under substantial criticism.
A number of national commissions advocated that removal be used only
as a last resort (American Bar Association 1977; National Commission
on Children in Need of Parents 1979). The efforts of these critics ultimately led the United States Congress to enact Public Law 96-272, the
Adoption Assistance and Child Welfare Act of 1980. That law established, as a matter of national policy, a preference for keeping children
with their parents whenever possible. Even before passage of the federal
law many states had adopted policies designed to reduce reliance on
foster care. Programs were established to provide special services to
parents, such as homemakers, crisis counseling, respite care for children, and training in parental skills. In part because of these policies, the
number of children in foster care declined from a high of 500,000 in 1977
to 273,000 in 1982 (American Humane Association 1984).

Is this reversal of policy wise? Obviously, children like the four pro-
filed earlier are not being cared for adequately, and to justify leaving
them at home it is necessary to assume that at home their lives can be
improved, or that foster care will not better their situation.[2] Evaluating
the wisdom of the alternative policies requires comparing information
about what happens to abused and neglected children following foster
placement with that for similar children left at home. Surprisingly,
there are very few data. The substantial changes in public policy that
took place in the 1970's were based more on ideological and fiscal considerations than on evidence about the impact of various types of interventions on the development of abused and neglected children
(Aber 1980). A strong belief in our society that biological parents

should not lose custody of their children unless absolutely necessary, the expense of foster care, and claims that foster care harms children by separating them from parents to whom they are psychologically attached or through unstable placements led policymakers to adopt a preference for keeping children with their parents.

This book presents the results of a research project that was designed to provide data for use by policymakers concerned with protecting abused and neglected children. The research compared the development, over a two-year period, of two groups of abused and neglected children. The children in one group were left in their own homes; the other children were placed in foster care. From their experiences we hoped to gain insights that would help decision-makers— legislators drafting new laws and judges or social workers deciding individual cases—make better decisions in the future about appropriate intervention.

The Study Design

The study grew out of one author's work in developing legal standards for protecting abused and neglected children (Wald 1976). He found that the paucity of evidence regarding the impact of different intervention strategies meant legislators, judges, and social workers had to adopt policies, or decide cases, largely on intuition. What was needed, therefore, was a study that would provide the necessary information.

As the coauthors were working on a study design, the California legislature adopted the California Family Protection Act, SB30 1977 (California State Legislature 1977). This legislation created an experimental project in two California counties, one purpose of which was to maintain abused and neglected children in their own homes by providing services to their families. One of these counties was San Mateo, located just south of San Francisco and north of Stanford University, our institution.[3]

Specifically, the legislation changed the legal grounds for placing children in foster care in the two experimental counties. It permitted removal in only the most serious cases of physical abuse or neglect or when the child evidenced severe emotional problems that the parents were unwilling to have treated. The standard for removal was left unchanged in the remaining California counties. In these counties, the law permitted foster care placement of abused or neglected children whenever the home environment was "detrimental" to the child, even if the child had not suffered serious physical abuse or evidenced severe emotional damage. The legislature also provided the experimental counties with a substantial amount of money to be used for services to the families of the children left at home. The services were designed to minimize the need for removal and to protect children left in their homes.

By comparing the development (physical, academic, social, emotional) of abused and neglected children remaining at home in San Mateo with those placed in foster care in the neighboring counties, we were able to explore the consequences of alternative intervention strategies. We evaluated sixty-five children, all of ages five to ten, for a two-year period following their identification as abused or neglected. Thirty-six of the children were at home; twenty-nine were in foster care. We came to know each of the children and their caretakers quite well. We saw the adults at least every three months, and the children at least every six months. We visited the children's schools, observed them at play, and talked with their teachers. We have extensive data on each child's initial physical, academic, social, and emotional condition, and on changes in each of these domains over the two-year period. In addition, we compared the development of all the abused or neglected children, both at home and in foster care, with a group of eighty-one children of the same age who were not abused or neglected.

The four children whose cases were cited at the beginning of the chapter were subjects in our study. Sean and Chris lived in San Mateo county and remained at home with their parents; John and Liz lived in adjacent counties and were placed in foster care.

Defining the Goals

The design of the research, our mode of analysis, and our presentation were dictated by our conception of the policy issues. Policy regarding the use of foster care is made at two levels. The first is legislative. Each state has laws establishing the *substantive* standards upon which removal is authorized. These laws provide guidelines that, in effect, reflect a legislative preference for home or foster placement (Wald 1976). For example, in some states the laws permit removal whenever it is "in the child's best interest," whereas in other states removal is allowed only if leaving the child at home would be "seriously detrimental" to the child; a legislature might go further and either require or forbid removal in specified situations.

A legislature also can adopt *procedural* rules that will affect the number of removals. In the legal system, decision makers never approach a decision neutrally. Rather, the law establishes burdens of proof that dictate which of the opposing advocates has to provide the more persuasive case. For example, legislatures can make removal more difficult by requiring that the social service agency prove the need for removal rather than by making the parents prove that removal should not occur. In addition, a legislature might specify the level of proof—"preponderance of the evidence," "clear and convincing evidence," "beyond a reasonable doubt"—by which a proponent must prove a case. The greater the burden of proof, the less likely it is that the party bearing the burden will prevail. Finally, a legislature can create presumptions favoring one option or the other. A presumption is often determinative where there is otherwise little evidence to guide decision makers.

Although legislatures establish the general rules regulating legal intervention, the actual decision to place a given child in foster care or to leave the child at home is made by a social service agency or court. A social worker or judge must determine, in light of the facts in a specific situation, whether removal is *permissible* under state law and *desirable* in terms of protecting the well-being of the child. Unlike the legislature, which adopts general rules designed to promote the interests of the majority of children, courts and social workers must make individualized decisions based on clinical assessments of individual cases.

Thus, to aid legislative decisions, research findings must at least indicate whether, *on average*, abused or neglected children do better in one setting or the other. A legislature can then adopt rules favoring the alternative that is better for *most* children. Even more helpful would be findings that showed the impact of alternative placements on certain categories of children—for example, abused versus neglected, older versus younger, children from single-parent versus two-parent homes. Using such findings, presumptions could be created favoring different options for different *groups* of children (or parents).

Decision-making is more difficult at the court and agency level. In each case a judge or social worker must determine, for the specific child, the costs and benefits of each option. Theoretically, the decision maker takes into account the full variety of factors—such as the extent of the harm the child has suffered, the attitude of the parents and their child, the availability of resources—that can help in predicting the likely impact of alternative decisions. In some instances the correct alternative may seem obvious; in others it may be extremely elusive. Although it is useful for judges or social workers to know what happens to an average child, they also need information relevant to the particular combinations of characteristics of parents and children to determine the likely impact of home or foster care on specific children.

In developing our study, because we hoped to obtain data that would be useful both to legislators and to judges or social workers, we looked for differences between our home and foster groups and also for factors that accounted for an outcome in individual cases. However, we present mostly group data. That is, we look at how the children at home and in foster care, *on average*, developed during the two years. Such group data are critical at the legislative level but are less helpful to judicial or agency decision makers.[4] Although we searched for factors that would explain why the situations of individual children became better or worse, we found few factors that predicted the outcome for individual children, either because of small sample size or because such factors did not in fact exist in our study population.

There are many ways we could present our data. It is tempting to try to tell many stories. We could have tried to identify the factors that accounted for the great variation in the well-being of the children when we first saw them, despite the fact that they had a common history of abuse and neglect, or to determine which factors most influenced the development of each child in the abused, neglected, and comparison groups over the two-year period. We have chosen to limit our presentation. We focus on describing the data most helpful to policymakers who must decide whether to prefer home or foster care as the means of protecting abused and neglected children. Analyzing that issue is complex enough, and we have kept to it. We do, however, present a substantial amount of statistical and clinical information about the children and their families, which provides some new insights about the general development of abused and neglected children.

The research also afforded us an opportunity to explore issues of importance to child development theorists. Like Zigler (1980), we believe that good research about child abuse must draw its methods and theories from the general body of child development research. Therefore, we have tried to address policy-relevant questions while being attentive to the theories and methods of basic child development research. As we discuss in Chapter 2, a major concern with the use of foster care is that separation from a parent with whom the child has an adequate "attachment" relationship may be very harmful to the child. Some theorists have asserted "better a bad home than a good foster home" (Bowlby 1965, p. 85). In contrast, proponents of foster care see foster homes not only as safer, but also as a better environment for socializing children. The relative importance of attachment versus other aspects of socialization is a central question in research in the development of all children. There is also a substantial debate about whether later experiences can overcome developmental problems resulting from poor parental care during very early childhood. We believe that our findings with regard to the foster children help illuminate these general issues.

We had one other major goal in conducting our research. We began with a strong belief that policymakers need interdisciplinary research to aid them in developing laws or public programs (Wald et al. 1983). However, we were aware of the substantial difficulties in conducting such research (Hobbs 1980; Cronbach 1982). Throughout this book, we discuss the ways in which we tried to ensure that our findings would be both valid and useful to policymakers. Yet we must candidly admit that in the end we were not able to arrive at findings as useful as we would have liked. Therefore, we detail the methodological problems that ultimately limited our ability to provide *answers* to policymakers. We hope that our experiences will prove helpful in understanding both the promise, and some of the limits, of policy-oriented research. Moreover, we hope that other researchers interested in studying abused and neglected children will be able to learn by observing the problems we encountered.

In the next chapter, we elaborate further the issues that must be addressed in developing policy toward foster care. We also discuss the limitations of existing research. Chapter 3 describes the design of the study. Deciding how to compare children at home and in foster care necessarily requires us to define the aspects of development we believe to be most important for children; our choices and the rationales for them are presented in Chapter 3.

In Chapter 4 we turn to describing the incidents leading to intervention and the backgrounds of the parents and children. Chapter 5 describes the children at the time we first saw them. In our description we compare the development of the abused and neglected children with the development of the comparison children. The chapter provides some indication of the impact abuse and neglect had on the children's development. As we shall see, for many children the impact appeared to be devastating.

In Chapters 6 and 7 we examine some of the events that affected the children's lives following intervention. We were, of course, concerned with the kinds of services delivered to the families and children. We also look at the functioning of the parents of the home children, the quality of the foster homes, the contact between children in foster care and their biological parents, and the stability of the foster placements. In these chapters, we show the many difficulties faced by both the home and foster children during the two years.

Chapters 8 and 9 look at changes in the children's development during the two years. We examine their physical well-being, academic performance, emotional health, social skills, and personal happiness. We also explore the "attachment" issue, trying to determine whether foster care met the children's need for emotional security. The picture that emerged was surprising in many respects. Most surprising, and disturbing, was the limited ability of either home placement (with services to parents) or foster care to significantly improve the children's well-being. In Chapter 10, we examine in detail the case histories of two children, in order to provide additional perspectives on the data presented in Chapters 8 and 9.

For reasons we discuss in Chapter 3, we were not able to do as complete an analysis of the impact of home and foster care on the black and Hispanic children in our sample as on white children. Thus, the major focus of the report is on the white children, though Chapter 11 contains a more limited analysis of the outcome for the black and Hispanic children. Their experiences turned out to be quite different from those of the white children.

In Chapter 12 we discuss some policy implications we believe follow from our findings, comment on themes that run throughout the study, and raise some questions about the wisdom of current efforts to avoid the use of foster care. We also suggest changes in the delivery of services to children and families.

Two

The Policy Dilemma

POLICY PREFERENCES for or against the use of foster care to protect abused or neglected children rest ultimately on value judgments.
Leaving such a child at home, even if the best treatment program is
available, always entails some risk.[1] Against that risk a legislature drafting a statute, or a judge in an individual case, must weigh any costs
associated with placement. Critics of foster placement tend to focus on
three factors: a preference for preserving biological ties or minimizing
government intrusion in the family; concern over the financial cost of
placement; and concern that foster care may actually be worse for children than living at home would be, even taking into account the risk
of reabuse or continued neglect for children at home (Wald 1976; Hubbell 1981). Some of these judgments can be illuminated by research.
Although it cannot be established how much weight should be given
to preserving biological ties, it is relatively easy to obtain data on the
financial costs of foster care. Similarly, studies can document the
amount of reabuse or continued neglect that is likely to occur within
maintaining families.

The hard problem is how to evaluate the third concern. What is
meant when it is said that foster care may be *worse* for children? It certainly does not mean that children are more likely to be abused or
physically neglected in foster care: it appears clear that removal lowers
the chances of reabuse or neglect. Although some children are injured
by foster parents, the rate of reported abuse by foster parents is lower
than that of the general population (Bolton, Laner, and Gia 1981) and
far lower than the rate of reabuse by those who have once abused a
child. Foster parents also are less likely to neglect children's physical
needs. For the most part, they do not leave children unattended; they

virtually always provide adequate food or shelter; they send foster children to school; their households tend to be stable and their care of the child regular. The attraction of foster care as a means of protecting children from further abuse or neglect is heightened by the relatively poor results of programs attempting to prevent reabuse by providing special services to parents. Several studies report reabuse in as many as 50 percent of all cases, even where the services to parents were intensive (Cohn and Collignon 1979; Herrenkohl et al. 1980; Magura 1981). Changing the behavior of neglectful parents may be even more difficult (Polansky et al. 1981). Thus, if the major goal is to protect children from further *physical* harm, this is most likely achieved through foster care.

If one is concerned with *emotional* harm, however, the calculus may change. A number of researchers have reported problems in the emotional development of foster children. If placement with foster parents does have a significant negative impact on the emotional or social development of children, a policy designed only to avoid the risk of further abuse or physical neglect may be unwise. It is of interest, therefore, to review the research on the impact of foster care in order to identify particular possible harms to children. It must be stressed, however, that there are serious limitations in virtually all of the studies that will next be described, especially if we wish to use them for making policy about placement of abused or neglected children. We will review the problems after presenting the research.

Research on Foster Care

THE CASE AGAINST FOSTER CARE

Awareness of the psychological impact of placement had its roots in the theoretical work of child analysts, especially that of John Bowlby, who asserted that separation from parents might have a negative impact on children, even children from "bad" homes (Bowlby 1951, 1965). Bowlby was instrumental in identifying the importance to every child of having an emotional bond with her parents (or other primary caretaker). He labelled this relationship "attachment."[2] It now has been well demonstrated that separation from attachment figures is extremely painful to children and, more significantly, may have long-term negative consequences, at least if the child is not able to establish an adequate new relationship (Bowlby 1965; Rutter 1972; Rutter 1976).

Attachment theory predicts several different ways in which removal from home may be harmful to a child. In addition to the pain of separation, which often is very profound, a lengthy separation from a primary caretaker may permanently impair the child's attachment to that person, even if the separation is not permanent. Perhaps the greatest threat, however, occurs when the child is separated permanently from an attachment figure and is either unable to develop a new relationship or is denied the opportunity to do so. Deprivation of a secure attachment relationship with a primary caretaker may impair a child's ability to form other adequate relationships, both as a child and as an adult. Deprivation of any attachment relationship also has been associated with diminished school performance and increased delinquency (Bowlby 1944; Rutter 1979), though "causal" connections are still undetermined. Moreover, the quality as well as the existence of an attachment relationship may be important to the child's development. Several studies have found that a child's intellectual curiosity, personality development, and ability to get along with peers (up to age five) are related to how *secure* an attachment she has to a primary caretaker (Sroufe 1983; Waters, Wippman, and Sroufe 1979).

It is well documented that foster care frequently neither lends itself to maintaining ties with the biological parent nor facilitates establishment of emotional bonds with new caretakers. Foster care *is supposed to be temporary*—a way station until the child's home can be made safe. Yet if foster parents are told their custody of the child is only temporary, it seems unlikely they will allow themselves to become emotionally involved with the child. Adults, like children, suffer pain upon separation. A foster mother who has cared for many children may protect herself against that pain by limiting emotional involvement. Foster fathers may be even less involved. Thus, the foster families may act in ways that impede the development of a secure attachment relationship between the child and foster parents.

The possibility that foster parents may remain emotionally uninvolved with the child is only part of the problem. The most common criticism of the foster care system focuses on its instability. The majority of children who remain in foster care for longer than six months are subjected to multiple placements (Knitzer and Allen 1978; National Commission on Children in Need of Parents 1979). It is common for a child to be in three or more placements in a one- to two-year period. Owing to this instability, foster children may be unwilling, or unable, ever to develop a trusting relationship with their caretakers (Van Der Waals 1960). It is argued that the absence of such bonds contributes to the low self-esteem, loneliness, and feelings of isolation that some commentators find among foster children (Littner 1974; Geiser 1973).

Foster care may put children at risk in other ways. Many commentators assert that children need continuity and stability of environment in order to have normal emotional development (Goldstein, Freud, and Solnit 1973). There also is clinical evidence that some children view foster home placement as punishment for wrongdoing or as rejection by their parents (Littner 1956). Weinstein (1960, p. 15) asserts that the "child [in foster care] may be confronted with three sets of adults [natural parents, foster parents, social worker], all of whom have some stake in caring for him and planning for his future. In the absence of clearly structured role expectations, both power and responsibility may sometimes be shared, sometimes competed for, and sometimes denied by one or more of the three." As a result, children placed in foster homes may experience identity problems, conflicts of loyalty, and anxiety about their future.

There also are studies showing high rates of behavioral problems (Bryce and Ehlert 1971; Littner 1974; Frank 1980; Bohman and Sigvardsson 1980), school problems (Canning 1974), and delinquency (Ferguson 1966) among foster children, though none of these studies compared rates of such behavior in non–foster children or presented evidence about the childrens' behavior prior to placement. In addition, several studies find that children in foster care retain strong emotional bonds to their biological parents, even after lengthy stays in care (Fanshel and Shinn 1978; Weinstein 1960). Even if foster children do not show developmental or social deficits, their preferences require some consideration.

Despite methodological problems with the research, there is reason to be concerned with the social, emotional, and academic development of children after they are placed in foster care, given the theoretical literature and the consistency of the clinical findings. If foster placement leads to substantial deterioration in these areas, it may be better to forgo foster placement and run the risk of further physical abuse or neglect by the biological parents, at least in situations where abuse or neglect is not life-threatening or likely to lead to permanent impairment.

THE CASE FOR FOSTER CARE

If all the negative findings and the theoretical objections to foster care were in fact valid, policymakers would face a painful dilemma.

How should the different type of harms be balanced? Is it worse to be beaten or to lack an attachment figure? The picture is more complex than an anti–foster care proponent might wish, however. Despite what seems to be a widespread acceptance of the "harms" of foster care, the evidence is by no means one-sided. In fact, a number of studies find positive results of foster care, even for children who have experienced multiple placements.

First, several studies of large numbers of adults who grew up in foster homes found no evidence of greater criminality, mental illness, or marital failure than in the general population (Theis 1924; Meier 1965). In a more recent study, Festinger (1983) interviewed 277 adults who had spent substantial periods of time in foster care in New York City and had been living with foster families or in group homes when they reached their eighteenth birthday. The majority of participants reported quite favorable views of their foster homes. Festinger concluded that "overall, [the former foster children] were not so different from others their age in what they were doing, in the feelings they expressed, and in their hopes for the future" (p. 294). Other studies have found that children in foster care do not have especially low self-esteem or poor self-concept (Seligman 1979; Lemmon 1975), nor do they have especially high rates of delinquency (Runyan 1985).

Moreover, several recent studies indicate that the impact of foster care may be positive, at least for some children. Kent (1976) reviewed case records of more than 500 neglected and abused children who were under court supervision in Los Angeles. The cases were chosen so as to have an equal proportion of physically abused, sexually abused, and "grossly neglected" children. Using information found in the case records (in itself a significant methodological problem), Kent found that a substantial number of children who had been in foster care at least a year were rated by their social workers as being better off, in both physical health and social adjustment, than at the time they entered foster care. Similar results, again using case records, were found by Palmer (1979) with respect to a decrease in "behavior problems" exhibited by foster children from the time of placement until discharge. Leitenberg et al. (1981) compared the school attendance and the police contacts of 187 neglected and "unmanageable" children, aged eleven to sixteen, some of whom were in their own homes, some in foster homes, some in group homes, and some in a state "reform school." The children in the foster homes exhibited the lowest level of problem behaviors. There is even evidence that children who remain in foster care exhibit fewer problems than children returned to their biological parents (Fanshel and Shinn 1978; Zimmerman 1982), and that some children prefer foster care over return to their parents. One study of seventy children, aged twelve to fifteen, found that 47 percent preferred foster care while 44 percent wanted to return home (Lemmon 1975). Bush (1980) found that of two groups of children, those remaining with foster parents described themselves as generally more satisfied than did those who were reunited with biological parents after living in foster care for a time.

The most important research is a longitudinal study done by David Fanshel and his colleagues at Columbia University (Fanshel and Shinn 1978). They assessed the development, over a five-year period, of 500 children aged six months to thirteen years, placed in foster care in New York City in 1966. The children were placed for a variety of reasons; approximately 13 percent were officially categorized as abused or neglected. Although their findings are complex, making it difficult to draw generalizations, careful analysis of their data indicates that the well-being of the majority of the children improved, in terms of physical development, IQ, and school performance, after a six-month period in foster care. Most children maintained improvement in these areas throughout the five years. The children did not seem to have "identity problems"; most did not show evidence of serious placement-associated emotional or behavioral problems. Moreover, the positive findings applied to children who experienced multiple placements as well as those in a single placement. There were, however, significant differences depending on the age at which the child entered care. Younger children adjusted better, especially if they had stable placements.

In considering the costs and benefits of home and foster placement it must also be recognized that the attachment relationship between abused children and their parents is often poor (Lamb et al. 1985; Schneider-Rosen and Cicchetti 1984; Egeland and Sroufe 1981; George and Main 1979), and that abused and neglected children at home evidence many social, emotional, and behavioral problems (Martin 1980; Kinard 1982; Egeland, Sroufe, and Erickson 1983; Jacobson and Straker 1982; Toro 1982).

In sum, the research presents a mixed picture of the impact of foster care. Because of methodological problems in most of the studies, it is difficult to draw firm conclusions from them or base policy on them.

Results vary by the age of the child, reason for placement, type of placement, sex, and race. Most of the studies did not focus solely on abused or neglected children. We discuss the limitations of the research in more detail in the following sections.

Limitations in Existing Studies

In what ways are the existing studies deficient for use by policy-makers deciding when to authorize or use foster care? To be policy-relevant, a study has to have the following characteristics: it should include comparable children at home and in foster care; the study population must be relevant to the policy issues being addressed; there must be adequate base-line information about the children prior to intervention and the study must be longitudinal; the measures of "doing better" or "doing worse" should be clearly defined and related to important aspects of a child's development; and the sample size must be adequate. No research to date meets all these requirements. In this section we explain why we believe they must be met.[3]

COMPARABILITY OF SAMPLES

To provide policy-relevant data, a researcher must compare the development of children left in their own homes with a group of children placed in foster care. If the two populations differ substantially in ways that may be systematically related to how foster placement affects a child, inferences about what might have happened to either group of children had the opposite placement decision been made are tenuous and filled with ambiguity. One could, as Fanshel and his colleagues did, describe the changes that took place in the children; their study provided a considerable advance in the quantity and quality of information regarding the development of children in foster care. But in the presence of large differences between children or their home environments prior to a placement decision, one cannot draw conclusions about the effects of that decision.

The problem is most obvious if there are differences in the extent of abuse or in parental characteristics related to the likelihood of reabuse. For example, if children are left at home only with those parents most amenable to receiving treatment, we cannot predict, by looking at what happens to these children, what might have occurred in other families where the parents were less amenable to treatment. Similar problems arise if the children are different from one another. If courts or agencies tend to place children with emotional problems with foster parents, studies that find higher levels of emotional problems among foster children tell us little about the impact of foster care.

RELEVANT POPULATIONS

In addition to comparability, sample selection must focus on relevant populations. There are many reasons why children enter foster care. Sometimes a child's biological parents are unable to take care of her—a single parent may be hospitalized, jailed, or physically unable to provide care. In other instances the child may have severe emotional problems, and foster placement can facilitate therapy for the child, relief for the biological parents, or both; the reason may be parent-child conflict in a biological family, the placement being a form of divorce. Finally, children are placed, usually against their parents' will, because of abuse and neglect.

The policy issues regarding foster placement are quite different for each of these reasons because the impact of placement is likely to vary depending on the reason for it. For example, a teenager in foster care as a result of parent-child conflict is likely to feel different about reunion with a parent than will a six-year-old whose mother has had to enter a hospital. Yet most of the studies previously discussed fail to provide information about reasons for foster placement; many do not report age, sex, or other factors that might relate to the impact of foster care on a specific group. Obviously, when one is concerned with the policy question of whether to place abused and neglected children in foster care, it is important to know the impact of placement on these children; data related to children whose parents are hospitalized or to teenagers fighting with their parents may not be germane to questions regarding abused and neglected children.

LONGITUDINAL DESIGN

Virtually all studies of children in foster care are cross-sectional; i.e., they look at any given child at only one point in time, even though they may deal with children of different ages. Cross-sectional studies can be misleading in several ways. First, they cannot tell us anything about the condition of the children at the time foster care begins. We cannot tell the impact of foster care on children unless we have baseline data about their condition at that time. For example, in the studies reporting that a large percentage of children in foster care exhibit behavior problems, we have no way of knowing whether the problems began after foster placement or were present at the time of placement. They may, in fact, have been mitigated by foster care. Since many studies show that the type of children who end up in foster care are likely to have problems in their biological families, the criticism that foster care is associated with emotional and behavioral problems must be treated quite skeptically.

In addition to lacking base-line data,[4] most studies are not longitudinal. It is essential to follow children for a period of time in order to take into account changes that are likely to happen the longer the child remains in foster care. Many children suffer short-term setbacks as a result of placement. In young children, the trauma associated with separation can cause loss of bladder control as well as sleeping and eating problems (Littner 1956; Robertson and Robertson 1971). These problems may disappear over time. In contrast, the behaviors of some children may be admirable soon after placement (this is sometimes called the "honeymoon effect") and then deteriorate as the placement continues.

For most children, the long-term negative and positive aspects of foster care may not become noticeable rapidly. For example, confusion about identity might be related to a child's growing emotional commitment to the foster parents or to decreased contact with the biological parent. Any negative consequences of multiple foster placements cannot be determined until the child has been in foster care long enough to experience multiple placements. Lengthy follow-up also is needed to measure positive outcome. While it may be realistic to effect sudden changes in a positive direction for some behaviors and attitudes (which may be only temporary), most positive changes will come about more slowly. For example, a rapid, significant change in school performance or lessening of emotional problems would not be expected, especially if the problems were severe.

A longitudinal design also is needed to assess the positive and negative outcome of leaving the child at home. The impact of treatment programs designed to alleviate problems in the biological parents' home cannot be determined by cross-sectional studies.

How long is "long enough" for an effective longitudinal study? Should the fact that the majority of children seem to be "doing better" in one or the other setting after six or twelve months be determinative of legal policy? Or is it necessary to follow the children for a longer time, even to adulthood? There are many reasons to believe that longer is better. Some theorists maintain that the consequences of broken attachments will show up in adolescence as increased delinquency and in adulthood as an inability to establish adequate emotional relationships (Rutter 1972). On the other hand, the main consequence of growing up in an abusing or neglecting family may be that the child becomes a poor parent. Thus, even relatively lengthy studies may provide only partial data.

SELECTION OF MEASURES

A fourth major deficiency of most studies is the utilization of inadequate measures. In part this is a problem of poor research. Many studies use undefined measures, such as "unfavorable behavior" (Baylor and Monachesi 1939), "aggressiveness" (Canning 1974), or "general well-being" (Weinstein 1960). In addition, many studies measure outcomes by referring to caseworkers' assessments of children. Such assessments, especially if they are drawn solely from these records, have consistently been shown to be unreliable. Casework records are not kept in a systematic fashion; different workers evaluate the same behavior differently; and retrospective judgments are particularly suspect. Overall, the reliability of the reported findings must be treated skeptically.

Beyond such obvious methodological problems is a more subtle problem in the choice of measures. If the only goal of intervention were reduction of the likelihood of reabuse or of continued physical neglect, choosing measures would be fairly simple. However, since concern about foster care focuses on its potentially negative impact on the child's emotional and social development, one must decide what areas of emotional and social development can and should be studied.

Choosing measures involves several important judgments. First, it must be decided what sorts of measures are likely to be relevant to policymakers. Will judges or legislators be less likely to support foster care if children given such care exhibit lower self-esteem or more bedwetting? Will they favor removal because children in foster care show greater social competence or increased IQ scores? It may well be that aspects of development interesting to child development scholars may not seem important to policymakers.[5] In addition, there may be measures that are of questionable relevance for policy purposes because the deficits being measured have few, if any, long-term consequences. For example, it may be that children placed in foster care evidence lower (or higher) self-esteem than other children, or that abused children left at home experience delays in gross motor development; however, it is far from clear what implications higher or lower self-esteem or delayed gross motor development have on the child's long-term well-being. This is not to say that studies should not look at these variables. The critical question is whether the measures chosen are of sufficient importance to justify their use as a basis for such an important decision as home versus foster care.

SAMPLE SIZE

The final problem with many studies is their small sample size. Even if we can develop adequate dependent variables, researchers still face the problem of dealing with the large number of independent variables that might account for differences in outcome in the two groups. The problem is not severe with regard to the basic legislative question of whether the law should favor home placement or foster care. If it turns out that there are clear-cut differences between the two groups on the most important dependent variables, a legislative body will have information directly relevant to the policy decision. Judges, however, must decide which option is better for a specific child. Even at the legislative level it would be useful to know whether the overall findings hold true for various subpopulations, such as children of a given age, gender, or ethnicity. Obviously, better policy could be developed if we understood under which conditions home or foster care were preferable, not just that on average one alternative seemed preferable. To achieve this requires studies of large samples, with well-defined subsamples.

We have elaborated these problems at some length for two reasons. First, the policy relevance of any study, including ours, must be assessed in light of the degree to which the study successfully handles these problems. As we discuss in Chapter 3, we were reasonably successful in meeting these criteria, although our sample was considerably smaller than we would have liked, our follow-up was only for two years, and we encountered problems in assessing sample comparability.

Second, we believe that these considerations are given inadequate attention by funding agencies, especially government agencies, that provide grants for policy-oriented research related to children, and by many researchers as well. The issue of child abuse is a prime example of the deficiencies of much government-funded research. Between 1974 and 1986 the federal government alone spent nearly $100 million for research relating to abused and neglected children. Yet a great deal of the research consisted of small projects exhibiting many of the methodological problems we have identified. It is therefore not surprising that a leading researcher recently concluded that "theoretical and empirical research efforts in the area of child abuse . . . still remain somewhat primitive and rudimentary. . . . Given the embryonic state of knowledge that currently exists, it is not surprising that the literature is as replete with myths at it is with well-validated facts" (Zigler 1980, pp. 12, 14). Without substantial changes in the policies of those who funded research we have little hope of significantly improving the lives of hundreds of thousands of abused and neglected children.

Despite their limitations, the studies previously described provided a useful framework for our research. They identified areas of concern about the well-being of children both at home and in foster care, areas upon which our study focuses.

Three

The Research Design

———

THIS CHAPTER DESCRIBES the basic design of our study, including sample selection and size, choice of variables, and definition of baseline conditions. It describes how we attempted to achieve the methodological desiderata discussed in Chapter 2. In keeping with our goal of demonstrating problems encountered in doing policy-oriented field research, we also discuss some efforts that were unsuccessful.

Selection of Subjects

FINDING COMPARABLE CHILDREN

The biggest gap in the existing research is the absence of studies with samples consisting of comparable children at home and in foster care. This gap is not surprising. In ordinary circumstances, there presumably will be systematic differences between home and foster children, since social work agencies and courts are more likely to remove the most seriously abused or neglected children. Therefore, a research project ideally should include random assignment of children to home and foster care. Only in this way can recruitment bias and the need to search for relevant (and largely unknown) variables that may distinguish the two groups be completely eliminated. Unfortunately, judges and social workers perceive insurmountable ethical problems with such a procedure, since it involves either leaving children in homes believed on a clinical basis to be dangerous or depriving parents of custody despite the social worker's or judge's belief that removal is not absolutely necessary.[1]

The passage of the California legislation, which established two counties for the experimental administration of special services for families keeping children at home and changed the legal standards to make removal more difficult in these counties, provided an opportunity to approximate comparability. We assumed that, as a result of this legislation, there would be a group of children left at home in San Mateo County who would have been placed in foster care in other California counties. Conversely, there would be children placed in foster care in other counties who would have been left at home in San Mateo. We therefore drew our home population from San Mateo County and our foster care sample from two neighboring counties, Alameda and Santa Clara, which were operating under the old law and offered fewer family services.

In deciding which cases to select, we recognized that not all children left at home in San Mateo County would have been placed in foster care in the other counties, nor vice versa. Child protection agencies investigate situations involving a wide range of actual or potential harms to children. Some situations are sufficiently serious that removal would occur in any county, regardless of the services available there or the existence of a particular law. Other cases are sufficiently minor that removal would be extremely unlikely in any county.

In selecting our groups, we defined comparability in three ways. First, we wanted the seriousness of the incidents leading to intervention to be comparable. The risk of reabuse or continued neglect may be greater in cases involving more serious injuries or more extensive neglect. In addition, more seriously abused or neglected children may have greater emotional or behavioral problems. If either of these assumptions is correct, and all children receiving foster care were the more seriously abused or neglected among the total, we would not learn how seriously injured children might fare if left with their biological parents.

Second, we wanted the home conditions and childrearing capabilities of the parents to be comparable. If the parents of the home children were more responsive and amenable to services, or had fewer problems associated with abuse and neglect (problems such as a history of alcohol abuse), findings about how their children fared would not tell us how other children might develop if left in more disorganized homes. Finally, we wanted children who were comparable in terms of the developmental aspects being studied. If, for example, the children in one group evidenced severe emotional problems initially, whereas the children in the other did not, any comparison of change in the two groups over time would be flawed.

The process of finding children who met these criteria involved several steps. First, we asked social workers in San Mateo County to identify every case of abuse or neglect in which, in their judgment, removal would have been probable without the new law. In the other two counties, social workers identified all new foster care cases in which, in their judgment, a child would have been left at home if the county offered services similar to those in San Mateo County. After receiving each case file, two of our senior investigators read it (the court or agency report) to determine whether, on the basis of each precipitative incident and any past history of abuse or neglect, the cases from the various counties appeared comparable. We did not accept any placement cases from Alameda or Santa Clara counties if we felt the extent of the physical abuse was so severe, or the history of neglect so exteme, that San Mateo authorities would also have removed the child. We excluded San Mateo County cases if the threatened harm to the child was relatively minimal and the parent was willing to accept treatment services, since we felt that Alameda and Santa Clara judges would also not consider removal in such situations.

The most serious problem in determining comparability related to information about the children. Agency intervention usually was based either on the nature of the injury to the child or the failure of the parent to provide adequate care. At the time of intervention social workers knew very little about the children. We did not see the children until after the agency was involved.[2] At that time, we knew only the child's age, sex, and ethnic background. Therefore, we had to assume that there would not be significant differences in the children's development if the seriousness of the incident and basic parental characteristics were similar. In making placement decisions, judges or caseworkers might be responding to child-related variables, but this seemed unlikely, since in most cases the children were seen only briefly (if at all) before the placement decision was made.

We did eliminate cases if the recommended resolution was placement in a residential treatment facility. In these cases, the children generally exhibited extreme behavior problems; therefore, it was unlikely that they would have been left at home regardless of the services available. We also excluded several other types of cases from our sample. In keeping with the policy focus of the study, we eliminated cases that did not present a real policy decision. For example, placement is always necessary when no parents are available (e.g., if the parents are in jail) or when the parents refuse to retain custody. We excluded sexual abuse cases because, when we began the study, the incidence rate of sexual abuse of children between five and ten years of age was too low to find a sufficient number of cases in each county.

We limited the study population in one other way. The final sample consists of children who were between five and ten years old at the time of the intervention.[3] Initially, we planned to include children between the ages of one and ten years old. There are very few reliable measures for children younger than one and such measures apply to only a limited range of child attributes. Many of the cases with children older than ten, while cast as cases of abuse or neglect, primarily involve child behavior problems, such as running away. Furthermore, older children's perferences often play a major role in the placement decision. We thought these cases would confound the basic study. After conducting a six-month pilot study including children aged one to ten, we decided to exclude children younger than five. This decision was made in part on the basis of cost; obtaining an adequate sample for the one-to-ten age range would have required a budget several times greater than the one available. More important, in the pilot study school attendance and performance, teacher ratings of the child, and interviews with the children themselves emerged as extremely useful measures. Therefore, we chose a sample consisting of primary-school-aged children.

SELECTION PROCEDURE

Using these criteria, we wanted a final sample of eighty children, half drawn from the experimentally funded county—San Mateo—who would have been removed from their homes if the special services (and laws) were not available, and half selected in the comparison counties, where they were placed in foster care but might have been left at home had the county implemented services similar to those found in San Mateo.[4] In Alameda and Santa Clara counties we reviewed the court records for every child judicially determined to be abused or neglected who was in our age range. We did not become involved until after court adjudication since we were asking for confidential information from the parents. We felt that parents worried about court proceedings would not provide accurate information. In addition about one-third of all cases filed by the county social services agencies are dismissed by the courts. Enrolling cases prior to adjudication would require spending limited resources on initial evaluations of a large number of parents and children who eventually would have to be dropped from the study.

The sample was obtained somewhat differently in San Mateo County, reflecting the different practices used to implement the special legislation. A special unit of the Department of Social Services was created to screen all children who were legally definable as abused or neglected, and for whom removal was a possibility. The workers in this unit decided whether to leave the child at home or file a court petition requesting foster care placement. Court petitions were used only when the agency sought removal. Theoretically, but for the special legislation, every child left at home by this unit would have been removed. Therefore, we reviewed every case selected by this special unit to remain at home. Our assessment differed somewhat from the workers'. We felt that some of the cases they included as "likely to be removed" without the special legislation actually involved situations where it was unlikely that a court in Alameda or Santa Clara counties would have authorized removal. We screened out these marginal cases.

THE FINAL SAMPLE

During a one-and-a-half-year period, the counties referred ninety-eight families whose children met our criteria to us for inclusion.[5] Of these, eighteen families refused to participate; we could not locate the parents of two children in foster care to obtain permission to include their children; and two families moved before the initial interviews were completed. Thus, we began the study with seventy-six families. Five families moved within the first year of the study and could not be located (if a family moved out of the area and we knew where they were, our interviewers went to the new location, even to other states), and four families withdrew during the first year.[6] This left sixty-seven children whom we were able to follow for two years. Thirty-seven of the children were left at home initially; thirty were in foster care.

This report focuses primarily on thirty-two of these sixty-seven children. We could not analyze the other thirty-five cases adequately *in terms of the purpose of the study* (comparing the development of children at home with those in foster care), because of two factors, confounding ethnic differences and movement of children between home and foster care during the two years.

Ethnic differences were a major problem because children of different ethnic groups were not evenly distributed between home and foster placement. The difference in ethnicity arose because blacks constitute only 5 percent of the population of San Mateo County but 30 percent in Alameda County, the county from which most of our foster cases came. Thus we had many more blacks in foster care than at home. The number of Hispanics at home seemed to be a case of random variation in sampling. Table 3.1 shows the number of children in each placement, including those who moved from home to foster care, or vice versa, during our two-year study, broken down by ethnicity. Only four black children were at home continuously and only one Hispanic child was continuously in foster care—numbers too small to permit comparison of home versus foster placement for these ethnicities. Moreover, there were systematic differences in the development of children from the different ethnic groups. If we had not found such differences, we could have analyzed a single multiethnic home group and a single multiethnic foster group. However, because black, Hispanic, and white children were rated so differently by parents and teachers, and rated themselves so differently, we could not aggregate the scores across ethnicities. Therefore, we had to exclude both blacks and Hispanics from the primary analysis of home versus foster care, though we are able, in chapter 11, to describe changes in the well-being of these children during the two years.[7]

The second problem was movement between categories. As previously indicated, we began with thirty-seven children at home and thirty children in foster care. If the world were a kind place to field researchers (and to children), we would be able to freeze our categorizations to study them. Unfortunately, the world is not a kind place. Fifteen children did not remain in their original placement category—that is, home or foster care: six children originally placed at home were removed from their parents during the two years and placed in foster homes, six children originally in foster care were returned to their parents. In addition, two children, one who started at home and one who started in foster care were ultimately placed in residential institutions.

Assessing developmental changes in the children who moved between home and foster care posed substantial methodological problems. For example, if a child spent eighteen months at home and then was moved into foster care, the measures obtained during the six months in foster care reflected only the initial impact of the move. In analyzing the data for children continuously in foster care, we found substantial change over time in many cases. Thus, data reflecting only three or six months of placement (or even a year) do not give a valid picture of the long-term impact of foster care. The same problem arose for the children initially in foster care who returned home. Following their return home, some children were quite happy and seemed to be

TABLE 3.1
*Distribution of Full Sample of Sixty-Seven Children
by Ethnicity and Placement Category*

Ethnicity	Continuously at home	Continuously in foster care	Part of time at home, part in foster care
Black	4	8	4
Hispanic	6	1	1
White	19	13	7
Other	2	0	0

doing well initially, but their well-being began to deteriorate after three or four months. Others showed the opposite pattern. In virtually all these cases, the children were not in a given setting long enough for us to obtain reliable data about their functioning in that setting. Therefore, we had to exclude these cases. We also excluded the two children who went into institutional care, since many of our measures were not appropriate for a child in residential placement.

Thus, the major focus of the report is on thirty-two white children, nineteen of whom were continuously at home, thirteen continuously in foster care. We discuss in a more limited manner the outcome for the black and Hispanic children since their experiences were quite different from those of the white children.

A COMPARISON SAMPLE

In addition to abused or neglected children, we decided to incorporate a comparison group of children who were neither abused nor neglected. Although inclusion of a comparison group is not essential to the central comparison of home and foster home placement, inclusion of such a group allows us to understand any differences found between the home and foster samples, in terms of normative behavior. For example, changes over time occurring at the same rate in both home and foster groups might yield no differences between them. Yet, if the comparison group children experienced a different pattern of change we would learn something about both home and foster placement that would otherwise be missed. Normative data are particularly important for understanding the information we obtained from our interview schedules and questionnaires, since there were no previously determined norms.

Ideally, we would have included in the comparison group a classmate of each abused or neglected child, matched to that child in age, sex, ethnicity, and parents' social and educational attainment, income, and marital status, the variables most commonly related to child development. For a variety of reasons this was not possible.[8] In fact, we have doubts that a true comparison group would exist. Parents who abuse or neglect their children have a combination of characteristics (see Chapter 4) that are not likely to be found in nonabusing, nonneglecting parents, even in those selected to be comparable in terms of socioeconomic and family structure variables.

Our comparison group consisted of children who attended three schools from which a large number of reports of abuse and neglect were received each year. In each county, one such school was designated for participation. Thirty children were randomly selected from the first through the fourth grades of each school, a group representing approximately the age span of our study children. This process yielded families generally similar in socioeconomic background to those of our study, although some differences were noted.[9] They will be described in more detail in Chapter 4. Interviews, questionnaires, and observations of the comparison group of children and parents were similar to those employed for the study sample. However, the comparison sample was assessed only two times, eighteen months apart, whereas the study sample was assessed at three-month intervals throughout the two years of our project.

Gathering and Measuring Data

SELECTION OF MEASURES

As we discussed in Chapter 2, one of the greatest weaknesses of most other research on foster care lies in the choice of measures. Therefore, we spent a substantial period of time selecting and testing our measures.[10] We based our measures on three considerations. First, we wanted to look at aspects of the child's well-being that would be of interest to policymakers. We assumed that legislators and judges are concerned with physical health and evidence of malfunctioning, such as poor school performance, severe emotional disorders, or antisocial behavior; thus we planned to make direct measures on these variables; in addition, through literature-reviews and discussion with colleagues, we identified other aspects of a child's development that would be predictive of these variables. For example, we decided to assess the child's peer relationships, inasmuch as a number of studies report that abused and neglected children fare badly in retaining friendships and adapting to peer expectations (Pavenstedt 1973; Sroufe 1983; Roff, Sells, and Golden 1972; Cowen et al. 1973); moreover, poor peer relationships in early childhood are a good predictor of later social problems (Hartup 1983).

We also wanted to examine the quality of the parent-child relationship and more specifically in the foster care literature. Finally, we sought to obtain the child's perspective on the impact of intervention. Although the child's views may seem of obvious interest, in fact they are given little weight in placement decisions. Many judges and child-care workers believe that they must determine the child's best interest independently of the child's views, since the child may want to remain in, or return to, a "bad" home. We believe that the children's views are important in and of themselves, since their happiness deserves consideration, even if following the child's desire may increase the risk of their causing social problems. Moreover, the child is the best source of information concerning the subjective impact of separation and living in a new family. Furthermore, in the chaotic world of many of the children, their caretakers, teachers, and social workers all changed frequently, leaving the child as the only constant source of information over the two-year period.

Our second goal was to select measures that would be appropriate to the age of our sample and employable on a repeated basis while still remaining valid as the child got older. We believe, like Fanshel and Shinn (1978), that it is very important to assess several different aspects of a child's development and to obtain evaluations from different informants about the child. We felt it unlikely that various interventions would affect a child's cognitive, social, and emotional development all in the same way; instead, it seemed likely that parents, foster parents, teachers, social workers, our interviewers, and the child herself would all have different perspectives on the child's development.

Third, we wanted to gather data about the child as frequently as possible. We interviewed the child's caretaker every three months, the child every six months, and the teachers and social workers yearly. We saw the caretakers (biological or foster mothers) every three months in order to keep up their interest and participation in the project and to have an ongoing account of what was happening in the child's life. We chose longer periods between interviews of the children and teachers because we were concerned about their tolerance for participation and wanted the interviews to be sufficiently far apart to minimize the "learning" effect of repeated testing or questioning.[11]

Four women inteviewers, who worked full time for three to four years on the study, personally interviewed the caretakers, children, and social workers. Each interviewer had previous experience working with children, with families, or with both.[12] Interviewers and subjects were matched by ethnicity. Each interviewer saw the same fifteen to twenty children and their caretakers throughout the two years. They came to know most of their families quite well—in fact, it was a constant ethical and emotional problem for them not to become active social workers for the families.[13] The interviewers also conducted yearly interviews with the social workers responsible for their children.

Teacher evaluations were obtained through questionnaires, distributed to each teacher personally but completed by the teacher alone and returned to us by mail. Additional school data were obtained by reading the child's cumulative school file. Finally, the children were given cognitive tests at the beginning, middle, and end of the two-year period.

We tried to obtain data about the children as soon after court or agency intervention as possible in order to have adequate base-line information. This did not pose a problem for most of the children left at home. In San Mateo County we received a case within two days of the time the social services agency became involved. In most instances we contacted the family within a week. Our interviewer would go to the parent's home, explain the purposes of the project, obtain permission, and, if the mother had time, do the first set of interviews. A second meeting would be set up for the following week, at which time the child was interviewed and tested. For the home cases the only delays came when we could not contact the parent immediately, when the parent wanted time to decide whether to participate, or when it was difficult to set a time to see the child. To minimize broken appointments, all our interviewing and testing was done in a specially outfitted van driven to the parent's home.[14]

The foster children posed a more difficult problem. In both Alameda and Santa Clara counties, all the children who were placed in foster care were removed from their parents at the time they were initially reported to the child protection agency. Thus, we could not see these children until they were already in an out-of-home placement. Furthermore, we decided not to contact any out-of-home cases until all court proceedings were completed, because the parents were reluctant to talk with us while proceedings were pending. The court process generally lasted between three and six weeks. It then usually took several weeks to contact the biological and foster parents, obtain their agreements to participate in the study, and arrange to interview and test the child. For those children who were moved to new foster homes upon completion of the court proceedings, we chose to wait an additional three weeks before interviewing them, to allow them an initial period of adjustment. Consequently, most initial interviews were conducted between six and twelve weeks after the initial removal. In five cases, the inital interviewers took place in the fourth or fifth months following placement, because of delays in the court process or difficulty in contacting the parents.[15] Thus, we face a difficult problem in interpreting the initial data about the foster children. To what degree do their scores on our various measures reflect the impact of foster care?[16] We deal with this issue in Chapters 5 and 11, after we describe the incidents leading to intervention, compare the characteristics of the parents of each group, and look at our initial child measures.

Specific Measures

PHYSICAL HEALTH

A number of previous studies[17] of abused, neglected, and foster children have emphasized the prevalence of medical problems in these groups (Martin 1976; Swire and Kavaler 1977; Gruber 1978). We used two approaches in assessing the children's physical health. To detect obvious problems we gave all children a physical exam and recorded their height and weight. The exam consisted of evaluation of six areas of physical well-being: (1) vision, (2) hearing, (3) respiration, (4) coordination, (5) skin, and (6) mouth and teeth. The exam was performed by our interviewers, who were trained by a physician to carry out these simple evaluations.[18] The exam was given at the beginning and end of the study, with the height and weight measurements being taken yearly. Our second health assessment came from caretakers' responses to specific health-related items on our interviews. The caretakers rated the child's health and provided a history of past medical problems, such as the number of illnesses or accidents, hospitalizations, and visits to doctors and dentists. Current health data were obtained yearly.

COGNITIVE DEVELOPMENT

Although we were more interested in actual school performance than in performance on cognitive tests, we did give each child a standard IQ test to help us identify children performing below expectations. There are conflicting findings about the IQ of abused and neglected children (Fanshel and Shinn 1978; Martin 1976); Fanshel has the only data on changes in IQ over time and these are only for foster children. We selected two cognitive tests that covered the age range of our sample: the Wechsler Preschool and Primary Scale of Intelligence (WPPSI) for ages four and five, and the Wechsler Intelligence Scale for Children–Revised (WISC-R) for ages six through sixteen. Both tests have been standardized on large samples. The WPPSI, which is similar in structure to the WISC-R, is merely a downward extension of the WISC-R, which enabled us to make comparisons across time and across tests. Tests were administered by two psychologists experienced in the testing of "problem" children. All tests for a given child were done by the same tester.

ACADEMIC PERFORMANCE

To assess academic performance, we gathered data from school records and the children's teachers. We read each child's full school record. These records usually included information on absenteeism, retentions, achievement test scores, and whether or not the children received special help or were enrolled in special classes at school. In addition, each year we asked the teachers to rate children's academic standing in the class.

SOCIAL DEVELOPMENT

There are a number of reasons why we wanted to give special attention to the social and emotional development of the children in our sample. Previous studies of abused or neglected children found noticeable deficits in the levels of their social functioning (Pavenstedt 1973; Martin 1976); and poor early social functioning may be predictive of later psychiatric problems or academic difficulties (Garmezy 1970; Jones 1976; Kohn 1977). Most of the literature that discusses problems with foster care focuses on social and emotional problems of foster children. If these children behave in a socially inadequate manner they may be harder to deal with, which, in turn, may influence both the stability and duration of placement. On the other hand, assuming that some growth and change are possible, foster placement may have a strong, measurable impact on a child's social behavior and interpersonal skills.

In assessing social development it is particularly important to have both multiple measures and more than one evaluator. Since a child is likely to act (or be perceived) differently at home and in school, we obtained assessments from both caretakers and teachers. Since children may get along better with either adults or peers, we focused both on adult-child relationships and behavior with peers. We wanted to measure each child's strengths as well as weaknesses. Unfortunately, no instruments that existed at the time we began the study seemed entirely appropriate to our sample. Therefore we developed two instruments, one designed to measure problem behaviors, the other to measure social competence. We obtained additional information about the child's behavior and peer relations in our general interviews with the caretakers and children. We will describe the specific items in each instrument in later chapters and at this point provide an overview of the aspects of development we wanted to assess.

Behavioral problems. Children identified as abused or neglected frequently exhibit behavioral problems, such as extreme aggressiveness, anxiety, or withdrawal (Martin 1976). These behaviors may lead to additional difficulties for the child, whether with outside authorities, in peer interactions, or within a home setting. Foster care also has been reported to be associated with behavioral problems such as bed-wetting, sleep disturbances, and anxiety.

We therefore developed a child behavior scale (abbreviated as CBS). The CBS contained forty-three problem behaviors, ranging from common behaviors in which all children may engage some of the time (e.g., crying, whining, pouting) to more serious behaviors (e.g., stealing, setting fires, running away). There also were questions about behaviors that indicate the presence of anxiety, withdrawal, and hyperactivity. The scale was first administered verbally to every mother participating in our study—both biological and foster mothers. Subsequent administrations, which occurred at six-month intervals, were given only to current caretakers. Using this scale, we examined whether foster placement alleviated any significant problems the child evidenced at intervention and whether it resulted in any other problems. Repeated use of the scale allowed us to determine whether certain problems associated with foster care, for example bed-wetting, were only temporary regressions. Finally, through this scale we could determine whether problems exhibited by children left at home were alleviated by intervention or the passage of time.

Social competence. The concept of social competence is an important one that has not been focused on in most studies of abused and neglected children. To remedy that, we assessed the social strengths of each child—competent behavior at school, with peers, and at home—and examined whether the presence of extreme incompetencies was stable across time or could be altered by the different interventions.

The social competence instrument we developed consisted of two scales,[19] one administered as an interview to parents or caretakers, the other as a questionnaire filled out by teachers. The parent/caretaker scale contained thirty items dealing with ways children behave in interactions with that person, and fifteen items asking parents to compare their child to other children on global traits and behaviors, such as friendliness, ease of being around, and general helpfulness.

The first thirty items were selected to fit with an a priori classification schema. After reviewing various studies of social competence, we identified five dimensions that had been used in defining a socially effective person. These were (with examples): *interpersonal resourcefulness*, asks for help when not able to do some task or activity; *social sensitivity*, leaves you alone when you look busy or occupied; *social effectiveness*, gets you to do things he or she wants; *normative adherence*, quiets down when asked; *autonomy*, stands up for own ideas and rights. Using a five-point scale, the parent or caretaker rated the frequency of occurrence of the behavior, from "never" to "most of the time," in a typical day. The scale was administered verbally to the child's current caretaker at six-month intervals, beginning with the second set of interviews (three months after the initial interviews)—which means that for the foster group it was completed only by the foster mothers.

Social behavior at school. Since prior studies (Pavenstedt 1973) indicated that abused and neglected children evidenced substantial deficits in social relations at school, we were particularly concerned with examining the children's classroom behavior, interaction with the teacher, and peer relations.

Most of our information was obtained from the teachers. Once a year, we asked each child's teacher to complete a questionnaire containing items describing the child's behavior at school. The scale sought to measure the same qualities—interpersonal resourcefulness, social sensitivity, autonomy, and normative adherence—as the parent/ caretaker social competence scale. However, the items pertained to behavior in the classroom setting rather than at home. We wanted to determined how well the child adhered to the rules, the degree of autonomy demonstrated by the child, and the ability of the child to successfully use the teacher as a resource. We also asked a number of global questions (how easy do you find it to be around this child?, how likeable is this child?) to see if the teachers' overall impressions of the children differed systematically according to placement in the foster, home, or comparison groups.[20] Finally, we asked the teachers to rate the child's peer relations. Although teacher ratings are not the ideal measure of peer relations, they are a reasonable way of identifying children with clear problems.

THE CHILDREN'S PERSPECTIVES ABOUT THEIR LIVES

Our final source of information was the children themselves. Each child was interviewed every six months. The interviews covered two principal areas. First, we asked the children to describe events of a typical day, and give us their views and evaluations of their particular circumstances and experiences. We explored several areas of the children's world: their neighborhood friendships, their attitude toward school, the availability of social resources (e.g., what the child liked most about the neighborhood, whom the child could talk to when troubled). We also explored the children's personal feelings about themselves and their caretakers. Many of the questions were adopted from Zill's national survey of children (Zill 1976).

These interviews were extremely useful. Most of the children were able to discuss their feelings about their experiences; their perceptions are a rich source of data. A portion of our success here may be due to repeated visits by the same interviewer, so that familiarity and rapport were developed. The children were willing to identify their preferred caretaker, talk about school and social problems, and indicate whether abusive or neglectful conditions were continuing. We used the information from these interviews to create three scales: one measuring child self-esteem; a second measuring the child's satisfaction with peer relations; the third measuring the child's school satisfaction. In addition, the interviews provided an overall picture of the children's happiness and their satisfaction with their family relationships.

EXPLANATORY FACTORS (INDEPENDENT VARIABLES)

In addition to describing differences in development of the home and foster groups during the two years, we hoped to identify any factors related to outcome for individual children. Many factors that might be relevant are obvious and easy to categorize. These include background variables such as age, sex, ethnicity; parental characteristics, such as age, marital status, education, income, history of pathologies; and variables related to circumstances of placement such as the reason for intervention, reabuse or continued neglect of the child, extent of relocations among the families of the at-home children, the number and nature of moves experienced by foster children, parental visiting of foster children, services or therapies given the parents and/ or child, and the status of the child at the end of two years (at home, adopted, or in temporary foster care).

We also looked at the emotional environment in the child's home. Previous studies have shown the importance of physical and social environments for cognitive growth and social development. Furthermore, one of the reasons often cited for placing a child in a foster home is to improve his physical and social environment. We focused on the three main aspects of the environment: the nature of the parent-child interaction, the parents' emotional state, and the organizational structure of the family.

We were concerned about parent-child relations because of our interest in attachment. Based on previous studies, we felt that abused and neglected children were likely to have poor attachment relationships, either at home or in foster care. Unfortunately, there were no standard measures of child-parent attachment for children aged five to ten at the time we began the study.[21] Therefore, we developed our own proxy measures.

We focused on the biological and foster parents' emotional states because there are many studies reporting that abusive and neglecting parents are socially isolated, have low self-esteem, and evidence little involvement with their children. As a result the parents may be poor socialization models or teachers for the children. Therefore, we attempted to measure these qualities in all the caretakers and to assess their impact on the children. Again, owing to the absence of standardized instruments suitable for our population, we developed our own measures of parental self-esteem and involvement with the children.

We also assessed the social climate and organization of the home, using five subscales of the Moos Family Environment Scale (Moos and Moos 1981). This widely used instrument assesses the cohesion, expressiveness, conflict, organization, and control in the family, on the basis of the respondent's answers to a series of questions.

We debated trying to obtain an additional measure of the quality of the foster home. However, we discovered only one existent scale (Fanshel 1966), and we felt it had not shown enough relationship to outcome for foster children to justify its use. Moreover, it is designed to be used by caseworkers familiar with the foster parents. We felt that in a large number of our cases the caseworkers did not know the foster parents well enough to fill out the instrument accurately. Although our interviewers had more contact with the foster parents, they doubted their ability to make the type of assessments called for by the Fanshel scale.

In addition to instruments that provided overall scores on certain dimensions of the home environment, we tried to obtain a naturalistic picture of the day-to-day life of each child. The most important source of this information was the intensive interview conducted with the primary caretaker every three months throughout the study. The interview format was open-ended and wide-ranging. Initially, the parents provided a full developmental history of the child. In later interviews, the caretaker was asked to describe any important events that had occurred since the previous visit, as well as ongoing experiences the caretaker and child had been sharing. To supplement the open-ended questions, we utilized a schedule asking whether certain events that might have major significance to the child had occurred. This schedule, which was filled out at six-month intervals by interviewers, recorded information gathered from a variety of sources—parents, caretakers, social workers, and the child. Items included events such as births, marriages, illnesses, deaths, changes in the child's placement or dependency status, and changes in social workers.

Finally, we assessed the quality of the physical environment. We developed an observational checklist that our interviewers filled out after their initial visit to the child's home and repeated yearly or whenever the child's residence changed. Both biological parents' and current caretakers' homes were rated. The scale measures the safety, comfort, density, and orderliness of the home.

Length of Follow-up

We gathered data about each child for two years from the time of the initial intervention. The two-year follow-up was chosen for several reasons. Previous research suggested that the likelihood of multiple placements increases the longer a child is in foster care (Wald 1976). On the basis of these data, a minimum of two years is needed to determine the negative impact of multiple placements. In addition, many states' laws allow a court to decide not to return children to their parents at the end of two years of foster placement (Wald 1976). Several commentators argue that two years is too long, and that decisions about termination of foster placement should occur between six months and one year in order to provide the child with a permanent new home quickly (Goldstein, Freud, and Solnit 1979). They contend that prolonging this decision beyond one year is harmful. We wanted to see if there was a negative change in the condition of foster children in the second year, which would support such contentions.

Unquestionably an even longer follow-up would have been desirable. Life was continually changing for both the home and foster children. We know that major changes took place just as some children left the study; for example, two children changed custody just at the two-year mark. The condition of several biological parents deteriorated dramatically at this time. In fact, for many of the children and parents in our sample, life consisted of a series of crises and it seemed likely that such crises would continue to occur throughout the child's minority. Thus any follow-up that did not last until adulthood would not give a full picture of the consequences of living in these families.

We would like to see longitudinal studies that followed children to adulthood, although we would not like to be the investigators. Eight years is long enough to be working on one project.[22] We believe, moreover, that it is reasonable to base policy on an assessment of impact over a two-year period.

In retrospect, we are reasonably pleased with our ability to carry out the study in a manner sufficiently rigorous to justify using the findings for policy purposes.[23] There are, of course, aspects of the study we would like to be able to do over. Most important, if we had anticipated the significance of ethnic differences, we might have focused only on white children (given the ethnic composition of San Mateo County), and searched for a comparison county that more closely approximated the ethnic makeup of that county. This would have created substantial administrative problems, however, since it would have required selecting a county farther from our research location. Another major change would have been to give all children a standard California Achievement Test on a regular basis. We relied on school records, which, as we discuss in Chapter 5, were woefully incomplete.

We believe that the extensiveness of our data, the inclusion of a comparison group, the longitudinal design, and the use of measures drawn from basic child development research enables us to provide important new information about the development of abused and neglected children, as well as about the impact of home versus foster placement. Unfortunately, even though our study was highly funded for a social science research project, we did not have enough funds to obtain a truly adequate sample size. Therefore, many of our conclusions must be more tentative than we would like. We hope that others will replicate, and expand upon, our efforts.

Four

The Home and Foster Samples: Precipitative Incidents, the Mothers, and the Children

IN THIS CHAPTER we describe the incidents leading to intervention, some personal characteristics of the mothers in our study,[1] and some demographic data for the mothers and children. We focus solely on the thirty-two white children—nineteen home and thirteen foster cases—since these cases could be compared over time. We look to see whether the two groups were similar enough for us to reasonably expect that had a child been in the opposite placement, her development would have been similar to that of the average child in that group. To establish comparability, we use the nature of the abuse or neglect causing authorities to intervene, the history of such incidents, and the background of the mothers on factors likely to be related to their parenting abilities.

The Precipitative Incidents

THE PROBLEM OF CLASSIFICATION

Chapter 1 began with vignettes through which we tried to convey a sense of the situations that led to intervention. Unfortunately neither vignettes nor statistics give a totally accurate picture. The terms abuse and neglect have no agreed-upon definition (Zigler 1980; Giovannoni and Becerra 1979). Child protection agencies become involved in abuse cases ranging from brutally beaten children with broken bones to children who have suffered spankings by hand, without visible injuries.

Neglect cases are even more diverse. Adding to the complexity, many cases involve a mixture of abuse and neglect. While the triggering incident may be of one kind or the other, which of the two it is is often a matter of happenstance. Moreover, if one takes into account a variety of factors that may be related to how seriously we should view the need for intervention, such as the actual or potential severity of the injuries, the parent's mental state at the time of the incident, the presence or absence of a history of abuse or neglect, and the parent's receptiveness to intervention, every situation can be seen as unique.

We nevertheless need to show where along the spectrum of abuse and neglect our cases fall in order to determine whether or not (a) the incidents leading to intervention were in the range of seriousness where the removal decision was a real possibility for both groups of children, and (b) the circumstances surrounding the abuse or neglect put both groups of children at similar risk in terms of general development and the risk of future injury. If the children in both groups were not at similar risk it would be inappropriate to predict what might have happened had the opposite decisions been made about their placements. We begin by describing the types of precipitative incidents and then try to categorize their seriousness.

THE BASIS FOR INTERVENTION

Looking only at the primary reason for intervention, of the thirty-two cases considered here, fourteen involved abuse, eighteen neglect.

Abuse cases. All but two[2] of the fourteen abused children showed some signs of being hit, i.e., welts, bruises, or impaired walking or sitting: seven children had head injuries, two had been hit on the back and other parts of the body, and three had bruises and welts on the legs and buttocks. Most of the beatings were by hand, but three parents had used belts, one a stick, and two had kicked and choked the child. The injuries usually were observed by outsiders; whereas three cases were reported by the parents themselves, four reports came from school teachers, six from relatives or friends, and one from a doctor. Although only two of the children received medical attention, in most cases there was a potential for more serious injury. Parents inflicted the injury in all but one instance, where the beating was done by the mother's boyfriend.[3] Although a specific prior event triggered the beating in all cases—for example, the child was accused of lying, not doing homework, or misbehaving—the beatings were not isolated incidents stemming from an unusual problem. In all but two cases there was a long history of severe physical treatment of the child.

In each of the fourteen cases a protective agency intervened solely because of the physical abuse; we later discovered that seven of these children also had been neglected. We categorized a case as "solely abuse" if it involved a physical injury but family life was not disorganized or chaotic, the child's physical needs generally were met, school attendance was regular, and the child was not left unsupervised. An example was Paul:

Paul, a five-year-old, was reported to the police by his step-grandmother, who noticed bruises on his buttocks and legs when putting him to bed. Paul's mother, who was divorced from his father, admitted that Paul had been hit with a belt at her request by her boyfriend because Paul had come home two hours late from school. She said that Paul did this often, which frightened and upset her. There were several previously reported instances of severe spankings by both the mother and her boyfriend, and a number of "accidental" injuries, including one instance resulting in a fractured arm. Paul was otherwise well-cared-for physically and his mother seemed concerned about his academic and social development.

A case of both abuse and neglect was Scott:

Scott, aged six, lived with his father, who was an alcoholic, and his mother, who was severely depressed and had a history of treatment for mental illness. He came to agency attention when his teacher reported that he came to school with bruises on his face and jaw. His father had hit him by hand in the face. In addition to a history of such "spankings," the home was extremely filthy and Scott frequently was left unattended.

Neglect cases. Like the abuse cases, the eighteen cases of neglect varied substantially. Neglect does not have a clear legal meaning, nor is there a consensus among child welfare professionals about what behaviors or situations constitute it. In general the study families failed to provide adequate child care in a number of areas. They usually had meager economic resources, and in most instances one or both parents had a history of alcoholism, drug problems, or mental illness. Many of the families had a long history of dysfunctional behavior, evidenced by frequent moves and little effort at supervising their children. Many of the children had a history of poor school attendance.

Although most cases of neglect involved multiproblem families, it was possible to identify two main types of cases. In eight cases the parent's housing was such that it was dangerous for the child to remain there. Four of these eight parents lived in cars, campers, or motels. All these parents also took poor physical care of their children, but intervention would have been unlikely were it not for the inadequacy of the housing.

Typical cases were:

Tommie, an eight-year-old, lived with his mother and sister. His mother had a history of severe depression dating from her divorce from Tommie's father. Her apartment was so filthy as to pose a health hazard, and Tommie and his sister were frequently left alone. Tommie was often ill, which caused him to miss a great deal of school. However, the mother was loving toward the children and never used any physical discipline.

Laurie, a ten-year-old, was the youngest of sixteen children, all but two of whom were adults living away from home. Both her parents had severe problems with alcohol. She came to county attention when police officers, responding to a neighborhood disturbance, found the house littered with broken glass, saw broken windows and exposed electrical wiring, and discovered a decomposing cat in the backyard. Her parents seemed concerned about the children but lacked the energy or motivation to clean the house, supervise the children, or involve themselves in the children's lives.

For nine children, intervention occurred because the parent was unable or unwilling to provide adequate supervision or care. These cases ranged from abandonment (two mothers failed to pick up their children at daycare centers) to leaving a young child unsupervised for many hours. In three cases the parent initially asked that their child be given foster care; two of these children were not attending school. In almost all cases the children appeared to be at risk of physical harm. All the parents had lengthy histories of inadequate care.

In addition to the two main types of neglect, one case of the eighteen involved emotional neglect. The mother paid no attention to the child or his infant sibling, who was diagnosed as a failure-to-thrive infant. Although the study child was not left physically unattended, he was emotionally abandoned, since his mother rarely spoke to him or interacted with him.

In contrast to the abuse cases, virtually all the neglect cases involved only neglect. Only two neglectful families showed any evidence of excessive physical discipline. In fact, many imposed no discipline at all. In all the neglect cases, if removal occurred, all the children in the family were removed.

COMPARABILITY OF HOME AND FOSTER GROUPS VERSUS PLACEMENT STATUS

Main reason for intervention and placement status. The main reason for intervention was different in the home and foster groups, with the home sample including more abuse cases, the foster sample more neglect cases:

Reason for placement ($N = 32$)	Home	Foster
Abuse	11	3
Neglect	8	10

Because there were some differences in the development of abused and neglected children at the time we first saw them, we examined these categories separately in all our analyses of change over time, although our ability to do a comprehensive analysis was limited by the small number of abused children in foster care.

Seriousness of precipitative event. The earlier description gave an idea of the types of abuse and neglect represented in our sample, but not the relative seriousness of home and foster cases. Did the process we used to screen these cases, as described in Chapter 3, produce comparable cases? That is, had the behavior of the biological parents of both the home and foster children put the children at the same degree of risk, in terms of their physical and emotional development and the likelihood of reinjury if left at home?

Abuse cases. To make this assessment in abuse cases it is necessary to look at more than just the severity of the current physical injury. The circumstances surrounding the abuse (e.g., was it a manifestation of the parent's mental illness or drug abuse, did the parent reject the child emotionally) and the extent of prior abuse are more likely to be related to the child's development (and future development) than is the particular injury that resulted in agency action.[4]

Based on these factors, we rated two of the fourteen cases, both in the home group, as serious. In each instance the child was injured with an object, there was a history of severe discipline, and the parents seemed to have little self-control. Seven other cases posed a more moderate risk to the child's general development. In these cases the current injuries were serious but the method of punishment was less dangerous (the parents used a belt, not a metal object) or the past history less abusive. Of these cases, five remained at home and two were placed in foster care. Finally, there were five relatively minimal cases. The current injuries were minor, all resulting from spankings by hand to the buttocks, and the parents worried about their use of physical discipline. However, in each of these cases the history of repeated physical punishment raised the possibility of emotional damage to the children, which justified agency intervention; four of these children were left at home and one went into foster care.

The types of abuse were distributed as follows:

Abused sample (N = 14), by type	Home	Foster
Serious	2	0
Moderate	5	2
Minimal	4	1

Neglect cases. Neglect is more diverse than abuse, making categorization of seriousness even more difficult. In general, intervention is premised on potential, not actual, harm. Because the types of harm that might result from neglectful parenting are not comparable, we believe that the appropriate measure for comparing the two groups is not the harm per se but the extent of poor parenting. To determine this we drew on five factors, recognizing that many others could be included. They are: a history of neglectful behavior by the parents; the failure of past intervention efforts; whether the neglectful behavior was related to a mental illness or drug or alcohol abuse; the parents' negative attitude toward keeping the child; and the parents' unreceptiveness toward services. A combination of factors, of course, makes the situation even more serious.

We describe the mothers' backgrounds more fully in the next section. All the families had a history of neglectful behaviors and many had been unable to make use of previous services. Based on the five factors listed above, we believe that these situations posed at least a moderately serious threat to all the children. However, ten cases were more serious either because of negative attitudes of a parent toward the child or because of the severity of a parent's alcohol, drug, or mental problems. Of these cases, six children were placed in foster care. Among the eight relatively more moderate cases, four children were left at home and four were given foster placement. Thus, in terms of seriousness the two groups were comparable. The types of neglect were distributed as follows:

Neglected sample (N = 18), by type	Home	Foster
Serious	6	4
Moderate	4	4

Overall, we believe that, based on the precipitative incidents and past histories, the two groups of children were likely to be comparable in terms of current development. In addition, though the home group involved slightly more serious abuse situations, in light of the history of abuse or neglect in the majority of cases in both groups, there was a substantial risk of reabuse or continued neglect for most of the children.

The Mothers' Backgrounds

RELEVANCE OF MATERNAL CHARACTERISTICS TO THE ISSUE OF COMPARABILITY

A mother's background characteristics, like the history of parental treatment just discussed, are likely to be related to the children's social, emotional, and academic development. Of course, the best evidence of the children's actual development would be measures obtained directly from or about the children themselves. However, for reasons discussed previously, we could not obtain developmental measures (other than historical information) through direct assessments of the children *prior to intervention.* Therefore, we used maternal background and family structure characteristics known to relate to child-rearing ability and differences in children's development as proxies for estimating comparability of the children.[5] If there were substantial differences between the two groups of mothers we would be concerned that the children in each group might not be comparable developmentally. In addition, if the mothers of the home group had possessed greater (or lesser) parenting skills than the mothers of children in the foster group, we would be unable to assume that any changes in the development of the home children over the two years would also have taken place among the foster children *had they been left with their mothers.*

The mothers of the children we studied had many characteristics that might have negatively affected the children's development. The majority were poor, poorly educated, divorced or separated, isolated from the community, and low in self-esteem. Many had long histories of drug or alcohol abuse or mental illness. A few more mothers of the children placed in foster care evidenced these problems. There were substantial differences between both groups of abusing or neglecting mothers and the mothers of the comparison children.

SOCIOECONOMIC CHARACTERISTICS AND FAMILY STRUCTURE

In general the mothers tended to be single and to have low incomes, but the mothers of the home children were more likely to be married, to have some college education, to have higher income, and to have more stable ties in their community than mothers of foster group children.[6] See Table 4.1.

PSYCHOSOCIAL CHARACTERISTICS

We assessed aspects of the psychological and behavioral characteristics of the mothers, which other studies have found to be either predictors of abuse or neglect or associated with a parent's child-rearing capabilities: a history of antisocial or maladaptive behaviors; a parent's self-esteem; and the degree to which the parent is socially isolated. In addition, we explored with the mothers some aspects of their childhoods, especially any childhood history of abuse or neglect. Finally, we sought to categorize the family environment in terms of conflict, cohesion, and general patterns of interaction, using the scale developed by Moos (Moos and Moos 1981).

To assess parental pathology we asked the mothers if they had ever had problems with the use of drugs or alcohol, psychological problems requiring hospitalization, or had spent time in jail. We also reviewed all court reports and agency reports for mention of these problems. It is likely that our figures are conservative, since records are not complete and some mothers may not have provided correct information. Because the backgrounds of parents whose children were removed were investigated more extensively by the child protection agencies, the likelihood that past problems would be noted somewhere in the case records for this group was higher than for parents of children who remained at home.[7] As shown in Table 4.2, the majority of mothers had a history of one or more risk factors.[8] Again it appears that the mothers of the foster children had more risk factors than the home mothers, though part of the differences may be accounted for by the more complete records for foster cases.

Our measures of self-esteem and social isolation also show the mothers of children placed in foster care to have been a more troubled

TABLE 4.1

Demographic Characteristics of Biological Mothers of Home, Foster,
and Comparison Children

Characteristic of mother	Home (N = 19)	Foster (N = 13)	Comparison (N = 42)
Age at intake (years)			
Range	21–36	22–57	—
Median	29	30	—
Age at birth of child (years)			
Range	15–36	14–47	19–35
Median	22	22	25
Marital status			
Presently married	47%	23%	71%
Divorced or separated	47%	62%	17%
Single, never married	5%	8%	0%
Widowed	0%	8%	12%
Education			
Did not complete high school	32%	75%	10%
Graduated from high school	42%	17%	50%
Attended college	26%	8%	40%
Employment			
Full-time	42%	25%	45%
Part-time	16%	0%	2%
Not working	42%	75%	53%
Monthly income			
<$500	28%	46%	8%
$500–$1,000	28%	23%	18%
$1,001–$1,500	22%	31%	36%
>$1,500	22%	0%	38%
Time in current residence			
1–3 months	16%	69%	2%
4–12 months	21%	0%	12%
13–24 months	63%	31%	86%

group. Self-esteem was measured by the mothers' responses to the following questions:

Most people see me as a warm and friendly person.
I usually feel happy and outgoing.
I often feel lonely.
I seldom take "no" for an answer.
I feel sad for days on end.
I am optimistic about the future.

TABLE 4.2

Past Problems of Children's Biological Mothers

Problem recorded for mother	Home children	Foster children
Drugs/alcohol	32%	50%
Mental illness	26%	17%
Imprisonment	16%	43%
N	*19*	*12*
One or more problems	53%	75%
N	*19*	*12*
Abused/neglected as child	53%	27%
N	*19*	*11*

NOTE: Each mother could have more than one problem.

The "embeddedness" or social isolation variable is composed of the following items:

Do you have relatives who you are in contact with regularly?
Do you have friends living in this area?
Do you have a good friend you can depend on when you are in need?
Do you have neighbors who you talk to regularly?
Do you belong to any church, club, or other organized group?
Do you regularly participate in group activities?
Do people ever call on you to help them out?
Do you know people who can help when you or your family are in trouble?
I often feel lonely.
Do you work outside the home?

A respondent's score on each measure is simply the number of items answered in a positive direction.

The mothers of the children placed in foster homes tended to fall in the lower categories of embeddedness and self-esteem. These differences probably reflect both actual differences between the two groups and the fact that the biological mothers of foster children answered the self-esteem questions shortly after their children were removed from their homes. Some of the mothers may have been feeling bad about themselves during that time. A mother's participation in a social network may also have been affected by the removal of her children; whereas agencies encouraged the home parents to establish and draw on social networks, these were less obviously valuable to parents whose children were removed. To place these scores in some context, we also

TABLE 4.3
Self-Esteem and Social Embeddedness of Biological Mothers

Scale (number of positive answers)	Home ($N = 19$)	Foster ($N = 13$)	Comparison ($N = 42$)
Self-esteem			
Low (0 to 3)	22%	39%	2%
High (4 to 5)	78	61	98
Parental embeddedness			
Low (-8 to -1)	11%	39%	0%
Moderate (0 to 3)	39	46	4
High (4 to 10)	50	15	96

administered the self-esteem and embeddedness scales to the mothers of the comparison children. There were significant differences between the two groups. In general the comparison parents fell at the high end of the scales; the parents of abused or neglected children showed much greater variation. Only one of the comparison group parents was in the low range of self-esteem; none scored in the lowest range on embeddedness. See Table 4.3.

Although the mothers of the foster children scored lower than home mothers, on average,[9] there was more variation within these groups than between them. Within both the home and foster groups, several mothers responded positively to all the embeddedness and self-esteem questions; in contrast, one mother in each group saw herself as sad, lonely, pessimistic, not happy, perceived by others as cold and unfriendly, and as lacking any social support system. The scores of the remaining mothers in each group tended to be spread along the full continuum.

We looked at one other aspect of the families that might be related to the child's well-being at the time of intervention. Through the Moos Family Environment Scale we assessed the nature of the relationship within the family as well as the management of the family system as a whole.[10] The scores of the home and foster groups were similar, with the only major difference coming in the area of parental control, where the home parents reported themselves as more controlling.[11] This is not surprising given that the home group had proportionally more abuse cases than the foster group. We would expect abusive parents to be more controlling than neglecting ones.

OVERALL MEASURE

To test further for differences between groups of mothers, we combined the three behavioral problem categories (drug/alcohol, mental illness, imprisonment), a history of abuse or neglect, low self-esteem, and low embeddedness variables to form one score, with one point awarded for each problem. We again find a high degree of similarity, with the home group containing more mothers with no risk factors:

Risk factors	Home (N = 19)	Foster (N = 12)	Risk factors	Home (N = 19)	Foster (N = 12)
0	26%	8%	4	0%	0%
1	26	23	5	5	8
2	26	38	6	0	0
3	16	23			

SUMMARY

Based on the mothers' backgrounds, we expected that the children who were placed in foster care would be worse off developmentally, to the extent that the socioeconomic and psychological factors we described are related to child development. However, abusing and neglecting parents differed in background characteristics. The neglecting parents tended to be poorer, less educated, and more "pathological" in terms of drug or alcohol use or mental illness. In fact, the group differences between the home and foster mothers, in terms of these variables, is accounted for by the larger percentage of neglect cases in the foster group. We therefore looked for differences in the development of the children depending on whether they had been abused or neglected.

The Children

As we noted earlier, we faced a substantial methodological problem inasmuch as we did not interview any of the children until after intervention and after placement of the foster children; we gathered data for one of our measures, the social competence scale, the second time we interviewed the mothers, three months after the initial interviews. For the foster children, the foster (rather than the biological) mothers completed this scale. Undoubtedly, the children acted differently in foster care than in their own homes.[12] Likewise, the teacher ratings were obtained three to five months after intervention. Thus, for the

TABLE 4.4
Age and Sex of Home and Foster Children

Category	Home (N = 19)	Foster (N = 13)	Category	Home (N = 19)	Foster (N = 13)
Age (years)			Age (years)		
4	5%	8%	9	16%	8%
5	16	24	10	5	15
6	16	8	Sex		
7	21	30	Male	69	62
8	21	8	Female	31	38

foster children, much of our initial data pertained to the children's experience in foster care.

Whereas most of the measures on the home children were obtained within three weeks of agency intervention (except for teacher ratings and the social competence scale), these data may not be a true "baseline" either. By then, social services had been initiated for most families, though it is unlikely that any services had substantial impact in only three weeks. In fact, it is more likely that at least some scores for home children were abnormally low, since this was a crisis period for most of the families and the children were being interviewed shortly after the event that triggered intervention. In addition, half the children had been placed in foster homes for a short period (one to three days) during investigation of the abuse or neglect report, an experience that upsets many children.

Even those initial measures that called for retrospective assessments by the mothers (for example, questions regarding the child's health since birth or the child's behavioral problems prior to intervention) may have been affected by the timing of the initial interventions. Obviously, past behavior is not affected by an intervention. However, at the time of the initial interviews, the biological mothers were not in comparable positions. The home mothers were living with their children, and their "retrospective" reports might well have been influenced by current problems. In contrast, the foster children had not lived with their biological mothers for two to four months; these mothers relied totally on memory and may have been remembering happier days (or bleaker ones). In addition, they were motivated to present an image of a happier situation since they were, for the most part, striving to regain custody of their children.[13]

Thus, many of our initial data were obtained at a time when there was already an impact of intervention, especially for the foster children. For certain measures, such as IQ and height, the timing probably made little difference. For other measures the impact of placement probably was quite pronounced. We cannot know, based on initial scores, if the children's development was comparable prior to intervention.

The two groups were similar in age and gender distributions. See Table 4.4. As we will show in Chapter 5, the children's scores on IQ tests and their physical health also seem quite comparable. However, on a number of other measures, at the time of our initial interviews, the foster children appeared better off than the home children. For example, foster children scored higher on our measures of self-esteem and peer relations. They were rated more favorably on social skills by their teachers. To judge from the descriptions of mothers, behaviors prior to removal were better among foster children than among the home children. We therefore face the question of whether the children in the two groups were different developmentally *prior to intervention*. We discuss this issue at the end of Chapter 5, after presenting the baseline scores broken down by home and foster placement.

Five

The Children: Initial Assessments

The Relevance of the Data

The social workers who first respond to reports that a child has been abused or neglected know little more about the child than that she has been physically injured, or left unattended, or neglected in some other way; rarely do they have information about the child's developmental status. Is the child healthy? Experiencing emotional problems? Academic problems? How does the child perceive her situation? Even by the time the child is placed in foster care or left at home under agency supervision, little information has been obtained about the child's development by the social worker.[1] The investigation process focuses mainly on the parents.

Thus, we first learned about a child's general well-being when we interviewed the children and their caretakers. We were concerned with the children's initial developmental status for two reasons. First, the initial scores provided the base-line for each child and each placement group, against which we measured change over time. Second, the children's initial status, seen in conjunction with data on the comparison children, provided some indication of the impact of the children's home environments on their development. The data in this chapter compare the thirty-two white abused or neglected children with the forty-two white children in our comparison sample.[2] The comparison children provided a norm for assessing the degree to which the abused or neglected children were at risk. In addition, changes in the comparison children during the two years of the study provided a trend-line of "normal" change against which we could measure change in the home and foster groups.

The General Picture: Preliminary Considerations

On first meeting the children, our field staff were surprised. Most of the children were attractive, appeared healthy, and talked readily with their new "friends." As they got to know the children better, the staff's initial impressions changed. The interviewers found many children to be frightened and anxious, and noticed subtle differences between the mistreated and comparison children in mood, demeanor, and cleanliness. We later discovered that many of the abused and neglected children had substantial social and academic deficits. As a group, the children clearly seemed damaged. Yet there was an enormous range in the well-being of the children. A few were doing reasonably well in most respects; four or five others were doing extremely badly in virtually every way. Most commonly, however, a child functioned well in one domain but poorly in another. Three children illustrate these points.

Larry, age nine, was doing poorly in all domains. He was referred to child protective services by school authorities when he came to school badly bruised. His mother had beaten him in the face and over his body with a belt. His parents stated that he had severe behavioral problems at home and would not respond to discipline. They reported a history of fire-setting, lying, stealing, fighting with siblings, and poor peer relations. Larry also felt that he had trouble making friends. He was unhappy in school and showed relatively low self-esteem. He stated that he got along badly with his parents. His teacher characterized him as hard to control and difficult to like and as having bad peer relations.

In contrast Tommie, age eight, whose mother was depressed and provided poor physical care, seemed to be doing reasonably well in most areas. Tommie showed high self-esteem, loved school, and felt he had good friends. His teacher liked him and said he was academically adequate, but felt that he had problems with peer relations. His mother felt that Tommie was well behaved, but was concerned that he was too withdrawn.

Rachel, age five, presented a mixed picture. She had been hit by her father when she tried to break up a fight between him and his girlfriend. He was under the influence of drugs at the time. There was a long history of parental neglect. Yet Rachel was well liked by her teacher and her foster mother, and seemed to be socially and academically adequate in school. She was well behaved in her foster home. However, Rachel was unhappy, was low in self-esteem, and felt that other children did not like her.

In the following sections a picture will emerge of the abused and neglected children as a group. In reading the descriptions, which are filled with group averages, it is important to remember that the range on many variables was great; abuse and neglect do not have invariable outcomes for children. There were nevertheless consistent differences between home and foster children. On most measures the foster children, on average, were rated higher, or reported as exhibiting fewer problems, than the home children. However, none of these differences was statistically significant. What accounts for these differences? Do they indicate that there were group differences prior to placement? Do they reflect a positive impact of foster care? Or are they just random variation? We discuss this issue at the end of the chapter.[3]

Physical Health

Since previous studies emphasized the prevalence of medical problems among abused and neglected children, we were suprised that our initial health screening revealed relatively few health problems among the children in either setting.[4] The children—particularly the home children—were of normal or above-normal height and weight; the mean height percentiles for the home and foster groups, respectively, were 64 and 55, and the mean weight percentiles 70 and 54.[5] A few children might have been at risk in terms of physical development: one home child and three foster children fell below the 35th percentile in both height and weight. Although these children's small statures might have been related to a history of malnourishment or poor care, this number of small children would be expected in any distribution.

The physical screening examinations also yielded relatively little serious pathology. Of the nineteen children in the home group three (16 percent) experienced vision problems, as did one (8 percent) of twelve children in the foster group.[6] As for hearing problems, the numbers were two (home 10 percent, foster 15 percent) for each group. The figures are similar to national norms for these ages.[7] An evaluation of coordination was done by looking at the child's ability to hop on one foot, walk a straight line, and do finger pointing, and by observing the child's gait. Pathology was noted if two tests were abnormal. Four home children (21 percent) and two foster children (17 percent) showed some sign of coordination problems; the U.S. norm is approximately 5 percent. We looked to see whether there were any children who evidenced several health problems; two home children (10 percent) and one foster child (8 percent) had two or more problems. There was some evidence of poor care and possible past abuse. Nine (47 percent) of the home children and five (38 percent) of the foster children had scars. Five (26 percent) of the home children and two (15 percent) of the foster children had rashes and bruises. However, none of the children seemed in bad current health.

The mothers' ratings of the children's current health also were generally positive for both groups of children. Although we might tend to discount such reports by abusive or neglectful parents, our more objective data support and give credibility to their assessments. About three-fourths of all mothers reported their child's present health as very good or excellent. Most mothers stated that the child's health in past years had been good. However, more of the abusing/neglecting mothers than comparison parents reported a history of at least one serious accident (six versus four, respectively), which we would expect of abused and neglected children.

To give some sense of the type of problems we found, we present a brief vignette of one child with relatively poor health.

Rachel, a five-year-old girl, entered the study because of physical abuse by her father. The father and mother were separated and Rachel was sent by her mother to live with her father despite his history of alcohol and drug abuse.

At the time of the county examination immediately following the abuse incident, Rachel's right eye was swollen and her right lower jaw was bruised. Otherwise she was described as a pretty, tiny, precocious five-year-old, self-sufficient and aware of her surroundings and in good physical health. At our examination sometime later she was described as looking healthy, though somewhat dirty from play. On questioning she stated that she felt good "but not all the time." She also stated "I get tummy aches when I eat, ain't very good about eating." Her height was at the 30th percentile and her weight at the 40th percentile.

The physical examination was normal except for mosquito bites on her legs. She did have difficulties with coordination and hearing. She was not able to walk in a straight line, nor jump while hopping on her left foot, and was inaccurate with pointing to her nose on the finger-to-nose test. She had difficulty with visual convergence and obviously squinted when she read the chart. However, vision was tested at 20/30 for both eyes. Her hearing appeared to be normal. In sum, she was a basically healthy child, somewhat on the small side with some minimal signs of neurological damage.

Several factors may account for the reasonably good physical condition of our sample, as compared with the findings in other studies: our children were older than those in most studies, thus failure-to-thrive cases were eliminated; our sample was not drawn from a hospital-based population, as is the case with many studies; we excluded from the study the most seriously abused children, who might have been in the worst physical condition. In all these respects our sample was more typical of the average case of reported abuse or neglect for this age group than most studies. Thus, our children's health and physical development may also have been typical of most abused and neglected children of their ages.

IQ

All the children were given Wechsler IQ tests. The majority scored in the normal range, as shown in Table 5.1. There were no differences between the home and foster groups on the verbal portion; the home children's average score was somewhat higher on the performance portion of the test.

Academic Performance

To assess academic performance, we gathered data from school records and children's teachers. Unfortunately there are many gaps in the data. To a large extent, the missing data evidenced the problems the children were having during the course of our study. Four of ten home children and three of the four foster children for whom we had adequate records were absent from classes more than 10 percent of the year preceding intervention. In contrast, only one child of the forty-two in our comparison group missed that much school. Because of their high rates of absenteeism, the study children often were not present when standardized tests were given. Some school records were incomplete or totally missing, either because some children changed schools so often that the system was unable to keep track of them or because of poor record-keeping by the school system.

Despite the gaps, we were able to piece together, through a variety of indicators, a picture of the children's performance over the two-year period. As we shall show in Chapter 8, most of the children had major academic difficulties throughout the two years. This was true regardless of placement. However, we have many fewer data about the children's initial academic status. We do not have measures of preintervention academic performance for half the home sample or for any of the foster children. One-fourth of the home and nearly half of the foster chil-

TABLE 5.1
Initial Scores of Home and Foster Children on IQ Tests

IQ	Home (N = 19)	Foster (N = 13)
Verbal		
Mean	95.9	94.1
SD	15.9	14.2
Median	100.0	95.0
Range	62–120	75–114
Performance		
Mean	103.1	92.2
SD	15.8	16.2
Median	105.0	92.0
Range	77–135	49–114
Total		
Mean	98.6	92.6
SD	15.7	14.1
Median	96.0	93.0
Range	68–126	63–114

dren were in kindergarten or preschool at the time of intervention. None of these children had grades or test scores. Moreover, the majority of the first-graders had either missed or not been given standardized tests. None of the foster children had taken any standardized tests in the years prior to intervention. It should be noted that even if we had had a complete set of grades for each child, comparisons would have been difficult. As Fanshel and Shinn (1978) discuss, grades from different elementary schools tend to be either meaningless or noncomparable. Some schools give only written reports, some use a pass–fail system, and others use letter grades. Some schools give all kindergarten and first-grade children A's. We therefore recommend that other researchers give children standardized tests if they want to assess school achievement.

Although we cannot tell much about either group prior to intervention, we know that shortly after intervention many of the children were rated at or near the bottom of their classes by their teachers. Despite the normal IQ distribution in both groups, only one abused or neglected child was rated above-average academically; thirteen home children (70 percent) and six foster children (46 percent) were considered below-average academically by their teachers. In contrast, twenty-nine (68 percent) of the comparison children were rated average or above. Three of the home children were in special education classes at the time of intervention and three of the foster children had previously had to repeat one year's courses owing to poor academic performance, which further indicates that children in both home and foster groups were at risk.

Behavioral and Emotional Problems

PAST AND CURRENT PROBLEMS

We were more surprised by the children's poor school performance than by the evidence that many children displayed problems in the psychological realm. Previous studies reported that a significant number of abused or neglected children evidenced emotional problems (Martin 1976). Unfortunately, our children were no different. According to the mothers, the majority of the abused or neglected children had been referred for psychological counseling and many had exhibited pathological behaviors.[8] We asked the mothers, "Has your child ever been referred to or seen by a psychiatrist, psychologist, or counselor for behavioral and/or emotional problems prior to the current county intervention?" An extremely large number of children had been referred. Fifteen (79 percent) of the nineteen home mothers and eight (62 percent) of the thirteen mothers of foster children reported referral. Abused children were more likely to have been referred than neglected children. In contrast, only twelve (28 percent) of the forty-two comparison children's mothers reported referral. This latter figure is consistent with epidemiological data on childhood psychological and behavioral problems.

We also inquired about certain behaviors that most clinicians regard as symptomatic of psychological problems. These behaviors were vandalism, fire-setting, stealing, running away, hoarding food, self-inflicted injury, tantrums, and daytime wetting. The mothers first were asked whether their child had *ever* exhibited such behavior. Seventeen (89 percent) of the nineteen home children, eight (62 percent) of the thirteen foster children, and twenty-five of the forty-two (59 percent) comparison children had exhibited one or more such behaviors at some time. The primary difference between the groups was that the abused and neglected children often evidenced multiple symptomatic behaviors, whereas most comparison children exhibited only a single such behavior, and, in most cases, only a single instance. Except with regard to tantrums, the abused children tended to exhibit more prob-

TABLE 5.2

Mother's Initial Reports of Children's Recurring Extreme Behavioral Problems in Past Year

Behavior	Home (N = 18)	Foster (N = 12)	Comparison (N = 42)
Vandalism	5 (28%)	1 (8%)	2 (5%)
Fire-setting	3 (17)	1 (8)	2 (5)
Stealing	4 (22)	1 (8)	2 (5)
Running away	2 (11)	0	0
Hoarding food	5 (28)	2 (17)	3 (7)
Tantrums	5 (28)	3 (17)	9 (22)
Self-injury	0	1 (8)	0
Daytime wetting	2 (11)	0	1 (2)

lems than the neglected children. To further survey symptoms, we asked if behaviors that might be indicative of depression had ever been exhibited, for example, staring into space, acting withdrawn, or being very fearful. Although twelve of the thirty-two mothers reported that the child had regularly exhibited one such behavior, only two children were reported to have exhibited two such behaviors.

To obtain current base-line data, we asked the mothers to report whether any of the symptomatic behaviors had occurred during the past twelve months, either once, episodically, or chronically. A smaller number of children exhibited one or more behaviors during the past year, especially with regard to fire-setting and tantrums, than had exhibited them at least one other earlier time. Still, the abused and neglected group showed somewhat more problems than did the comparison children, and the home mothers reported more problems than the mothers of the foster children. See Table 5.2. Two-thirds of abused/ neglected children's mothers (twenty-one of thirty-two) also reported that the child was overactive and easily distracted.

Finally we determined the number of children in each group who were reported to be in therapy at the time of entry into the study.[9] Seven home children (37 percent) were in therapy; two other children were in special education classes because of psychological problems. In the foster group, two children (16 percent) were in therapy, and one child was in a special education class.

The following vignettes provide some flavor of the children evidencing more severe emotional problems.

Robert, an eight-year-old, was reported to protective services by the manager of the motel in which he lived with his mother, father, and older brother. The manager noticed that Robert was extensively bruised. Both children told police that they had been beaten with a heavily-buckled belt and had previously been kicked, choked, and beaten. School records indicated that Robert was considered hyperactive. His mother described him as high-strung, with a strong temper and a short fuse. Besides hyperactivity, she cited as serious problems his refusal to obey, screaming, tantrums, lying, and arguing with and hitting other children. In the past few months, Robert had regularly engaged in vandalism and stealing, set four or five fires, and hoarded food. Robert had low self-esteem and poor peer relations.[10]

Maryanne, six years old, was reported to protective services by the school nurse, who noticed numerous bruises, scratches, and black-and-blue marks on her back, arms, buttocks, and thighs. These injuries were from punishment administered by her mother, with a paddle, because Maryanne had gone to school with "her hair messed up." At least three previous episodes of neglect and/or beatings had been reported to authorities. Her mother reported that she hit Maryanne because she had no effective means of controlling Maryanne's behavior, especially her propensity to wander away from home on her own. She also reported that Maryanne stole, had tantrums, and hurt herself by pulling at her hair; and further described Maryanne as pouting and complaining a great deal. She noted that she was irritable, easily distracted, refused to obey, and lied. Many of these behaviors also were reported by the foster mother at the time Maryanne entered placement.

INITIAL IMPACT OF FOSTER CARE ON CHILDREN'S EMOTIONAL FUNCTIONING

One of the most commonly voiced concerns over foster care is that the trauma of separation will cause emotional problems for children, which will be reflected in acting-out behaviors, sleep or eating disorders, excessive fear, or withdrawal. To examine this, we asked the foster parents to describe any emotional problems the children were exhibiting. Although they could report only open manifestations of adjustment problems—and were probably predisposed to find good adjustments[11]—they did relate important information regarding the emotional well-being of the children.

We were able to compare the foster parents' reports with the biological mothers' reports of what the child was like prior to removal. Thus, we were able to see if foster placement appeared to cause problems, or if problems were a continuation of past behaviors. We looked first to see if the children appeared to become withdrawn or depressed following placement. Although foster placement may have resulted in such behaviors for some children, there was a diminution of them in other children. Four foster mothers indicated that the child was often fearful, unhappy, worried, or prone to stare into space. No child, however, exhibited more than one such behavior; three had not evidenced these problems at home, according to their mothers. There were also four children who exhibited one or more of these problems at home but not in foster care.

A similar pattern emerged with regard to acting-out behavior. As previously discussed, such behavior was frequently reported by the parent of the abused and neglected children. Six of the thirteen foster parents reported the child to be "very active," easily distracted, or excessively fidgety. According to their biological mothers, three of these six children had behaved in this manner at home; three others reported no such behavior. Three children exhibited the behavior at home but not in foster care. With regard to the extreme behaviors of stealing and vandalism, four children exhibited such behaviors following placement; two of the four had done so in their original homes as well. Three other children had exhibited these behaviors at home but did not in foster care.

Overall, foster care did not seem to generate problem behaviors in the majority of children, though some such behaviors seemed to emerge for about a quarter of the children. Foster placement did seem to affect some aspects of the children's well-being, however. Consistent with reports in other studies, many of the children evidenced regressive behaviors, such as bed-wetting, nightmares or sleep problems, and eating problems. Four children began bed-wetting at night and two became daytime wetters. Six children initially had eating problems, including one who hoarded food (for three of the six children this had ceased to be a problem by the time of our interview). Several children also experienced sleep problems. Clearly, the children were showing signs of emotional stress.

Social Behavior: Home and School

A number of studies report that abused and neglected children are socially immature, unable to engage in give-and-take, and often make excessive demands on others (Egeland, Sroufe, and Erickson 1983). Other studies show high levels of parent-child conflict in abusing families (Burgess and Conger 1978). Because poor social behavior can affect children's relations with peers and teachers, as well as lead to abusive parental behavior, we were interested in the child's social development. Both the parents and the teachers gave the children low ratings on social competence and likeability; the teachers also reported that the children had problems with peer relations. In light of the literature reporting substantial initial adjustment problems for foster children, we were surprised that, on average, the foster children seemed to be adjusting reasonably well.

PARENT-CHILD RELATIONS: SOCIAL BEHAVIOR AT HOME

Problem behaviors. Our measures of the children's behavior at home came from interviews with the mothers. These provided only maternal perceptions of the child's behavior. As a result, we cannot know whether children who were said to "nag a lot" by their mothers actually behaved differently from other children. It may well be that abusive or neglectful parents have distorted perceptions of their children's behavior. They may view common behaviors such as crying or whining as more offensive or problematic than would other parents. However, whether the behavior is "real" or perceived, the parent's perceptions are likely to affect the child's world. There is likely to be more family conflict if the mother perceives the child as difficult. In addition, children seen as difficult may be at increased risk of being abused, neglected, or emotionally rejected. Thus, whether one child's behavior actually differed from another's, or the mothers' perceptions differed, a mother's view of her child might tell us something about whether the two groups of children were at equal risk of further maltreatment. It must be remembered, though, that the biological mothers of the foster children rated them retrospectively, after they had been in care for some time. We do not know how much, or in which direction, this affected their responses.

Using the child behavior scale described in Chapter 3, we sought to determine whether the mothers were experiencing problems arising from common behaviors expressed by all children at some time. These behaviors were crying, whining, pouting, complaining, yelling or screaming, disobeying, and lying. We asked the mother whether her child exhibited each behavior a lot, a little, or not at all during the past month (for the foster children, their biological mothers were asked to think back to the month before placement).[12] If the mother said that the child evidenced a behavior "a lot," we asked her to describe the conduct more fully and indicate whether the behavior was a problem for her. We counted only behaviors the mothers considered to be problems.

TABLE 5.3

Initial Reports, by Biological Mothers, of Problematic Child Behaviors

Number of behaviors	Home (N = 19)	Foster (N = 13)	Comparison (N = 42)
0–1	8 (42%)	11 (84%)	33 (79%)
2–3	4 (21)	1 (8)	8 (19)
4–7	7 (37)	1 (8)	1 (2)

NOTE: Seven problem behaviors were identified: crying, whining, pouting, complaining, yelling, disobeying, and lying.

Most home mothers found their children's behaviors problematic. This was not true of the mothers of the foster children. Table 5.3 shows the number of behaviors reported as problems, and their distributions. Almost three-fifths of the mothers of the home children reported two or more problem behaviors. Over a third reported four or more. Surprisingly, there were no abuse-versus-neglect differences: we had expected that abusive parents might report more problems. In contrast, most mothers whose children were in foster care remembered them as well-behaved: 84 percent (eleven mothers) reported one negative behavior or none. Were these children in fact better-behaved while at home? It seems unlikely that they had as few behavioral problems as the comparison children, given that their mothers reported that many of the children had evidenced psychopathology and extreme behaviors. It may be that "absence made the heart grow fonder" or that, with respect to acting-out behaviors, out of sight meant out of mind.

We do have some evidence that the children who entered foster care may, in fact, have been somewhat less prone to such behaviors as crying and whining. After the children entered foster care, the foster mothers rated them on these behaviors. We compared the biological mothers' reports with those of the foster mothers. The reports were generally consistent. Like the biological mothers, the foster mothers saw the children as well-behaved. Only one foster child was described as exhibiting as many as two problem behaviors. Of course, the children may have behaved better in foster care. It is also possible that the foster mothers, who were paid to deal with children's behaviors, might have been less likely to categorize a given behavior as a *problem* for them. Several of the foster mothers told us in general conversation that the child had been lying a lot or refusing to obey. However, they rarely listed these as problems on the CBS. Thus, we cannot assume that the

TABLE 5.4

Caretakers' Initial Ratings of Children's Social Competence

Measure	Home (N = 19)	Foster (N = 11)	Comparison (N = 42)
Mean	3.2	3.2	3.6
SD	0.5	0.6	0.5
Range	2.3–3.8	2.1–4.1	2.8–4.4

coincidence of reports proves that the foster children were better behaved *prior to intervention.*

Social competence. Our second instrument looking at the children's behavior focused on the child's potential interpersonal strengths, as well as weaknesses. We asked the home children's mothers and the *foster* mothers[13] to rate the children on thirty behaviors reflecting social skills. The items examined the child's willingness to follow rules, to help others, to take the initiative, to show independence, and to be considerate toward others. The scale also contained some negative behaviors, such as unwillingness to quiet down, nagging, or whining. Thus it overlapped, in part, with the child behavior scale. Each behavior was rated on a 1–5 scale, 5 denoting the most competent. A principal-components analysis yielded twenty items that were highly correlated. The twenty-item ratings were summed and averaged to yield a single composite score.

The average social competence scores of the abused and neglected children, which were the same for the home and foster groups, were somewhat lower than those of the comparison children. See Table 5.4. However, the overall averages mask important information. The lower scores of the home children were accounted for primarily by low ratings on items that looked at parent-child interaction, for example, taking too long to do a job or picking the wrong time to ask a question. The lower scores of the foster children were due primarily to low ratings on sharing items; for example, the foster children were reported as unwilling to share toys or food. Surprisingly, there were no group differences on the items related to initiative, autonomy, or task persistence. This pattern continued over time (as discussed in Chapter 8). We have concluded that this scale is more a measure of parent-child interaction than of a more general set of social skills displayed by the child.[14] The mothers' responses to this scale indicated again that the home children experienced more negative parent-child interactions than the foster children.

TEACHER-CHILD RELATIONSHIPS:
SOCIAL BEHAVIOR AT SCHOOL

Social competence at school. Children must, of course, interact with teachers and other children, as well as with their caretakers. In order to assess the children's social functioning at school, we asked the teachers to fill out a questionnaire (the social behavior scale) similar to the caretaker social competence instrument, except that the items pertained to the classroom setting.[15] There were twenty items. Typical questions were: "Does the child work on class activities and assignments independently?"; ". . . quiet down when asked?"; ". . . need help or suggestions to get started in a task, activity, game?"; ". . . misbehave when you don't let him/her have his/her way?"; ". . . nag or whine until he/she gets something?" The responses, which could range from never to most of the time, were scored on a 1-to-5 rating scale. The scores were summed and averaged to get a composite score. A higher score meant greater skills.

We also asked the teachers five questions that were combined as a measure of how likable the teacher found the child. The items were: "Some children are easy to be around. How easy do you find it to be around the child?" "Some children are more physically attractive than others. Compared to most children you know, how attractive do you find this child?" "Compared to most children you know, how hard do you find it to deal with this child?" "Some children are very likable. How likable do you consider the child to be?" "Children don't always want to do what is asked of them. Compared to other children you know, how often does this child not do or refuse to do something you ask?" Each item was scored +2 or −2, with a possible range of +10 to −10.[16]

On both measures, the home children received lower ratings than the foster and comparison children. See Table 5.5. The difference was more pronounced with regard to likability. The similarity between the foster and comparison children was surprising. The home–foster differences may have been confounded by abuse–neglect differences. The three abused children in foster care were extremely well liked by their teachers. Among the neglected children the foster children were rated higher than the home children, but the differences were small.[17]

Peer relations. The teachers felt that the abused and neglected children functioned poorly in their relations with other children (in fact the teachers had a much more negative view than did the children—

TABLE 5.5

Teachers' Initial Ratings of Children's Social Behavior and Likability

Measure	Home	Foster	Comparison
Social behavior			
Mean	3.2	3.5	3.8
SD	0.5	0.7	0.6
Range	2.0–4.1	2.3–4.5	2.6–4.7
N	*18*	*8*	*42*
Likability			
Mean	1.1	3.6	3.9
SD	4.3	4.5	4.2
Range	−8–+7	−3–+9	−7–+9
N	*17*	*8*	*42*

TABLE 5.6

Teachers' Initial Ratings of Children's Peer Relations

Measure	Home (*N* = 17)	Foster (*N* = 8)	Comparison (*N* = 42)
Mean	−1.9	−0.3	1.6
SD	3.9	3.1	4.0
Range	−10–+5	−6–+3	−10–+8

see the following section). We asked the teachers: "How well do you think this child gets along with other children?" "How friendly and outgoing among playmates do you consider this child to be?" "How liked and accepted by peers is this child?" "How often does this child direct and lead others?" "How effective is this child in getting his way around other children?" Each item was scored +2 to −2 with a possible range of +10 to −10 for the total score.

The abused and neglected children were rated well below the comparison children. See Table 5.6. Only one child of the seventeen home children for whom we had scores was ranked in the top 40 percent of her school class in social rank. The picture was just slightly better for the foster children. In contrast, thirty-two of the forty-two comparison children were ranked in the top 40 percent of their classes. The low ratings by teachers seem to indicate that most of the abused and neglected children, both at home and in foster care, either developed negative interpersonal behaviors or failed to develop positive behaviors, which carried over to their conduct at school.

Children's Personal Satisfaction

Their parents found many of the children difficult to deal with. Their teachers felt that they lacked social and academic skills. The majority of children had been referred for psychological help. By any standard, most of the children had suffered more than their share of pain, inattention, and physical and emotional deprivation. In light of all this, how did the children see their lives?

We asked the children questions exploring how they got along with peers, how they liked school, and whether they felt happy, lucky, and capable of doing things well. Their responses reflected the negative impact of their environment. Although there was substantial variation within each group, overall the abused and neglected children were less happy with their lives than the comparison sample. We must note, however, that the children's responses varied significantly over time. Their responses to the items on our self-esteem measure seemed particularly affected by temporary situational factors.

SELF-ESTEEM

We adapted our measure of self-esteem from Zill's index of self-esteem, which he used on a national sample of children (Zill 1976). The children were asked twelve questions that looked at both general happiness and feelings of competence in interpersonal relations. The items were:

I am lucky.
I often wish I were someone else.
I'm easy to like.
I'm happy most of the time.
I really don't like being a boy/girl.
Kids usually follow my ideas.
I feel lonely.
I can do many things well.
I am always getting into trouble.
I sometimes feel I can't learn.
I like being the way I am.
I do many bad things.

Each item was scored $+1$ or -1, allowing possible scores of $+12$ to -12. Although there was substantial overlap in the scores of the children from all groups, the abused and neglected children, especially in the

TABLE 5.7
Children's Initial Self-Esteem Scores

Measure	Home (N = 17)[a]	Foster (N = 13)	Comparison (N = 42)
Score intervals			
−12−0	8 (47%)	3 (24%)	6 (14%)
1−6	8 (47)	8 (60)	17 (40)
7−12	1 (6)	2 (16)	19 (46)
Mean score	0.8	3.6	5.2
SD	4.7	4.8	4.7
Range	−8−+8	−4−+12	−8−+12

[a] We do not include data for two children who were sufficiently incoherent during their interviews that we judged the interviews to be unreliable.

home group, clearly had poorer self-images. The children's self-esteem scores are shown in Table 5.7.

Based on the average scores, the home and foster groups appear quite different. However, the scores of the abused children differed from those of neglected children, with abused children having much lower scores. When we controlled for the different ratio of abused-to-neglected children in each group, the foster children still perceived themselves somewhat more positively than home children did, but the difference was smaller. Looking at all the children, the most striking finding is the absence of high scores among the abused and neglected children, regardless of placement, relative to the comparison group: nearly half the comparison children scored in the highest range of the scale, in contrast to 6 and 16 percent, respectively, of the study's home and foster children. The abused and neglected children generally were most pessimistic about themselves and their lives. In particular, they were much more likely to report that they "did many bad things" and "got into trouble a lot."

PEER RELATIONS

We assessed the children's peer satisfaction based on their responses to the following questions: How do you get along with kids in this neighborhood? Do you ever feel lonely and wish you had more friends? Do you like most of the kids in your class? Do most of the kids in your class like you? Do kids usually follow your ideas? Each item was scored +2 or −2, creating a scale that ranged from −10 to +10. Overall, the abused and neglected children were not positive about their peer rela-

TABLE 5.8
Children's Initial Ratings of Peer Relations

Measure	Home (N = 16)	Foster (N = 12)	Comparison (N = 42)
Mean	1.3	2.5	4.2
SD	4.8	4.0	4.2
Range	−10−+10	−6−+7	−10−+10

tions, though they did not see their situations as bleakly as their teachers did. Nevertheless, these children perceived their relations more negatively than the comparison children did. See Table 5.8. In particular, the abused and the neglected children were much more likely to feel that "kids don't follow my ideas" than were the comparison children. The abused (but not the neglected) children also were more likely to report that other children did not like them. All abused children, both at home and in foster care, reported more negatively about relations than did the neglected children. When we looked at responses of abused and neglected children separately, we found no differences correlating with foster or home placement; the higher average score for foster children results from the greater proportion of neglected children in foster care.

SCHOOL SATISFACTION

The children were doing poorly in school, academically and socially. Thus, we might expect them to dislike school. Many foster children had been in several schools by the time we saw them. To test the children's attitudes toward school we asked them four questions: "Do you like your teacher?" "Are you interested in your school work?" "How do you feel about going to school?" "Would you rather go to another school?" Each item was scaled +2 or −2, creating a scale ranging from −8 to +8.

The majority of children in all three groups seemed to like school.[18] There was no evidence that their poor school performance, the multiple placements experienced by the foster children, or the frequent change of schools experienced by many of the home children created a negative attitude toward school. Perhaps children of this age are not prepared to criticize school. Whatever the reason, this aspect of the child's world did not seem to be affected by their home environments or by foster placement.

Contrasting the Abused and Neglected
with Comparison Children

Except in a few cases, the abused and neglected children seemed damaged, not destroyed. Although nearly half the children came to the attention of state officials because of physical abuse, few children evidenced significant physical harm. Based on the parents' past behavior it seemed likely that at least four or five families might seriously abuse the child absent intervention; in the remaining cases the threat of future serious physical harm to the child seemed relatively minimal.

Many more of the children were threatened emotionally. Half had been referred for psychological counseling, even prior to the incident that brought them to our attention; many still showed psychological problems. At least a third of the parents considered their children to be problems. The teachers reported that a majority of the children were not accepted by their peers or liked by the teachers themselves. Many children, despite general satisfaction with their schools and neighborhoods, had low self-esteem, reported problems with peers, and showed signs of depression, anxiety, and fear. Very few abused or neglected children, at home or in foster care, showed positive development when measured against the comparison children. On most measures no more than one or two abused or neglected children ranked in the top 25 percent of the entire group of seventy-four children (thirty-two abused and neglected and forty-two comparison). Finally, though the data were sparse, it seems clear that most of the children were doing very poorly academically, although the majority had average IQ's.

Although the comparison children generally showed more positive development, we cannot attribute the poor development of the abused and neglected children solely to their having been abused or neglected. First, these children had experienced more than abuse or neglect. They came from homes in which there was a great deal of parental conflict; many parents had been divorced and some were mentally ill; studies have found that parental conflict, divorce, and mental illness put children at risk. The comparison sample contained more families with higher incomes and parents who tended to be better educated. Some of the differences in the status of the children were attenuated when we controlled for family structure and income; even then the abused and neglected group was worse off. We could not control for all other possible differences. Because there may be a number of explanations for differences between the children, our findings do not establish the impact of abuse and neglect on the children's development; rather, they show some possible relationships.

Individual Variability

A child experiencing difficulties in one aspect of development was not necessarily doing poorly in others. Five children, all at home, were having troubles in virtually all aspects of development. Most other children presented a mixed picture. Many apparently interacted differently with their parents and their teachers. Not all children with psychological problems had low self-esteem. Children doing poorly academically and socially sometimes had relatively high self-esteem. The varied development of these children emphasizes the importance of our multimeasure approach.

We looked at a number of factors to see if they were related to all the children's initial status. The abused and neglected children were worse off than the comparison children regardless of their parent's income, marital status, or education. Within the abused and neglected group, abused children tended to have lower overall well-being than neglected children, primarily owing to their low self-esteem and low assessment of their peer relations. They also had more extensive histories of emotional problems. Their parents' marital status, the mother's age when the child was born, and the mother's report of problems with the birth and early care of the child also were related to the abused and neglected children's development. Within this group, children whose mothers were very young at the time of the child's birth were somewhat worse off. This finding is consistent with research indicating that very young parents have limited child-rearing skills. In addition, abused and neglected children from two-parent families had lower ratings than children from single-parent homes. Although initially surprising, the relationship makes sense. In most of the two-parent families of abused or neglected children, there was substantial conflict between the parents, which may have negatively affected the children.[19]

The mother's assessment of pregnancy, delivery, and early caretaking experiences with her infant might be related to problems in early bonding or attachment.[20] We asked the mothers whether they desired the pregnancy, whether the infant was premature, whether there were problems with the delivery, whether there was anything wrong with the infant at delivery, and whether they had been able to care for the child as they desired. The children of the mothers who reported not wanting the pregnancy and problems during pregnancy or delivery had the lowest socioemotional status, based on the child's self-report and the reports by teachers.[21] In addition, the mothers of the five lowest-rated children (all at home) were the only mothers to indicate that the child had been a lot of trouble to raise and that they sometimes wished that they did not have the child to worry about. Two of these mothers also indicated that they did not feel close to the child. Whether this emotional rejection caused the child's problem, resulted from the child's poor behavior, or was a combination of both, we cannot tell. It does seem clear that there was a relationship between the children's well-being and their mothers' feelings about them, which may have dated from the time of pregnancy.

Comparability

At the time of our initial interviews, there were differences between the home and foster groups in the *average* scores received by the children on teacher ratings and in the children's scores on self-esteem and peer relations, though none of the differences were statistically significant. The biological mothers of the foster children reported considerably few *past* problem behaviors (e.g., crying, whining) and somewhat fewer psychological problems. The groups were similar with regard to physical health (although the home children were taller and heavier), IQ, past academic performance, social competence, and school satisfaction.

We have no way of knowing for certain whether the group averages would have been comparable if we had seen the children in each group prior to intervention; obviously, it is possible that, on any given measure, the scores might have been the same, lower, or higher. Can we draw any conclusions from the fact that the foster children had higher initial average scores on a number of measures, including those based on the mothers' reports of how the children behaved prior to the intervention? Were the groups different prior to intervention? Was there an initial positive impact on foster care?

We doubt that such conclusions can be drawn. The higher initial average scores of the foster group do not necessarily mean that the home and foster groups were noncomparable, either prior to intervention or at our initial assessments. None of the differences was statistically significant. They may be accounted for primarily by random fluctuations, which we would expect in any sample of this size. Even though the foster children scored higher on all school and personal satisfaction variables, this may reflect only the fact that these variables are not entirely independent. Moreover, the fact that the group means might have changed significantly for some variables if we had included those children initially at home who were later put into foster care, and the children in foster care who were later returned home, lends support to the view that the differences were more likely random than systematic.

On the other hand, it is possible that the foster children were, in fact, better off prior to intervention. In support of this argument, it might be contended that not only were their initial teacher ratings and personal satisfaction scores higher, but their mothers also rated them as better behaved on the retrospective items. However, there are several reasons to reject this hypothesis. The incidents leading to intervention were similar. So were the background characteristics of the mothers, after we controlled for the difference in the ratio of abused and neglected children in each group. But we do not place much emphasis on the difference in reports by the biological mothers. As discussed previously, we believe that the home group mothers reported more problems than the foster group mothers did because children were living with the home mothers and problems were salient. Problematic behaviors probably were far less salient to the mothers of the foster children, who had not lived with their children for several months. The timing of the initial interviews was another confounding factor. Many caseworkers report an initial "honeymoon period" following placement and our data are consistent with this idea. In contrast, the low personal satisfaction scores of the home children might reflect the fact that we saw these children at a particularly bad time: we were questioning them very shortly after the incident that led to intervention.

A third possibility is that had we tested the children prior to intervention, we might have found that the children who went into foster care were actually in worse shape than those remaining at home. Under this hypothesis, the differences noted during the initial interviews are assumed to reflect the impact of foster care. Some of the higher scores may be related to an initial positive impact of foster care, others to differences in the way foster parents and abusing and neglecting parents perceive (or report) children's behavior, others to biases of the teachers in favor of foster children. The exact timing of the interviews may also account for some differences. Still another, quite different hypothesis is that there might have been real differences between the home and foster groups prior to intervention and the foster children might have shown even higher ratings prior to removal. By this hypothesis, foster care would have had a negative impact, bringing the two groups closer together after intervention than they were before.

Finally, it is possible that some combination of these hypotheses is true and that the children differed—systematically or randomly—on some variables, and were the same on others, with the differences reflecting an impact of foster care, timing, or some other factor(s).

There is no scientific way of determining whether the children were, in fact, comparable prior to intervention. Regardless of which explanation is accepted, the abused and neglected children clearly were at risk of continued poor development. Thus, we are justified in being concerned not only with the risk of reabuse or continued neglect, but also with the impact of intervention on the children's overall development.

Six

Major Events in the Children's Lives During the Study

IN THIS CHAPTER, we look at several aspects of the children's lives during the two years following agency intervention. We describe, in a general fashion, the quality of the home and foster care environments. We also look at the services provided to the home and foster families, the stability (or instability) of the foster placements, and the amount of contact between the foster children and their biological parents.

We focus on these aspects of the children's world because previous research indicates that each of them may be related to the child's development. Moreover, provision of services, stability of placement, quality of foster homes, and visitation by biological parents are of special interest to policymakers, since, to a greater or lesser degree, they can be affected by alternative public policies. We hope that our discussion helps readers picture the complexity of predicting the outcome of intervention.

Services to Caretakers and Children

We were not able to do an extensive evaluation of the services provided to each family. There were too many different types of services, given for varying lengths of time and in different combinations, for us to do any complex analysis given our limited sample size. Moreover, though we kept a record of the types of services offered, we did not attempt to evaluate the quality of the services. We did not have the resources to make such assessments. Indeed, the agencies were willing to participate because we were *not* trying to assess quality of services. Finally, we did not know of any instruments by which we could measure quality of services. Therefore, we present only a basic picture of the types of services offered in each county and a relatively rough estimate of the quantity of services each family received, distinguishing those who received some services from those who received none.

TYPES OF SERVICES FOR HOME CHILDREN

Following the passage of the experimental legislation, San Mateo County assigned each family a family care worker, who was responsible for direct work with the parents, the child, or both. In some instances, the family care worker actually moved into the client's home for as long as four or five days at the time of the initial intervention. In most cases, the worker visited the family weekly or biweekly for six months, helping the mothers with household organization and child-rearing skills. Many of the family care workers also took the children on outings. The county provided a number of other services: out-of-home child care during the evening as well as during regular working hours, emergency respite care (whereby the child could be cared for in another home for up to forty-eight hours), mental health therapy for individuals and couples, housing for families without adequate housing, medical care for parents and children, and specialized school programs for emotionally disturbed children. Nine children received psychological therapy. It is our impression that the quality of services offered was very high. It is unlikely that any public social services system provides significantly better services. Most do worse.

Of course, not all the families received all, or even any, of these services. Three parents moved from the area before services could be provided or completed. Other families did not require all possible services. Moreover, under the experimental law, services could continue for only the six months following intervention, except in special circumstances. Therefore, most families were without services for eighteen of the twenty-four months.

We have divided the cases of our study into three broad groups: (1) families who received a high level of services, (2) those who received a low level of services, and (3) those who received none. A high level of services means that the parent(s) and child regularly received counseling and support, such as daycare (for children) or a homemaker (an assistant for the parent), for at least a six-month period, although the parents generally received far more services than the children. Many parents received much more, for example, income support, housing, and extensive contact with a family care worker. A low level of services generally meant just biweekly counseling for the parent(s), by either a social worker or a therapist at a mental health agency. In only one of the low-service cases did the child receive any services.

Overall, eleven of the families were high-services recipients, seven were low- and one mother and child, who moved from the area shortly after intervention, received none. The highest levels of services seemed to go to the parents and children with the most problems.

SERVICES TO FOSTER PARENTS, FOSTER CHILDREN, AND BIOLOGICAL PARENTS OF THE FOSTER CHILDREN

Services in both Alameda and Santa Clara counties tended to be typical of those reported in foster care systems throughout the country. For the most part, they consisted of biweekly or monthly visits by a social worker to the foster parents. These visits were not designed to provide direct counseling to the children. Generally, the workers offered advice to the foster mothers and checked the child's appearance. Four foster children received psychological therapy from a mental health professional, two in combination with their foster parents. As was the case with the home children, the "problem" foster children received the most services.

Only four of the biological parents of the foster children received extensive services, owing in part to limited availability of such services. However, the high mobility and lack of interest evidenced by the majority of biological parents made service delivery impossible in most cases. As we discuss in the Appendix, a parent's receptivity to services was a key factor in whether the child was returned to the parent.

Major Problems in the Home Children's Environments

Abusive or neglectful behavior was only one problematic aspect of the lives of the children who remained at home. Many mothers had a history of drug or alcohol abuse, mental illness, constant mobility, and family conflict. Unfortunately for their children, these problems persisted despite intervention. We describe here major problems, other than actual abuse or neglect, for the nineteen white home children's families.

FAMILY CONFLICT AND DIVORCE

The most prevalent problem was family conflict, manifested between the parents as well as between them and their children. Eight mothers had been divorced prior to intervention. Eight others divorced or separated during the two years. In sixteen of the nineteen families there was substantial conflict between the parents, whether they were living together or not. The parents of five children were involved in custody disputes; several of them had been in and out of court for years. At least eight mothers lived with a new boyfriend during the two years; three of these had several live-in boyfriends during this period. A number of recent studies have documented the potentially harmful impact of divorce on children (Wallerstein and Kelly 1980; Hetherington, Cox, and Cox 1982). In trying to understand the developmental problems the children evidenced initially (many of which continued), it is impossible to separate the effects of abuse or neglect from those related to divorce and family conflict.

ONGOING PARENTAL PROBLEMS: DRUGS, ALCOHOL, MENTAL ILLNESS, AND JOB LOSS

At least nine mothers continued to experience severe problems related to drugs, alcohol, or mental illness: one was committed to a psychiatric facility for a two-month period during the two years; one spent several weeks in an alcohol-detoxification program; one attempted suicide; and one used drugs heavily and changed residences almost weekly. The remaining five cases were not quite as severe, but their problems did greatly impair these mothers' ability and in some cases, desire to care for their children.

Seven parents lost their jobs at least once during the two years. In each case this was followed by depression and, in two-parent families, intense conflict.

EMOTIONAL REJECTION OF THE CHILD

Twelve mothers continued to express hostile or ambivalent attitudes toward their child: four mothers clearly rejected their child, regularly indicating both to our interviewers and to the child that they wished to be rid of the child; the other eight, not as openly hostile, were nevertheless constantly critical of, or paid virtually no attention to, their child.

SEPARATIONS

Four children were separated from their primary caretaker for substantial periods (one to two months) during the two years. One mother repeatedly sent the child to her former husband, who lived in another city, because she felt unable to provide care. Sometimes the child remained with his father for days, sometimes for weeks. A second child lived with his grandparents for two months while his mother was treated at a psychiatric facility. A third child was regularly left with a variety of caretakers because her mother did not want to provide care. A fourth child stayed in a foster home temporarily, while his mother joined an alcohol-detoxification program.

DISORGANIZATION OR CHAOS

All the factors just described created disorganization or chaos in the children's lives. We did not have any specific measures of family disorganization, nor have we constructed a quantifiable index of home chaos, because the kinds of disorganization were not always equivalent. Six families, however, seemed especially disorganized, as evidenced by frequent relocations, poor physical surroundings, ongoing drug or alcohol abuse or mental illness, and continuous family conflict. We describe one such family to provide a sense of the poor quality of some of the homes:

Mrs. R had been known to the child protective services for years. Both she and her husband had low IQ's and histories of mental illness. The parents were separated; the children lived with the mother. The father continued to visit and often took care of the children when the mother worked.

During the two years of our study, the parents separated and reunited several times. At first the mother lived in a house, which was always filthy and in disrepair. She was eventually evicted and then lived for a time with the children in a car. She later resumed living with the father—the whole family lived in a motel room. At one point, the father attempted suicide.

Following another separation was a two-month period in which the study child went to live with his grandparents while the mother was in a psychiatric halfway house. After her release they moved back into a motel. During most of the two years the child felt responsible for caring for his mother and he worried continually about her emotional condition.

Though the R's were extreme, the majority of families experienced similar problems. Only three or four families were relatively free of major problems during the two years.

Stability of Foster Placements

Were the foster children better off? Throughout the two years we recorded every change of placement for each foster child, the child's relationship to each new caretaker, and the length of time of each placement. Thus it should be easy to describe the stability or instability of foster care. However, placement patterns are quite variable. Therefore, before cataloging it, let us explain in what ways movement is a problem.[1]

CATEGORIZING "MOVEMENT PATTERNS"

There are a number of reasons to be concerned about movement. Any child who moves to a different home must adjust to a new school, new peers, and a new neighborhood. Each adjustment may be difficult. The parents of our home-group children also moved from place to place, requiring their children to adjust to new schools, peers, new neighborhoods. Neglectful parents, in particular, tend to be highly mobile: eleven of the home families changed residences at least once during the study period; eight moved three or more times. There is a major difference, however, when *foster* children are moved from home to home. The children have to adjust not only to new surroundings, but to new caretakers as well. This may be far more difficult than relating to new peers or a new school. A child who lives with a series of different caretakers may never have the opportunity to form a psychological relationship with an adult. In addition, the child may view each move as a rejection by the foster parent, which in some cases is true.

Therefore, we believe it important to assess the implications of the move for the child's psychological development. Most studies of foster care report only the total number of moves children experience, but looking only at the total number of moves over a two-year period does not give an appropriate picture. All moves may not require the same psychological adjustments. For example, one of our study children spent her first year living in the home of an older sister. At the end of the year she was moved to the home of an older brother. She had known both all her life. A second child spent one year living with non-relative foster parents and then was moved to another non-relative foster home. Even though both children moved twice, psychologically their movement patterns may have been quite different.

There are other ways in which movement patterns differ, even though the number of moves is the same. The following vignettes describe movement patterns of three children, each of whom experienced four placements in the two-year period. The timing of the moves and the degree of stability ultimately achieved differed for each child.

George was placed first in an emergency (temporary) foster home where he stayed for ten weeks. He was then placed in another emergency foster home, staying for twelve weeks. He was next placed in a permanent foster home, where he stayed for eight months. At that point he was moved to a fourth foster home, where he stayed for eleven months.

Tony was placed in an emergency foster home for one week. He was then in another emergency home for four weeks. He moved to a supposedly permanent foster home, but this lasted only for three months. He then moved to a fourth home, where he remained for the last twenty months of the study and by whom he was adopted.

Rachel was placed in an emergency foster home for two weeks. She then spent three months living with her grandparents. She then returned to her father, where she remained for six months. She was again removed and placed in the children's shelter for eight weeks. Finally, she was placed in a relative's foster home for fifteen months.

These are just some of the many movement patterns we observed, each of which may have a different meaning to, and psychological impact on, the child. Therefore, in addition to the number of moves, we focus on whether the child was primarily in one foster home over the two-year period or in several homes without any "permanent" placement.

TOTAL NUMBER OF MOVES

Most studies of children's movement in foster care provide data on the average number of moves. Average numbers can be very misleading. Some children, once placed, do not move at all; others move a great deal. Therefore, we need data on the movement of individual children. The number of moves our children experienced after the initial placement was made (including periods of shelter care) may be tabulated as follows:

Number of moves	Number of children	Number of moves	Number of children
0	2	2–3	6
1	2	4–5	3

Obviously, if measured by the number of moves, foster care did not provide stability. Two-thirds of the children had two or more moves; three children moved four or five times.

TOTAL LENGTH OF TIME IN A SINGLE HOME

The number of moves provides a misleading picture of the total stability the children experienced over the two years. Most children moved several times shortly after intervention and then had a stable placement. Although some children never had a long placement, the number of such children is smaller than one would imagine if we looked only at the total number of moves.

All but one of the children spent the majority of the two years in a single home; nearly half spent eighteen months or more in a single home, as the following tabulation shows:

Months in longest placement	Number of children	Months in longest placement	Number of children
24	2	12–17	6
18–23	4	<12	1

Most children initially were placed in several emergency foster homes, pending the outcome of court proceedings. Then they were placed in a permanent foster home, where in many cases they remained. When placement changes occurred, it generally happened in the first year of foster care. Only three children were moved from one foster home to another in the second year.

Looking at the entire two-year picture, we can categorize the children into three groups. The first group, comprising six children, experienced basically one stable placement for the entire two years: two were never moved, and three of the other four lived in a single home for at least the last twenty of the twenty-four months. A second group, consisting of three children, experienced several placements but basically had two main caretakers over the two-year period: all three were living with a second main caretaker at the end of the study, in what appeared to be a permanent arrangement (one had been adopted, one was with legal guardians, and one was with an older brother). Finally, four children moved from one foster family to another, experiencing three or more placements, though three of the four did have one long placement during the two years. Thus, half to three-fourths of the children had reasonably stable placements.

REASONS FOR MOVEMENT

It was not a goal of our study to account for foster care movement patterns. However, some aspects of these patterns shed light on the impact of foster care on the children and provide additional information about the children's behavior while in foster care. Therefore we will discuss them briefly.

There were four main reasons why children moved. The most common was built into the foster care system. Each of the counties placed children in temporary homes pending the disposition of court proceedings. Movement from a temporary to a long-term foster home accounted for at least one of the placement changes in every case in which there was a change. It was the only reason for movement in three cases.

The second major reason was a foster parent's request that the child be removed because of behavioral problems. This occurred for five children. It is interesting that whereas these children did have behavioral problems in the foster home from which they were removed, for four of them behavior was not problematic in the next placement, at least from the new foster parents' perspective. In fact, all five children were either adopted by, or moved permanently into the home of, the foster family that assumed custody immediately following the previous foster parents' request for removal. Whereas one child's behavior clearly improved in the second placement, in the other four cases it seemed that the major difference was in the foster parents' attitudes, rather than the child's behavior.

Third, some children were moved because the foster parents gave up custody for reasons unrelated to the child's behavior. The reasons varied. Two foster parents disliked dealing with the biological parents. Two other foster parents were having trouble dealing with the child's siblings, or with other children in the home, and requested removal of all children. In one case a relative who initially intended to provide long-term care decided that she could not do so. Finally, two children were returned home and then removed again during the two years. Each of these children twice went through the process of being placed in a temporary home and then a long-term foster home, which meant that each made five moves (including the temporary return home).

Contacts Between the Biological Parents and Their Children in Foster Care

VISITATION PATTERNS

Parental visitation has been linked both with the likelihood that the parent will eventually resume custody and with the well-being of the child during and after placement (Fanshel 1975; Weinstein 1960). Because of the perceived importance of visitation, we regularly gathered information about visiting patterns from the children, the biological parents, and the foster parents.

At the time of our initial interviews, usually six to twelve weeks following placement, the majority of mothers were visiting on a regular basis, although two parents had not visited at all. Seven mothers were visiting weekly or biweekly, which usually was as often as permitted by the social services agencies. After one year of placement, this picture had changed considerably. Only four parents now saw their child regularly; nine had little or no contact. After two years the rate of visiting had declined even further. Although the majority of parents still kept in some contact with the child, for most this consisted only of occasional phone calls; only two parents saw their children as often as once a month. See Table 6.1.

Viewed over the entire two years, four mothers visited rarely or never; only two visited regularly throughout the period; the other seven mothers visited relatively frequently in the first six months, but had little contact with their children after that.

CHILDREN'S ATTITUDES TOWARD VISITATION

The failure of the parents to visit was very painful to the children. They all wanted more visits initially. Twelve of the thirteen continued to want more visits throughout the two years. Even when parents had not contacted the child for months or years, the child never gave up hope. As one seven-year-old boy who had not heard from his mother in two years said: "Every time the phone rings I hope that it's her."

The continued emotional ties to parents, plus the multiple placements, undoubtedly affected the children's emotional ties to their new caretakers. We believe that a critical measure of the success or failure of foster care must be whether the child who is not returned home is able to form a close emotional relationship with "new parents." As we show in Chapter 9, the child's willingness to form a new relationship was influenced by the amount of parental visiting.

TABLE 6.1
Frequency of Visits by Biological Parents of Foster Children

| Frequency of visits | Number of parents ($N = 13$) | | |
	Initially (at 6–12 weeks)	At 1 year	At 2 years
Weekly	3	2	0
Biweekly	4	2	1
Monthly	2	1	1
Less than monthly	2	1	2
Occasional phone call only	0	5	6
None	2	2	3

The Foster Care Environment

The quality as well as the stability of a foster home undoubtedly influences the impact of foster care on a child. Many factors about a foster home can affect the child: the match between the needs of the child and the skills of the foster parents, the presence or absence of other children in the home, and the attitude of the family toward the particular child are a few.

Each foster home is unique. Since how well a given home and a given child will match is very difficult to predict in advance, the success or failure of placement is often a matter of luck. However, though each foster home had unique characteristics, they all tended to be systematically different from the children's parental homes. This section describes some of the major differences. We are unable to determine which, if any, of these differences might have influenced the development of any particular child. We present these data solely to provide greater understanding of the foster care experience.

ECOLOGICAL VARIABLES

All but two of the thirteen white foster children lived in more than one foster home. The data described here compare the biological family environments and the initial foster family environments.[2] The new families differed from the children's previous families in a number of ways. Four of the children were placed with relatives: three with grandparents and one with an older sister. None of the four had lived with these relatives before, and the three grandchildren had not had much prior contact with the grandparents. The remaining nine children were in non-relative homes. Four children were placed along with a sibling. Most children moved from single-parent to two-parent families, inasmuch as only three of the biological mothers were married and all but one of the foster mothers were married (the exception was a child's grandmother). The foster families tended to be larger than the biological families: several had foster children other than the study child; most had natural or adopted children as well.

The foster mothers had a median age of forty-five compared to a median age of thirty for the biological mothers. All the foster families had incomes of more than $1,500 per month. Nine of the biological families had incomes of less than $1,000 per month; none had incomes greater than $1,500 per month.

THE OLD AND NEW PHYSICAL ENVIRONMENTS

Placement in foster care almost always resulted in improved physical surroundings for the child. The foster families lived in more affluent neighborhoods. Moreover, since all the foster housing had to meet minimum space and safety requirements in order to be licensed, and many of the children had been removed because of poor conditions in the biological household, the physical quality of the child's environment usually improved significantly. Nearly all foster families resided in detached, single-family houses; only two of the biological parents did so. The foster family's house also tended to be large, which meant that even though the actual number of people per household was greater in the foster families, most children moved into less crowded surroundings.

Each foster household was rated by our interviewers in terms of crowding, orderliness, safety, cleanliness, and comfort.[3] The lower the score the better: a house that was "ideal" scored a 1 on each dimension, or 5 overall. A totally disorganized residence would score 25. Twelve of the thirteen foster homes scored 15 or below on our scale, which meant that they were clean, safe, and orderly. In contrast, eleven of the thirteen living environments of the biological parents received scores of 20 or more. The living environments from which some of the children were removed included a condemned apartment building where the family resided in a garage with no windows; two apartments and one house described in the court reports as "filthy," roach-infested and littered with garbage but containing no food; a car; and a motel room.

THE PSYCHOLOGICAL ENVIRONMENTS

The fundamental changes achieved through foster placement were psychological. Living with "new parents," even relatives (though the transition may be easier), makes substantial demands of foster children's adaptational skills—the demands are undoubtedly more severe when the psychological environments of the two families are very different. Therefore, we examined some psychological dimensions of the settings.

Mothers' psychological health. A caretaker's psychological status is likely to affect her ability to care for and relate to her child. We assessed the self-esteem and social embeddedness of both the biological and the foster mothers and attempted to identify caretakers with clear emotional difficulties. Not surprisingly, the foster mothers seemed considerably healthier emotionally than most of the biological mothers.[4]

With regard to "self-esteem," described in Chapter 4, there were considerable differences between the groups. All the foster mothers scored 5 or 6 on our scale, with 6 being the most positive score. Ten of the thirteen biological mothers scored 4 or less. Most expressed feelings of loneliness, sadness, ineffectiveness, and inability to be with people; the foster mothers almost never indicated problems in these areas. Congruent with these feelings, the biological mothers reported themselves as considerably more isolated socially than the foster mothers. On our social embeddedness scale, 80 percent of the biological mothers indicated that they were extremely isolated. In contrast, most foster mothers had high levels of involvement with family, friends, and community groups. Two-thirds of the foster mothers categorized themselves as highly embedded; only two, both grandparents, scored in the lowest end of the scale.

As discussed in Chapter 4, many of the biological mothers of foster children had a history of severe emotional problems or drug or alcohol abuse. On the other hand, most foster mothers were highly integrated into a wide network of friends and relations. For the children, the difference in the social worlds of the adults was an opportunity and, perhaps, a hurdle.

Family environment. In addition to assessments of the caretaker's individual well-being, we examined the overall functioning of the family in terms of the five dimensions of the Moos Family Environment Scale. Differences were generally in the expected direction: that is, foster families scored higher on cohesion, expression, and organization, and lower on conflict. The difference was greatest with respect to organization. This makes sense in terms of what we learned in our interviews with foster mothers; for most of them the creation of an organized living environment was a high priority. Foster care gave most children a more defined structure for family life and more opportunity for open expression of feelings within the family. One needs to keep in mind that this is a reported, not observed, assessment. However, these differences were corroborated by our interviewer's opinion of the families.

Activities, rules, and discipline. We expected that just as the foster mothers' lives differed from those of the biological mothers, so would their methods of child-rearing. Without extensive observations it is difficult to obtain reliable information on child-rearing style. We did not make these observations. In order to gain some idea of the basic modes of parent-child interactions as the children sensed them, we asked the children questions about activities and rules in both the biological and foster families.

The move into a foster home seemed to alter the type of activities in which a child engaged. At least initially, the foster children tended to play indoors more than they did when they were at home, perhaps reflecting the foster parents' reluctance to let a new child wander around the neighborhood. In addition to relatively restricted activities, the foster children reported that they had more rules to obey. The children stated that their foster parents had more restrictions than their biological parents had about such things as "watching TV whenever you want" and "staying up as late as you want." Perhaps more important, the child saw greater consistency of enforcement in the foster homes. Eleven of the thirteen children reported that their foster parents made them follow the rules all or most of the time. Only seven of the children said that their biological parents had enforced the rules all or most of the time, when they lived at home. The rest said that the rules were enforced only sometimes or never.

All foster mothers claimed to engage the children in a number of family activities. Most reported such activities as reading, going to movies, visiting relatives, and playing games with the children. In addition, eight of the thirteen reported regularly setting aside time to be alone with the child. Most of the children said that the foster caretakers spent more time with them, took them to more places, and bought them more things than had their biological parents.

In summary, it appears that the foster homes provided a setting with more structure and fewer extremes. And even though foster child status may create uncertainty for the child with regard to many aspects of adult-child interactions, at least with regard to behavior, foster homes in our study generally provided a clearer set of expectations for such interactions than did the biological families.

VARIATION IN FOSTER HOMES

During the two years, the thirteen foster children lived in a total of twenty-four different foster homes. Although all differed from the biological homes, they also varied greatly from one another. The homes ranged from "emergency foster homes," where the foster mother frequently cared for four or five children, whom she expected to keep for no longer than eight weeks, to the homes of grandparents who expected to raise the child to adulthood. As previously indicated, we did not try to assess the quality of the foster parenting, though we did look at whether the foster family was prepared to keep the child permanently or wanted to do so. We discuss this aspect of the foster home in Chapter 9. Although we cannot rate quality, we can give some idea of the major differences in the caretakers' attitudes toward the placement.

Five of the children lived with relatives for at least part of the two years; three with grandparents, one with an older sister and then an older brother, one with an aunt. All the relatives took the child willingly, but not necessarily enthusiastically. Each family found placement a major disruption. This was especially true for the older sister. Only twenty-two years old and newly married, she had to assume the care of two younger sisters, one of whom was difficult behaviorally (the child in our sample), and one with a severe kidney problem requiring regular dialysis. The placement created a great strain on the marriage. The study child resented living with her sister, complaining that she had to do all the work for her older sister.

The three sets of grandparents were quite different from one another. One family was well-to-do, eager to have the child, and highly involved with their grandson. A second family, paternal grandparents, were older and less willing to become involved with the child, though it was clear they would keep him permanently. The third child lived with a widowed paternal grandmother, who was very hostile toward the child's mother but quite ambivalent about keeping the child. She had limited economic resources; various other relatives moved in and out of the house during the two years. The fifth child lived for six months with an aunt, who always viewed the placement as temporary.

The variation was as great among the non-relative foster parents. Several children lived in homes where the foster parents viewed themselves solely as "professionals" willing to take care of the child for as long as necessary, but not planning to keep the child permanently. Most of these families were providing care for several foster children;

children were constantly entering and leaving these homes. Several study children expressed concern that the foster mother did not have enough time for them. In contrast, one child lived with a family he "picked." Initially he was with a foster mother who disliked him. Although only six years old, he managed to persuade the parents of one of his schoolmates to take him from this foster home. These new parents were totally devoted to the child and his younger brother. They provided a very warm, close, supportive environment, ultimately becoming guardians of both. This case was unusual because, like the foster parents who were related to the child, these foster parents assumed the role only to provide a home for a specific child. All the other families were regularly licensed foster homes, providing care to many children. Several had been foster parents for years; for three families, however, the study child was among their first batch of foster children.

In addition to experience, commitment to the child, and the number of other children in the home, all the foster families differed in such things as the extent of the foster father's involvement (from quite minimal to highly involved), the degree to which the foster parents facilitated or impeded maintenance of a relationship with the biological parents, the extent of the foster parents' involvement in the child's school life and peer relations, and the degree to which the child was integrated into such family activities as vacations. All these factors undoubtedly influenced the child's satisfaction with the foster parents' home and sense of integration into the family.

Summary

Obviously, neither home nor foster placement should be thought of as a static situation. In both settings, the children in our study constantly had to adapt to changing environments. In this respect, their worlds were quite different, we believe, from those of most children. In the following chapters, we will see that in the two years following intervention, some children showed developmental gains while others lost ground. In light of their differing worlds, such variation is not surprising.

Seven

Outcomes for the Children, I: Reabuse and Continued Neglect, Permanence of Placement

———

IN REPORTING the outcomes for the children during the two years, we look first at reabuse or continued neglect for the home children, and failure to find a permanent home for the foster children. Both must be considered in conjunction with the children's physical, social, emotional, and academic development. Obviously, reabuse or continued neglect keeps a child at physical and developmental risk, and the failure to find a permanent home, when the child cannot be returned home, threatens the child's long-term development. Although we lack good evidence relating unstable foster placement to specific developmental problems, all child welfare experts agree that children need a stable parental figure for adequate psychological growth.

Reabuse or Continued Neglect

THE DEFINITIONAL PROBLEM

Determining reabuse or continued neglect is difficult. Although some conduct clearly constitutes either abuse or neglect of a child, not all physical harm or parental inattention does, at least for the purposes of permitting state intervention. In our study we found no abuse cases in which physical punishment ceased entirely when the child remained at home. In no case did a neglectful parent start to provide *very* good care. As is clear from our discussion in Chapter 6, life remained chaotic for many of the children. Yet not all the physical discipline or inadequate care came within the legal definition of abuse or neglect. We must draw some fine lines.

Initially all the abuse cases involved an incident of severe discipline that came to public attention. In some cases, the parental action was clearly life-threatening or could have led to serious physical injury. In other cases (usually involving spankings on the buttocks or arms), there could have been disagreement among child care professionals or judges as to whether the parental conflict amounted to abuse. Thus, we had to decide what degree of physical punishment would constitute reabuse. Would we only consider cases in which the nature of the parental action was of the same magnitude as that leading to the initial intervention? With that definition, less severe spankings would not be counted as reabuse. Or would any new incident that might be sufficient to justify state intervention be considered reabuse, even though it was less serious than the initial incident?

Similar, perhaps even greater problems, arise with respect to neglect. In almost all cases, the neglectful parental behavior had existed for some time. As might be expected, there were no cases where the parents totally altered their life-style. All improvement was a matter of degree: the home conditions became less of an immediate hazard to the child's safety, or were a hazard less often; the degree of supervision increased even though there were still times of inattention; or parental care for the child improved even though it was still lacking in many respects. Even in the one category in which a total change was possible—lack of an adequate home—the fact that a parent who had been living in a car moved into adequate housing did not mean that childcare became ideal. The initial lack of an adequate living environment generally reflected a degree of disorganization that affected all aspects of childcare. The immediate cause of intervention was gone, but some degree of neglect usually continued.

We opted for an approach using the standard that supervising agencies use in defining abuse or neglect. We tried to determine whether a child protection agency would have instituted a court action to protect the child because of the parents' actions. For example, we include among the reabuse cases a family in which the father continued to hit the child in the face with a belt, but do not include a family in which the child was spanked for smoking and made to eat a cigarette, even though we believe that the second parent's action was unreasonable. In the first case we believe the hitting, in light of the past history of abuse, justified legal action (though none was taken). Legal action would be unlikely in the second case. For the neglect cases, we included only those situations in which, during the two years, there was no significant improvement in the level of parental care. If there was improvement we do not include the case, even though the care of the child often became only minimally adequate.

RATES OF REABUSE OR CONTINUED NEGLECT

Home children. The relevant sample is not merely the nineteen white children who remained at home throughout the two years. Originally, twenty-three white children were left at home, but four were later removed during the two years, two because of reabuse and two because of continued neglect. These failures must be considered in deciding on the desirability of home placement. Thus, home placement clearly was unsuccessful in at least 20 percent of the cases involving white children.

Among the eleven abused white children who remained at home throughout the two years, five were physically abused one or more times in the two years following intervention: one was hit in the face; the parents of the other four continued to spank their children severely, but generally on the buttocks or legs, and to reject them emotionally. It must be noted that none of these children received an injury serious enough to require medical treatment, though one child's gums were bloodied when his mother brushed his teeth for him as punishment for inadequate brushing. None of the discipline was done in a manner that was life-threatening or likely to break bones or impair functioning. However, each of these children lived in fear of physical punishment.

We learned, after the study was completed, that two other children among the nineteen at home were sexually abused during the two years of the study—one by an older brother and one by an uncle. In both instances the mother's lack of concern for the child undoubtedly contributed to placing the child at risk for this abuse.

With regard to the eight neglect cases, there was no significant change in four: two children continued to miss substantial amounts of school and frequently were left unattended for entire days, one family continued to live in substandard housing, and one mother continually threatened to kill her son, told him he was worthless, and provided little physical care. Even in the four cases in which we saw improvement, only two changed substantially. In the other two, the parental care tended to fluctuate, with some periods of relatively good care and others when the child's needs were largely ignored for weeks at a time.

Thus the majority of children left at home were not in an ideal situation. Only a very few actually suffered, or appeared to be in danger of suffering, serious physical injuries through either abuse or inadequate care. However, most of the children received only adequate-to-marginal physical care, and many were subject to either active emotional abuse or the lack of parental concern and care. As we indicated in Chapter 6 the families of these children received various services designed to prevent reabuse and neglect. Although we did not evaluate these services in depth, our findings are not encouraging: as is evident from the foregoing discussion, the families changed relatively little, especially the neglecting families. We found no relationship between receipt of services and reabuse or continued neglect. Services clearly helped in some cases and had negligible impact in others.[1]

Foster children. The least we can expect from foster care is that the children will not be abused or neglected. Unfortunately, this was not uniformly the case. California law forbids foster parents to use corporal punishment of any kind; many foster parents, however, do spank children. Two children in our study were abused or grossly neglected by their foster parents. One girl was in a home where the foster mother used excessive physical punishment, pulling the girl's hair and slapping her. This girl also claimed to have had sexual contact with the foster father. Although these allegations were not made until the girl had moved from the home and were never substantiated by a social agency, we feel reasonably certain that both types of abuse occurred. The second child was a victim of emotional abuse. His first foster mother intensely disliked him and verbally abused him regularly. She provided adequate physical care but no emotional involvement. Eventually this child, who was only six, asked to be moved to another home and the foster mother readily agreed.

Our statistics on abuse and neglect in foster care are comparable to the few reported studies, which find ratings of alleged abuse for between 5 to 10 percent of the foster population (Bolton, Laner, and Gia 1981). In all the other placements, including the short-term ones, we found no evidence of abuse or gross neglect, though the quality of the emotional care was not always ideal. As previously discussed, five children were moved from a foster home at the request of the foster parents because of the latter's unwillingness or inability to cope with the child's behavior. In a few of these homes the foster parents had minimal emotional involvement with the children, though they provided adequate physical care.

Permanence of Placements

In Chapter 6 we reported that by the end of a year only five of the thirteen parents were visiting the child regularly, and that by the end of two years the number declined to two. It was quite clear in at least nine cases that the child would never return home.

We accept the view that children need permanent homes and need the stability of feeling secure, wanted, and loved. If a child was in an unstable foster placement at the end of two years, we considered this a negative outcome. Even if the child had benefited from foster care during that time, there was a reason to be concerned with the long-term well-being of the child in an unstable placement. As said earlier, however, such a child would not necessarily have been better off with her parents, since home placement can be worse than even unstable foster care. But instability is a cost that cannot be ignored.

We have already described the number of children who were given multiple placements. Indeed, in the first year, foster care did not provide stability for most children in our study. The picture changed, however, by the end of two years. Of the fourteen children[2] who remained in care, ten were in apparently permanent homes. We report this with some trepidation, since we have evidence within our study that predicting is a precarious business. For example, one girl was removed from her mother's home and placed with her father and stepmother. Throughout the study she reported that she was extremely happy with this arrangement and planned to make it permanent. At first she did not wish to visit with her mother and later did so with some reluctance. Yet at the end of the two years she decided to go back to her mother, who wanted her. The girl had been experiencing increased conflict with her stepmother. Our prediction only a week before she returned to her mother would have been that the girl preferred permanent foster care.

Despite such prediction problems, there are good reasons to support our conclusion about the ten apparently permanent foster placements. In one case the child had been adopted, in four cases the foster parents had become legal guardians, and two children lived with relatives. In most of these cases the original custodial parent was gone

TABLE 7.I

Placement of Foster Children at Two Years

Placement	Number of children
Permanent (new home)	
In adoptive home	1
Guardianship established	4[a]
With a relative	2
With a nonrelative	3
Impermanent	
With a relative	1
With a nonrelative	2

[a] One guardian was a grandparent.

from the scene or had accepted the placement as permanent. In three other cases the children had been in their present foster home for twenty-two, -six, and -eight months. Their biological parents had disappeared and the foster parents were committed to keeping them, even though legal guardianship had not been established.

Of the remaining three children, two were returned to their parents within six months of the end of the study. However, it was questionable whether these parents could provide adequate care. The other child seemed destined to experience a series of placements, since her mother kept regaining custody and then relinquishing it. (The foster child who had been placed in a residential institution, and therefore was excluded from our other analyses, also eventually resumed living with his mother.) The status of the children at the end of the two years is shown in Table 7.I.

In terms of permanence, the outcome for our sample of foster children seemed better than that generally reported in the literature. Approximately 70 percent were in seemingly stable placements and the remaining children were returned home—albeit to unstable homes. In fact, in terms of stability the foster children seemed in as good shape as the home children. We also tried to assess the likelihood that the home children would have to be removed in the future. We focused on the level of the mother's commitment to the child and the degree of continued abuse or neglect. Again, such predictions are hazardous. Yet the situation in four of the nineteen families was so disorganized and the level of parental commitment so low that we thought future placement likely, and indeed placement did occur in two cases after the study period ended.

It must be stressed, however, that a foster placement "objectively" judged secure by us was not necessarily one the child viewed as secure or desirable. We explore the children's feelings about placement, at the end of the two years, in Chapter 9. As will be shown, some children in "secure" settings seemed strongly bonded to new parents, but others continued to express a strong desire to return "home."

Eight

Outcomes for the Children, II: Developmental Measures

Measuring Change

We now turn to the children's development, the main focus of our research. We regularly assessed the children's health, cognitive development, academic performance, social skills, and personal satisfaction. Initially, many of the home children evidenced substantial problems in most of these areas. Following intervention virtually all the home parents, and half the home children, received counseling and other services. Yet, as we described in Chapter 6, the lives of many of the families remained in turmoil. Half the children were reabused or subject to continued neglect. Were they able to overcome their initial deficits despite these ongoing problems?

The foster children, as a group, were somewhat better adjusted socially and emotionally at the time we first saw them, though they were not without problems. Most of the children were in stable placements by the end of two years. However, their lives certainly had not been trouble-free in the intervening time. How did they cope with multiple placements, rejection by foster parents, decreased (lost) contact with their biological parents and siblings, and the need to adjust to new schools, foster siblings, and peers?

We assess change in a number of different ways, depending on the particular variable and the available data. Whenever possible we examine whether at the end of two years the children in each group were, on average, doing better, worse, or about the same as initially. For some measures, for example the number of children evidencing psychological problems, we report the percentage of children with problems over time. For variables that are based on scales or indices we compare initial group means with the final group means. Generally we present only initial and end data rather than interim measurements.[1] The choice of our end point is of course arbitrary. However, although specific details might have been somewhat different, the basic picture would not have changed had we used another end point. The trends in each group were consistent, though the amount of individual variation on some measures was greater among the home children than among foster children.

We also present, where appropriate, mean aggregate scores over the two years for all the children in each group. Aggregate scores provide a picture of the average well-being of the children in each group during the entire two years, revealing different cumulative experiences that might not be reflected in initial or end scores.

Both initial–end and aggregate measures look only at group ratings. As would be expected, group averages masked substantial individual variations. On most measures, some children in each group improved during the two years while others deteriorated. Therefore, we indicate the number of children who showed change on each variable.

Finally, for each aspect of development we identify a group of children we defined as "at risk." For purposes of deciding whether to favor home placement or foster care it might make a difference to policymakers whether the children in either setting were functioning normally or below normal. For example, assume that the average foster child did "better" (in terms of a variable we are measuring, such as self-esteem) over the two years than the average home child. Does this mean that policymakers should favor foster placement? In deciding this question, a policymaker might want to know if the children in both settings were functioning within a normal range, with the foster children at higher levels, or if the foster group went from below normal to normal. The case for removal and foster placement would be considerably stronger in the second situation.

On some variables we defined "at risk" in terms of specific problems, for example, poor vision or psychiatric problems. We look to see if children who initially had such problems continued to have them (and if some children developed such problems during the two years). On scaled variables, we define normality in relation to the comparison children. We considered the bottom 25 percent of the comparison sample "at risk" and determined the percentage of children in the home and out-of-home groups who initially were rated below this score. We then see whether there was change in the *proportion* of home and foster children below this mark at the end of the two years.

Viewed independently, each measure is subject to varying deficiencies: we dealt with small samples, missing data, and on some measures (for example, child self-esteem) substantial individual variability over time.[2] We warn against drawing conclusions from a single measure. Taken together, however, they provide a reasonably consistent and, we believe, accurate picture at the group level. The differences between the home and foster children hold steady across variables and over time. Different ways of analyzing the data all provide the same picture.

In terms of individual children, the most striking finding is that there was little change, for the majority of children, on most variables. There was a group of children who appeared to be doing badly on most measures throughout the two years and a few children who did well throughout. Most children started and ended doing adequately in some domains, poorly in others. There were a few children who showed substantial change. However, we were not able to account for a child's doing poorly or well, perhaps because of the small sample.

The Measures

PHYSICAL DEVELOPMENT AND HEALTH STATUS

At the start of the study most of the children were at or above national norms in height and weight and only a few showed signs of major health problems. Over the two years, many home children received only marginal physical care. Foster care, on the other hand, generally provided the children with adequate physical surroundings, proper nutrition, and regular medical care. Thus, we expected to find improved physical development and health among the foster children. However, since both the home and foster children were generally in good physical condition at the time of intervention, we did not expect dramatic changes. Our expectations were confirmed. Growth patterns were reasonably stable over the two years of the study. As a group the foster children gained somewhat more in both height and weight. This might be attributable either to better nutritional care or to a general regression toward the mean (or average) height and weight, since the foster children were smaller and lighter initially—and therefore would be expected to gain more than the taller, heavier home children.

We repeated our brief physical screenings for vision, hearing, and coordination problems at the end of one and two years. Throughout the two years the majority of children continued to fall within the normal range. Approximately 60 percent (twelve) of the home children and 70 percent (nine) of the foster children never evidenced these physical problems. Among the children in each group who had initially abnormal findings, similar proportions of each either remained abnormal or improved. Given the very small number of children with initial problems, we could not determine if placement in foster care improved the chances that abnormal vision, hearing, or coordination would be identified or corrected. Several home children originally classified as being normal later developed pathological signs. In contrast, no initially normal foster child developed problems. The foster children had fewer rashes or bruises at our final examination, which might indicate somewhat better care.

In sum, the major differences between the home and foster groups was that a larger proportion of the home children developed minor pathological signs. However, none of the signs was major and none of the changes over time was so remarkable as to warrant concluding that the children were at risk for physical disability.

COGNITIVE DEVELOPMENT

After intervention, social service agencies provided no special academic help to either the home or foster children in our study. At the time of our initial testing, the two groups of children had comparable overall scores on the WISC, though the foster children scored lower on the performance portion of the test. As a result of placement, the majority of foster children moved from lower-income, less structured environments to higher-income, more structured homes. To the extent that such environments contribute to test performance, we might expect higher scores in the foster group. We tested all children three times; some children were also tested at school. These repetitions, the children's greater familiarity with the tester, and their more settled status at the final measurement all should have led to improved scores.

Both groups of children did show a small but definite improvement in the performance portion of the WISC, the foster children to a greater extent. There were no group changes in the verbal scores.[3] See Table 8.1.

The picture that emerged from group data is supported by the individual changes. On the verbal portion of the test 61 percent (eleven of eighteen) of the home children and 75 percent (nine of twelve) of the foster children had higher scores. On the performance portion of

TABLE 8.1

IQ Scores of Home and Foster Children, Initially and at Two Years

	Home (N = 18)		Foster (N = 12)	
Score	Initially	At 2 years	Initially	At 2 years
Verbal				
Mean	95.7	96.8	92.4	94.4
SD	16.4	15.6	13.4	13.6
Performance				
Mean	102.4	109.7	90.6	104.7
SD	16.0	17.0	15.9	13.3

the test 78 percent (fourteen of eighteen) of the home children and 100 percent (twelve) of the foster cases had higher scores. If we use the more stringent criteria of counting only those cases where the change is greater than fifteen IQ points (one standard deviation), only one home and one foster child improved on the verbal portion and one child in each group declined. On the performance section, four home children improved and one had a lower score; two foster children showed improvement and none had lower scores. Using this more rigorous definition of change, there were no group differences over the two-year period.

ACADEMIC PERFORMANCE

There is reason to believe that placement ought to affect a child's academic performance. Before intervention many children were often absent from school, and many biological parents had shown little interest in the child's schoolwork. To the extent foster care resulted in greater school attendance and more adult support, we would expect better performance. On the other hand, because of placement changes, foster children frequently changed schools, which may have negated positive aspects of foster care. The following tabulation shows the number of schools attended by both groups of children following intervention.[4]

Number of schools	Home (N = 19)	Foster (N = 13)
1	10	3
2–3	6	5
4+	3	5

Unfortunately, assessing change over time proved quite difficult. As previously discussed, schools did not use the same standards in rating children. Standard test scores were missing in the majority of cases. Five of the foster children had not been in an academic program in the year before intervention, so we could not do prior-year assessments. We therefore had to piece together a picture of change from limited sources of data. It is clear that the majority of children had academic problems throughout the two years. There is some evidence, however, that foster placement increased the chance that a child's academic performance would approach her academic potential.

Attendance. One area in which foster care clearly benefited children was in school attendance. From the school records, we estimated each child's attendance during the two years preceding and two years following intervention.[5] We obtained similar absenteeism data for the comparison sample. Before intervention, the abused and neglected children were absent from school much more frequently than the comparison children. Following intervention, many of the home children continued to have high absentee rates.[6] Their parents generally failed to take responsibility for getting the child to school; some children were kept at home to help their parents. In contrast, the attendance of the foster children improved dramatically. All the foster parents saw that the children attended school. During our two-year study the percentages of children absent more than 10 percent of the time were: home ($N = 15$), 40 percent; foster ($N = 9$), 11 percent; and comparison group ($N = 42$), 2 percent.

Performance measures. We used four measures of school performance: the children's grades; scores on standardized tests; teacher ratings of the child's academic performance; and retentions at a previous grade level or placement in a special education class owing to academic problems. However, because grades between schools were noncomparable and the children missed so many of the standard tests, we will report only retention rates and teacher ratings.

Based on retentions and placement in special classes, the abused and neglected children both at home and in foster care were at considerably greater academic risk than were the comparison children. Fourteen (44 percent) of the thirty-two abused/neglected children were retained or placed in a special class at some point in their school career *because of academic deficiencies.*[7] Since eleven of these fourteen children had average or better WISC scores, their poor school performance seems related to other factors, most likely their home environments. Although thirteen (32 percent) of the comparison group also were retained, their retentions had a different character. Most were doing well academically and were retained for social rather than academic reasons.[8] Their parents and teachers supported retention in order to give them the opportunity to develop socially. Only 10 percent (four children) of the comparison sample were retained or placed in special classes because of academic problems.[9]

Retention rates demonstrate the overall academic problems of the abused and neglected children, but cannot be used to assess the impact of placement. In fact, we included in the retention statistics children who were retained *before our study* so as to give a full academic picture of the children; focusing on postintervention retention would yield a misleading measure of the impact of placement for three reasons. First, the foster group was at less risk of retention following intervention. Three children had already been retained and three did not begin school until they had been in care almost a year (these children had been in preschool at the time of intervention). Second, retention of a foster child does not necessarily indicate a failure of foster care. School performance is based on the cumulative experience of the child. It is unreasonable to expect that three, four, or five months in foster placement will make up for prior deficits. Moreover, foster children by virtue of placement may have been enrolled in schools in which higher standards were applied. Those children who moved from poor neighborhoods to middle-class settings may have done worse than their new schoolmates even if they were doing better than they had done previously.

Intervention may have resulted in more retention among the home children as well, even if their school performance was not worsening. Through intervention the children came into contact with counselors, social workers, new teachers, and others concerned about their welfare. Placement in a special class or retention in a grade may have been the result of surveillance by concerned people. (This is also true of foster children.) Therefore, we conclude only that, based on retention rates and placement in special classes, many children in both groups were doing poorly academically.

Our other measure of school performance did allow us to assess change over time. We asked the child's teacher to rate the child's academic performance each year. We obtained teacher rankings for the comparison children as well. All these were postintervention rankings, so we cannot be certain if the teachers saw improvement from the time before intervention. However, we can determine if each group showed improvement or deterioration during the two years.

TABLE 8.2

Teachers' Academic Ratings of Children, Initially and at Two Years

Rating	Home (N = 10)		Foster (N = 9)		Comparison (N = 41)[a]	
	Initially	At 2 years	Initially	At 2 years	Initially	At 2 years
Above average	0%	0%	11%	22%	46%	54%
Average	30	40	44	33	22	29
Below average	70	60	44	44	32	17

[a] One teacher failed to report an academic rating in the second year.

We will look only at children who were in regular classes and not retained during the two years, since scores in special classes are not comparable to scores from regular classes and we might expect a child to do better in the year following retention. There was extraordinarily little change in all the children's academic ranks, especially for the abused and neglected children. Among the ten home children in regular classes, four improved somewhat, four declined somewhat, *but no child was rated above-average at the beginning or end of the study.*[10] Among the nine foster children who met the criteria, one child was rated above-average both years, one child went from average to above-average, and the remaining children were average or below throughout the two years. Both groups were consistently rated more poorly than the comparison children; more comparison children improved over time. See Table 8.2.

Few abused or neglected children rated higher over time, but some evidence shows that foster care may have benefited a particular group of children. We examined the relationship, for children in regular classes, between the child's *average* verbal IQ scores and the *average* teacher rank over the two years. As Figure 1 illustrates, for foster children there was a very strong relationship between average verbal IQ and average academic rank by teachers. All the children judged by the teacher to be performing at average levels or above had IQ scores above the group average. The converse is also true. Thus, over the two years, the foster children generally performed at their "expected" level.[11]

The children who remained at home, however, do not show such a pattern. In Figure 1, we see that there were four high-IQ children whose teachers rated them very low academically. These children were performing far below expectations.[12] It seems likely that, for some or

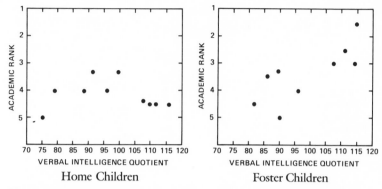

Fig. 1. Relationship of average academic rank to average verbal intelligence quotient.

perhaps all these children, their failure to live up to their potential was, at least in part, attributable to problems in the home environment or to frequent absences.[13]

EMOTIONAL PROBLEMS

When we first encountered them, many of the children appeared to be at risk psychologically. Most had at some time been referred for mental health evaluation and treatment. Seven of the nineteen home children and two of the thirteen foster children were in treatment at the time we first saw them.

If we consider the fact of being in therapy as one index of psychological pathology, the children in both the home and foster groups remained highly troubled during the two years. All but one of the children initially in therapy were still in therapy at the end of two years (the exception was in the home group). In addition, three home and three foster children entered therapy during the two years: this did not necessarily indicate a worsening of their emotional status, because in four of the six cases, the child initially exhibited problems, and the biological or foster parents tried to deal with these themselves. They involved mental health professionals when their own efforts failed. However, two children, one at home and one in foster care, entered therapy following intervention because of intensifying emotional problems.

Although nearly half the children continued with or commenced therapy, as a whole the group showed fewer extreme behaviors over time (relatively few children exhibited specific behaviors either at the

TABLE 8.3
Mothers' Reports, Initially and at Two Years, of Children's Recurring Extreme Behavioral Problems

Behavior	Home ($N = 18$)		Foster ($N = 12$)		Comparison ($N = 39$)	
	Initially	At 2 years	Initially	At 2 years	Initially	At 2 years
Vandalism	28%	22%	8%	17%	5%	3%
Fire-setting	17	6	8	0	5	0
Stealing	22	11	8	8	5	3
Running away	11	0	0	0	0	3
Hoarding food	28	11	17	8	5	8
Tantrums	28	33	17	8	18	10
Self-injury	0	6	8	0	0	0
Daytime wetting	11	6	0	0	3	0

beginning or the conclusion of our study). Among the home children only vandalism and tantrums (which may not be indicative of general emotional problems) remained significant problems; only vandalism remained a problem among the foster children. The groups were comparable with regard to all behaviors except tantrums; five home children were reported as engaging in tantrums at the end of two years; no foster children were. See Table 8.3.

Examining the data by cases, 79 percent (fifteen) of the home mothers initially reported one or more extreme behaviors. After two years, 68 percent (thirteen) reported the presence of at least one extreme behavior. Sixty-two percent (eight) of the foster children were reported as exhibiting at least one extreme behavior initially; 54 percent (seven) of their caretakers reported such behaviors at the end of the study. In most cases the children initially reported as exhibiting extreme behaviors also exhibited them at the end of the study, though typically a different set of behaviors. In the case of the foster children a different person reported at the beginning and end since the initial reports were by biological mothers.

Although there was little overall change in the two groups, two children showed clear improvement and two showed deterioration in terms of psychological problems. We base this conclusion on the interviewers' and social workers' notes about the children, as well as on evidence from our measures. The following vignettes describe one child who improved and one who seemed to become significantly worse.

Jennifer, a nine-year-old girl, evidenced considerable improvement during the two years of the study. Her family came under agency supervision because

Jennifer had been beaten, by belt and by hand, by her stepfather for a period of several years. At the time of intervention, Jennifer and her mother had been in psychiatric therapy for one year. Her mother sought counseling for Jennifer because Jennifer had been hearing voices at night, running away from home, and exhibiting uncontrollable behavior at home. The psychiatrist reported that there had been no progress during the year of therapy. He recommended that Jennifer be placed in a residential institution. Following a brief foster placement, the psychiatrist decided that, owing to Jennifer's close attachment to her mother, she should remain at home.

At the initial interview, Jennifer's mother described Jennifer as crying a great deal, whining, easily distracted, and worried. Jennifer told our interviewer that she was not well liked, not happy, always getting into trouble, not able to learn, and doing bad things, and that she did not like the way she was. She had many problems with the other children at school. Her teacher, who found Jennifer unlikeable, reported that Jennifer had substantial emotional problems and did not relate well to peers.

At our six-month interviews, Jennifer's mother reported that Jennifer followed rules more easily, was more outgoing, was getting along better with other children, and appeared to take more pride in what she did. However, Jennifer reported that she did not like school, that she felt lonely, that she could not do things well, and that she got into trouble frequently. Although her stepfather had left the home, Jennifer remained frightened of him. At this time, Jennifer was receiving weekly counseling with a new therapist.

At the end of a year, Jennifer's mother was increasingly positive about Jennifer's behavior. Moreover, Jennifer was now reporting more positive feelings about herself. She was also viewed more favorably by her teacher, though the teacher reported that Jennifer was not effectively dealing with other children.

By eighteen months, Jennifer's mother reported delightful changes in Jennifer. She indicated that Jennifer helped prepare dinner after school and was communicating better by discussing problems. Jennifer's academic performance had improved; she was now spending some time in a regular class.

At two years, Jennifer's mother remained quite positive. She saw Jennifer as more independent and able to stand up for her ideas in an acceptable fashion. Jennifer's responses to our questions indicated an increase in self-esteem, though she still reported occasionally getting into trouble. At school, her new teacher thought her likeable, easy to be around, independent, and a leader of other children. She placed her in the upper half of the class in social skills. Jennifer's scores on the performance part of the WISC increased substantially.

In summary, Jennifer appears to have made considerable progress in her social behavior in the classroom, in relationships with her mother, and in her own assessment of her self-worth. Therapy, plus greater structuring of the home environment, the removal of the stepfather from the home, and the mother's increased emotional stability all appeared to facilitate Jennifer's improvement.

In contrast to Jennifer, Diana, an eight-year-old girl, appeared to become more psychologically disturbed during the two years. Although she was initially experiencing problems, she appeared to be able to cope with her situation when we first saw her. Despite provision of services to the family, over the two-year period she became increasingly depressed, withdrawing from many of her social relationships.

Diana came to the attention of child protective services when her mother sought to place her in foster care. Upon investigation, it appeared that her mother, who was overweight (300 pounds) and had a history of alcohol abuse, was providing only marginal care and supervision for her five children. Her husband seemed to be totally removed from the children. Through the provision of homemaker services to the mother, Diana was able to remain at home.

At our initial interviews Diana presented herself as a bright, reasonably contented child who scored in the almost superior range on intelligence tests. In answering the questions on our self-esteem and peer relationship measures, she described herself as happy and satisfied with her current situation both at home and at school. However, in general conversation she indicated that she had few friends and experienced difficulty with the neighborhood children. Diana's mother described a more problematic situation. She saw Diana as overweight, a compulsive eater, and "lethargic." She also indicated that Diana frequently stuttered, especially under stress. Diana's teacher noted still different qualities. She saw Diana as sad a good deal of the time, as having few friends, and as too compliant in her contact with others. She placed Diana in the lowest quintile of her class on both academic and social measures.

In the six months following intervention, services were provided to the family, especially to Diana's older and youngest brothers, both of whom had severe behavioral problems. Her mother received household assistance and individual counseling. However, Diana received no direct services other than those provided to her by her teachers at a parochial school.

Diana's situation worsened somewhat in the first year following agency intervention. Her mother was called to school by the principal because of three episodes of stealing by Diana. Her teacher, who had known her from the previous year, noted that Diana remained sad and depressed, had few friends, and continued to do very poorly in her academic work. Diana continued to have high self-esteem scores, however, and reported that her peer relations were very good, though she still said she had very few friends.

At our final meeting, Diana was overtly depressed and made statements to the effect that she did not like who she was, thought herself bad, felt lonely, and was unhappy. Her mother corroborated this picture, adding that Diana had severe arguments with her brothers and on one occasion had set a fire.

Her current teacher, different from the earlier-reporting teacher, while expressing feelings of liking for Diana, described her as a sad, lonely child without social contacts. Nonetheless, Diana improved somewhat in her academic performance and was now ranked by the teacher in the middle of the class, though still in the lowest quintile on social ratings.

Although Diana undoubtedly had emotional problems from the time we first saw her, she initially seemed to be coping with her situation. Her positive responses to our questions may have reflected self-denial, or she may have been unwilling to express her feelings to a stranger. By the second year following intervention, she no longer erected a facade for herself or toward our interviewer. She openly reported her unhappiness, her inability to concentrate in school ("I just stare off into space"), her loneliness, and her feelings of being worthless. Based on her mother's and teacher's reports, she was adding acting-out behaviors to her previously depressed, withdrawn conduct.

During the course of the study we thought that her problems were primarily caused by a lack of emotional support from her mother and father. However, six months after the study was completed, we learned that Diana had been sexually molested by her older brother during the time of our study. Thus, there were probably multiple reasons for Diana's deterioration.

SOCIAL BEHAVIOR IN THE SCHOOL SETTING:
TEACHER RATINGS

When we began studying the children, we were surprised by the extent of their academic problems. We were not surprised by their problems in social development at school. Many of the children were deficient in peer relations and showed inappropriate behaviors in the classroom. In fact, the most puzzling aspect of the initial scores was the relatively high ratings of the foster children. Whereas the home children received low ratings on social behavior, likability, and especially peer relations, the foster children rated similarly to the comparison children on both social behaviors and likability.

Whatever the reason for the initial differences, we expected no improvement for home children, in light of the possibility of continued abuse or neglect of the children and the instability in the lives of their parents. We were uncertain what to expect for the foster children. Some theorists argue that inadequate social behavior grows out of deficiencies in the parent-child relationship in the early years of life and that these behavior patterns are very hard to alter. Other experts believe that change in the parent-child relationship can significantly improve a child's general behavior. The foster children clearly had better role models and received more attentive treatment from their foster parents. Yet multiple placements, causing changes in school, peers, and caretakers, might have undermined any benefits from better role models.

As discussed in Chapter 5, the teachers rated three aspects of the child's behavior at school: specific classroom behaviors, including the child's ability to conform to classroom routines and work independently; the child's likability; and the child's peer relations. The ratings were highly correlated. In general, the home children's ratings declined over the two years. The foster group was more mixed, though their relative well-being, when measured against the comparison children, also declined.

Classroom behavior and likability. In terms of classroom behavior and general likability, the picture that emerged was one of both stability and change. At the group level there was relative stability in the mean scores of each group on both measures, though the home children were rated somewhat lower than the other groups on likability over time. At the individual level, however, there was substantial variability in both the home and foster groups; some children showed significant improvement, whereas others were rated considerably lower at the end of the two years. However, because there was more improvement among the lowest-rated foster children, the foster children as a group were less "at risk" by the end of two years (risk being defined in relation to the comparison children). In general, the abused children were rated lower at the end of two years, whereas the scores of the neglected children remained stable.

We looked at the teachers' ratings in several different ways in reaching these conclusions. First, we obtained an average group mean over the two years by taking *all* individual scores received by each child and computing the mean. Most children had three scores, each from a different teacher. However, because of missing data, some children had only two scores or even just one. The foster children, who were rated higher to begin with, rated higher, on average, for the whole two-year period. These children's scores resembled the comparison children's. See Table 8.4. Because these averages include all scores, regardless of the number of times the child received ratings, they do not tell us whether the home and foster groups changed over time. We therefore compared the initial and end scores for those children in each group for whom we had both scores. See Table 8.5. On classroom social behavior, there was little change in group scores over time, though in-

TABLE 8.4
Teachers' Ratings of Children's Social Behavior and Likability:
Group Means Aggregated over Two Years

Measure	Home (N = 19)	Foster (N = 12)	Comparison (N = 42)
Social behavior			
Mean[a]	3.2	3.6	3.7
SD	0.3	0.4	0.5
Likability			
Mean[a]	1.0	3.6	3.8
SD	2.6	2.7	3.3

[a]On 1–5 scale, 1 = low.

dividual children did improve or deteriorate. Most of the neglected children in both groups were rated slightly higher at the end; equal numbers of abused children were rated higher and lower.

The picture was somewhat different with regard to likability, for which all three groups had lower average scores at the end of two years than initially. The average score of the home children declined the most. This was due to two factors. Among the neglected children, equal numbers of children at home and in foster care had increased or decreased scores; however, the magnitude of the increase among the foster children was somewhat greater. More important, ten of eleven abused children were rated lower at the end of two years (scores were missing for the remaining three abused children). As a result, the average score of the home group, which contained more abused children was significantly lower than that of the foster group at the end of the two years. See Table 8.5.[14]

We also estimated the percentage of children in both the home and foster groups who were rated below the 25th-percentile score of the comparison children.[15] Using this standard of "at risk," there is reason to be concerned with the situation of the home children. Both initially and at our final measurement, the foster and comparison groups had a similiar distribution of likability scores, with approximately equal percentages of foster and comparison children at the lower end of the total distribution. In contrast, proportionately more home children were in the bottom range initially and this percentage increased over time. By the end of two years, the majority of the home children received scores in the range of the lowest 25 percent of the comparison children. Thus, the majority of home children were substantially below "normal" on this measure.

TABLE 8.5

*Teachers' Ratings of Children's Social Behavior and Likability,
Initially and at Two Years*

Measure	Home		Foster		Comparison	
	Initially	At 2 years	Initially	At 2 years	Initially	At 2 years
Social behavior						
Mean	3.2	3.3	3.5	3.6	3.8	3.7
SD	0.6	0.4	0.7	0.3	0.6	0.5
N	*18*	*18*	*8*	*8*	*42*	*42*
Likability						
Mean	1.5	−0.3	3.6	3.3	3.9	3.7
SD	3.8	3.0	4.5	3.7	4.2	3.8
N	*16*	*16*	*8*	*8*	*42*	*42*

Teacher assessments of peer relations. The differential impact of foster care was most pronounced with regard to teacher ratings of the children's peer relations. The rating of the home children, which were low initially, grew worse over time. Fifteen of the eighteen home children received very low scores at the end of two years. The abused children were doing even more poorly than the neglected children. The foster children showed a more mixed pattern. About half received relatively high ratings; the others had low to very low scores. Two foster children showed substantial improvement over the two years; two others were reported as having considerably poorer peer relations.[16]

By the end of two years, over 70 percent of the home children were rated below the 25th percentile of the comparison children (initially 50 percent were so rated). It is harder to derive an accurate estimate for the foster children because of the small numbers and missing data. A reasonable approximation is that 40 to 50 percent of these children were at risk initially and that the proportion of children at risk declined somewhat at the end of two years.

Overall assessment: school behavior. Our data certainly support the conclusion that, with respect to social development in the school setting, foster care did not harm most children and may have benefited some. Several factors might account for the improvement. The foster children attended school more regularly than the home children. Some of the home children came to school poorly groomed. Both factors might independently have influenced teacher evaluations. The child's appearance may also have helped with peer relations. Several home children reported being teased at school about their clothes or their smell. In addition, the foster children may have acquired new skills that enabled them to better relate to peers. They may have developed these skills by learning from their foster parents or by having to live with other children in the foster home.

Any conclusions regarding improvement must be tentative. The two groups were different at the time of initial measurement. Unless we assume that the foster children made rapid changes in skills relating to task performance, initiative, and in peer relations, the children may have been different before intervention. Moreover, we dealt with a very small number of foster children on these measures (eight). Four additional children entered school after a year in foster care; two of these received low ratings on all three measures in their first year of school and their ratings declined the following year. Still, the majority of the home children evidenced major deficiencies in social development initially and their situation either worsened or did not improve over time. Thus, our best guess is that foster placement tended to be a positive factor in the area of social development.

PARENT-CHILD RELATIONS

We look next at how the biological and foster parents perceived the children's behavior in the family setting. Each child's caretaker regularly completed our child behavior (CBS) and social competence scales. The CBS focused exclusively on negative behaviors, such as crying, whining, or complaining. The social competence scale contained items related to the child's skills at task performance, autonomy, and initiative, and some items related to interpersonal interactions. Because the only items that distinguished the three groups of children (home, foster, comparison) were those relating to parent-child interactions, our interest in the social scale is as it measures interaction rather than child behavior. Therefore, we view the caretakers' ratings on both the CBS and the social competence scale primarily as indicators of the quality of the parent-child relationship. We use these scores, the children's reports of how they were getting along with their parents or caretakers, and the parents' responses to the conflict and cohesion sections of the Moos Family Environment Scale, to develop a picture of familial interaction and atmosphere. Undoubtedly, both interaction and its context influenced the children's general behaviors and were in turn influenced by them.

Because the foster children were in multiple placements, we have different reporters at different times. We cannot tell whether changed scores reflect changes in behavior, a different match of foster parent and child, or merely differences in the tolerances of the different foster parents. Obviously, for the children who changed caretakers successive scores do not measure a progression within a relationship. Instead, the assessments reflect the initial phases of a relationship, which often changed—for better or for worse—as time passed.

Parental perceptions of a child's behaviors. At the point of initial intervention, more than half the home mothers reported two or more problem behaviors on the CBS. The majority portrayed their children as difficult to get along with—whining, complaining, or lying. This was not true of the foster mothers. At the time of our initial interviews, only one of the thirteen foster parents reported as many as two problems.

For the home children, the initial pattern generally maintained itself over the two-year period. At our last interviews, approximately half the mothers reported two or more problem behaviors; 21 percent (four mothers) reported four or more. See Table 8.6. The pattern in individual cases was fairly stable: seven mothers reported two or more behaviors throughout; five reported none or one throughout. There was change in one-third of the families: only two mothers reported worsening behavior and four reported substantial improvement. Thus many of the children were in conflict with their parents, at least from the mothers' perspectives.

The situation in the foster homes is harder to categorize. If we look only at the foster mothers' responses to the CBS, it would appear that the foster children were extremely well behaved. Foster mothers rarely described a child's behavior *as a problem.* However, we believe that the CBS understates both the amount of "problematic behavior" by the child and the degree of conflict, or difficulty, between the foster parents and the child. In our interviews, the foster mothers reported that the children exhibited similar types of behaviors as those reported by the home mothers. However, the foster mothers did not view these behaviors as posing *a problem.* The foster parents, at least those not relatives of the children, viewed themselves as "professionals" who were supposed to deal with the child's behavior problems. They often attributed behavior to the child's previous environment and felt that it was their responsibility to help the child cope.

TABLE 8.6

*Biological and Foster Mothers' Reports of Problematic Child Behaviors,
Initially and at One and Two Years*

Category	Number of behaviors		
	0–1	2–3	4–7
Home (*N* = 19)			
Initial report	42%	21%	37%
Report at 1 year	56	27	17
Report at 2 years	48	32	20
Foster (*N* = 13)			
Initial report	92	8	0
Report at 1 year	92	8	0
Report at 2 years	84	16	0
Comparison (*N* = 42)			
Report at 1 year	79	19	2
Report at 2 years	93	5	2

NOTE: Seven behaviors were identified: crying, whining, pouting, complaining, yelling, disobeying, and lying.

Yet we have evidence indicating that many of the foster parents did find the children's behavior problematic for them. As previously discussed, five children were moved from one foster home to another because the foster parents asked that the child be removed.[17] Each of these foster mothers reported substantial problems in our general conversations, but only one of them reported problem behaviors on the CBS or social competence scale. Four of the five children spent between six months and a year with foster mothers who viewed them as difficult. In addition to these five children, the caretakers of two other children, who remained in a single home throughout the two years, indicated that the child was very difficult to manage, although they did not label specific behaviors as a problem on the CBS.[18]

It must be stressed that we cannot assume there was parent-child conflict whenever a foster parent reported a behavior as a problem or described difficulties with the child. Several foster parents seemed able to remain very close to the child, and to respond with appropriate limit setting, regardless of the child's behavior. However, there were situations where the child's behavior generated substantial hostility from the foster mother.

The social competence scale provides additional evidence that the abused and neglected children initially had problems interacting with their caretakers, but that the problems seemed to lessen over time for the foster children.[19] There were clear differences between the abused and neglected and the comparison children in ratings on those questions that measured parent-child interaction, as, for examples: "Does the child quiet down when asked?"; ". . . stop before he/she goes beyond your limits?"; ". . . misbehave when you don't let him/her have his/her way?" Initially ten home children scored quite low on these items. Eight mothers of these ten remained dissatisfied with these aspects of their children's behavior throughout the two years.

The picture was somewhat different for the foster children. Whereas the foster children initially received low scores on items relating to adult-child interaction, at the end of the two years there were no group differences between the foster and comparison children on any items. At our last interviews, the foster mothers reported considerable improvement in the children's willingness to help around the house, to share toys with other children, and to give up something when asked to do so. It must be remembered that the final scores do not necessarily indicate a progression in the child's behavior since, for many children, the reporters were different. Whether it was changed behavior, or changed perceptions, three of the six foster children initially rated low improved substantially. Only one of the seven children initially rated high declined substantially.

The picture of higher conflict in the home families also emerged in the mothers' responses on the conflict and cohesion scales of the Family Environment Scale. The home mothers, on average, reported significantly higher levels of conflict and less cohesion than the foster mothers or mothers of the comparison children.

In sum, about half the mothers of the home children reported problems in dealing with their children throughout the two years. There was little change in the families with the most problems. About half the foster children were perceived as problems during the first year. This declined to approximately 25 percent at the end.

The children's perspective. We also tried to obtain the child's perceptions of the relationship. It is difficult to get accurate assessments of caregivers from children. They are generally reluctant to tell anyone, especially a stranger, of negative feelings. Thus, the children may have provided a rosier picture than actually existed. The children also may have had higher expectations of getting along with their biological parents than with foster parents; a moderately good relationship may have pleased the foster children. Still, some children in both settings were willing to report poor relations—and when they did, their assessments virtually always coincided with a parent's or foster parent's report.

We asked each child, "How are you getting along with your parents (caretakers)?" We divided their responses into two categories, "good" and "not-so-good" (these tended to be the words they used in answering the open-ended question). Of the eighteen home children who responded to this question at various times throughout the two years, nine (50 percent) reported not-so-good relations at least one time; five (28 percent) felt this way most of the two years. For example, one boy said "My mother is always sad—and always yelling at me." Another boy said, "Me and my dad fight. I don't like that; he always hurts me." Of the thirteen foster children, seven (53 percent) reported not-so-good relations at least once; three (23 percent) felt this was true during most of the two years.[20] One child mirrored the statements of the home children, saying he didn't like foster care because "I don't like to fight with Grandma, and Grandpa gets a board and threatens me." Thus, from the children's reports parent-child relations were, on average, about the same in each setting. In contrast, only fourteen (33 percent) of the forty-two comparison children reported poor relations once; just three (7 percent) did so twice.

Overall assessment: parent-child relations. Based on the average scores on the CBS, social competence scale, and Family Environment Scale, the mothers' reports of whether they found their child likable, and the children's responses about "getting along" with their caregivers, we believe that between eight and eleven home children were in families where parent-child relations were very poor for much of the two years. Eight mothers reported substantial behavior problems on two or more measures; four of these eight also said that they found their child unlikable. Four of the eight children in these families corroborated this, reporting poor parent-child relations. In addition, the three home children reported poor relations though their mothers did not.

The foster children are more difficult to categorize, inasmuch as they changed placements. We tried to develop a picture that encompassed their experiences in different homes. Looking at all our measures, we believe that three foster children spent most of the two years in homes where they did not get along well with their caregivers; two of the three lived with relatives. Two others spent half the two years in homes where they did not get along well with the foster parents. The eight other foster children generally got along well with their caretakers, though several spent a small amount of time in a foster home where they experienced difficulties.

Thus, as a group the foster children seemed to have established relations with their caregivers that were no worse than those of the home children. To the degree that the adults' reports reflected actual behavior, the foster children also were somewhat more likely to have acceptable behavior. It must be recognized, however, that the fact that a child reported "getting along" with a caretaker did not necessarily mean a warm, supportive relationship, or that the caretakers were meeting all the child's emotional needs. We explore these aspects of the relationships in Chapter 9.

THE CHILDREN'S SATISFACTION WITH SELF, PEERS, AND SCHOOL

By any standards, the study children did not lead easy lives either before or after intervention. During the two years, many of the home children were reabused or neglected; lived in families with conflict between parents as well as between parents and children; were doing poorly academically; and were viewed negatively by their teachers. Under the circumstances, one might well expect the home children to report worse feelings about themselves, their peer relations, and their school satisfaction at the end of the two years.

Prediction is harder for the foster children. Certainly the multiple placements, loss of contact with their biological parents, and generally poor academic performance did not enhance their lives. However, they were better fed, had more material goods, and lived in better physical surroundings than they had previously. The majority were liked by their teachers. Their caretakers were less disorganized. At least half the group lived with caring, committed adults by the end of the two years. Thus, we might expect a mixed picture for these children.

The picture that emerged from our interviews was surprising. In general, all three groups of children—home, foster, and comparison—reported increased satisfaction with themselves, their peer relations, and their schools at the end of two years. Moreover, with respect to self-esteem and peer relations, the children in each setting had quite similar levels of satisfaction by the end of two years, except for a small group of home children who were quite unhappy for most of the two years. With regard to school, the foster children, as a group, were the most satisfied, with every foster child reporting high satisfaction; but most home children also seemed to like school.

Before looking at the data from which we drew these conclusions, we must provide a warning. On both the self-esteem and peer relations measures, there was considerable variability in many children's responses from one time to the next. Their attitudes seemed to be greatly affected by situational factors; for example, a child who reported good peer relations on one occasion might report poor relations the next if she had recently quarreled with her best friend. Because of variability, small sample, and missing data, there were several large fluctuations in the group means at the five measurement periods. We also believe that the initial self-esteem scores of the home children were unusually low, possibly reflecting the fact that we saw these children at a time of particularly high family stress. On the other hand, both the home and foster groups showed a great increase in self-esteem at our last interview, which might have been related to the special nature of that interview, which took place at popular fast-food restaurants (the well-known "burger effect").

Both the individual variation and the impact of missing cases resulted in substantial variability in the group means at different measurement periods. The trend in each group, though higher, was not linear. Owing to the variability of means at different times, we do not base our conclusions solely on the group means at our last measurement. The critical factor is that *the trends and the comparative position of the home and foster children remain the same* no matter which time periods we examine. It would be unnecessarily confusing to present all the group means at each time period since the number of children responding varied. We present data from the start and end of the study, since this is the time frame we have used for other variables, and these periods reflect the general trends.

Averaging all scores over the two years for all children, regardless of the number of times a child responded, the home children clearly were, on average, the least satisfied group and the comparison children the most satisfied (except with school satisfaction, where the foster children seemed highest). See Table 8.7. In essence, these averages reflect the fact that the home children started out and remained the least satisfied, the comparison group started and remained the most satisfied, and the trend for all groups was the same.

With respect to change over time, the average score of each group increased on the measures of self-esteem and peer relations. A substantial majority of the children in each group were more satisfied at the

TABLE 8.7

Children's Self-Esteem, Peer Relations, and School Satisfaction:
Group Means Aggregated over Two Years

Measure	Home (N = 18)	Foster (N = 13)	Comparison (N = 42)
Self-esteem			
Mean[a]	2.7	5.0	6.2
SD	3.8	3.6	3.2
Peer relations			
Mean[b]	2.5	3.6	4.6
SD	3.0	2.4	3.2
School satisfaction			
Mean[c]	2.8	4.2	3.3
SD	2.5	1.3	2.0

[a] On −12–+12 scale.
[b] On −10–+10 scale.
[c] On −8–+8 scale.

end. There were no statistically significant changes in school satisfaction. See Table 8.8.

There were no group differences in the slope of the trends with regard to self-esteem or peer satisfaction. And whereas the mean scores for the foster and comparison groups increased on the school satisfaction during the two years while the home group stayed the same, equal proportions of all three groups went up and down over the two-year period. Thus, the pattern was the same on this variable as well. Interestingly, among the home group, the abused children showed much bigger gains on both self-esteem and peer relations than did the neglected children. This was also true of the three abused children in foster care. In fact, the abused children, who had the lowest scores initially, had the highest average scores at the end of the two years. This finding is particularly surprising since their teachers reported substantial declines in the peer relations of the abused children.

We must stress again that even though children had high scores at the end of the second year, many had experienced periods of great unhappiness. It seems safe to conclude, however, that neither removal from home, even when resulting in multiple placements, nor continued abuse or neglect of the home children, generally led to lower self-esteem or less satisfaction with peers or school. The children were able to maintain a self-concept not shared by their parents or teachers.

TABLE 8.8

*Children's Self-Esteem, Peer Relations, and School Satisfaction,
Initially and at Two Years*

	Home		Foster		Comparison	
Measure	Initially	At 2 years	Initially	At 2 years	Initially	At 2 years
Self-esteem						
Mean	0.7	5.7	3.4	7.0	5.2	7.2
SD	4.9	5.3	4.9	3.4	4.7	3.4
N	16		12		42	
Peer						
Mean	1.5	3.9	2.6	4.7	4.3	4.9
SD	5.0	4.2	4.2	4.4	4.2	3.7
N	15		11		42	
School satisfaction						
Mean	2.8	2.9	3.3	3.8	2.9	3.7
SD	4.0	2.6	1.6	3.5	2.6	2.2
N	15		8		42	

We have been unable to uncover any factors that consistently distinguish the high-esteem from the low-esteem children. Based on our clinical knowledge of each case, we believe that we can explain many of the big fluctuations in scores by specific events. For example, one child (a six-year-old boy) with a highly variable self-esteem score had a mother who was extremely hostile, very emotional, and unstable. His attitudes seemed to reflect his mother's current condition. Another child's attitudes went up and down depending on the support available from a teacher she liked. Because different factors affected each child, no factor emerged as a significant predictor.

A child's unhappiness or concern did not, however, always show up in responses to the questions that make up the three scales. Many children expressed their worries and fears in the talks with our interviewers. Among the home children, the primary fears were of being hit, of being unloved, and that possible harm might come to their parents. The foster children expressed many of the concerns and fears reported in other studies of foster children. Perhaps their primary concern was for the well-being of their parents. Some children did not want to enter foster care because of a conviction that their parents needed them. While in care more than half the children mentioned fears that parents might die or injure themselves. These fears often were based on an awareness of the parents' shortcomings. For example, one boy was afraid that his father "might go to jail for drinking on the freeway," whereas another boy said, "Mom has an apartment now—I think she has everything together but herself."

The possibility of being abandoned was another common theme among the foster children. Those children who were not visited by their biological parents were hurt and sad. The children also worried about the instability of foster care. One child said, "I'll probably be gone [from the foster family] at Christmas. I've never had a Christmas because we go to live someplace else. I never get good gifts." She went on to say she thought she would have to leave her foster family because "my mother doesn't want us anymore" (and therefore a permanent foster home would have to be located). Another girl, in an adoptive home after a year and a half, said, "I'm very happy—glad that I don't have to go to any more foster homes. It's a hard thing to do and then you have to forget them." Several children expressed fear that they would be evicted from the foster home if they misbehaved. This was not unreasonable; in three cases, the siblings of a child were removed from a foster home because of misbehavior while the study child was allowed to remain. These children, who missed their siblings, were especially fearful. Even children in seemingly stable placements faced the threat of being moved, sometimes being told by other foster children in the home not to count on staying there. The fact that they had little control over their own fate added to some children's worries. One girl, who wanted to return home, said, "The court and the judge will decide if I will go home but they don't tell me these things."

Four of the thirteen foster children exhibited short-term behaviors showing the stress of separation adjustment to a foster home, or both. Two children had nightmares for a time, one cried in bed each night, a fourth child rocked in bed each evening and had nightmares. Other children whose behavior revealed stress included one who was afraid of playing outdoors and another who was upset because her schoolmates teased her about being a foster child. Most of the symptoms or problems were temporary, but the fact that five children needed ongoing psychological therapy indicates that the children's emotional states might not have been as good as they portrayed them.

Thus, we have a mixed picture. Although most of the children seemed to be coping, they were a troubled group. Neither home placement with services nor foster care provided a burden-free setting.

Changes in Individual Children

In the previous section we ignored individual children and emphasized group results. Now we will try to find individuals in this mass of data. Our goal is to determine whether, in terms of changes in the *overall* well-being of the children, the home or foster group did "better" over the two years. We address three issues: first, were there individual children who functioned particularly well or particularly poorly in several areas of development throughout the two years? Second, were there children who showed substantial improvement, or deterioration, in several areas of development over the two years? Third, can we identify factors that account for why children did well or poorly, improved or deteriorated? In particular, any such factors related to placement?

Developing a composite picture of each child's "well-being" proved difficult. Although we expected that there would be some relationship between a child's developmental status in each of the various domains we examined—physical, academic, social, emotional, and personal satisfaction—a substantial body of research indicates that children may function adequately in one aspect of development but poorly in another (Maccoby 1980). Clearly there is no reason to believe that a child doing poorly academically necessarily will have poor peer relations. Perhaps less obvious, children often have better relations with their teachers than with their parents, or vice versa.

In fact, we found that, for most children, there was only a moderate relationship in their development across domains.[21] Even on measures we expected to be closely related, for example, the children's self-esteem scores and their assessments of peer relations, or the teachers' ratings of a child's social behavior and likability, we found children who scored high on one measure and low on another. In general, we found no relationship between the child's physical health or academic performance and the child's socioemotional development or parent-child interaction.

Since most of the children had adequate physical health and almost all showed academic deficiencies throughout the two years, we exclude these factors from our overall assessment. We also ignored whether a child experienced reabuse or continued neglect, and whether a foster child wanted to return to her parents. Although these factors might not be irrelevant to policymakers, we are interested in assembling the socioemotional components in less obvious ways. Thus we looked for children who consistently did poorly or well in terms of teachers' assessments of their social skills, maternal assessments of the children's behavior, the presence or absence of emotional problems, and, finally, the children's assessments of their general satisfaction and their peer relations. In determining a child's overall status, initially and at the end of the two-year period, we began by converting their scores on each of our different measures into a "standard score," which allowed us to compare where each child stood *in relation to the other abused and neglected children* on each of the measures.[22] We also considered whether the child had shown significant problems not captured by these measures.

At the time we first saw them, only one child's well-being was very high on *all* measures; his scores were in the top 25 percent of the abused/neglected group in every respect. No child ranked in the bottom 25 percent of the group on *all* measures. Since all the children but one were functioning well in some areas, about average in others, and relatively poorly in still others, we assessed the children in terms of their *predominant* pattern of well-being at our initial and final measurements. The children fell into three groups: those who appeared to be functioning well in relation to the other children (top 25 percent), those who appeared to be functioning poorly (bottom 25 percent), and those who were generally "average." This last group included some children who were in the middle of the entire sample on almost all measures and other children who were doing quite well in some areas and poorly in others.

Initially six children, all at home, fell into the low group. Seven children, three at home and four in foster care, were in the uppermost group. The remaining nineteen children had mixed or average patterns. A case example will illustrate some of the difficulties and complexities encountered in attempting to come up with a summary score on the socioemotional status of each child:

Jim, a seven-year-old, was referred to child protective services because his mother was reported to have beaten him with a stick. On investigation, the family was found to be living in a filthy home. Jim's mother, a single parent, was chronically ill with arthritis.

At the beginning of the study, his mother described Jim as a very active child, always in motion and not capable of sitting long enough even to watch TV. She reported that he disobeyed her and teased his babysitters so much that she found it difficult to keep them. She reported that Jim showed repeated episodes of vandalism, fire-setting, and food hoarding. In contrast, Jim's teacher said Jim was likable, exhibited reasonably good social behavior in school, and was well liked by his peers. In his self-description, Jim scored quite low on self-regard and even lower on peer relationships.

Jim was referred to a counselor and received some help for several months. At the end of the two years, his mother described him as less hyperactive and more inclined to follow her requests. There were few problem behaviors. In sharp contrast, his new teacher gave him low ratings on social behavior in school, likability, and peer relationships. Jim's statements about himself continued to be negative.

When we examined change in overall patterns, it was quite clear that only one child functioned uniformly well in all areas of development through the two years. Each of the six other children who rated high initially showed significant problems in at least one area of development at our last measurement period. Three of these six children still functioned reasonably well, though they rated quite low on one measure. Surprisingly, the other three children were doing quite poorly overall, and had gone from the best-functioning to the worst-functioning group. Of the six children functioning worst initially, one improved significantly, three showed improvement in some aspects of development but were still at substantial risk, and two children did not appear to improve at all.

The nineteen children whose development was initially average tended to stay the same or to improve. Three children improved significantly; they were functioning quite well by the end of the two years. Most of the other children still had major problems in some aspects of development, but generally seemed to cope.

Thus, overall, the abused and neglected children stayed much the same during the two years. There was little change in either the home or foster group relative to the comparison children; the overall status of the abused and neglected children continued to be poor. As stated earlier, this assessment does not include school performance, which generally remained low even for those children showing the most improvement in the socioemotional area.

We now turn to our third question: Can we identify factors that account for why particular children generally did well or poorly, improved or deteriorated? The clearest finding is that the worst cases tended to change little over time. All were children living at home. All received services. In only one or two cases did these services significantly improve the child's well-being. Because there were no low-group children in foster care initially (except for the one child who ended up in institutional placement), we cannot tell whether foster care would have helped the worst-off children. Of the seven children who were in the uppermost group initially, two of the three home children moved to the average group and one to the low group. Of the four highest-group foster children, one remained high, one was functioning poorly, and two became more mixed (average) in development. Of the nineteen children initially showing average development, both the home and foster children remained about the same over the two-year period.

It appears that we cannot expect much improvement for children left at home, especially those most at risk. Foster placement may have resulted in somewhat greater chances of improvement, but there was a danger of deterioration in both settings. By statistical means we examined a number of factors to see if they predicted the child's *final overall status*. The only factor that did so was the child's *initial* status. The following factors proved unrelated to the child's final status: mother's initial marital status, mother's history of pathologies, mother's age at birth of the study child, whether or not the mother had been abused as a child, the mother's education, the child's initial age, IQ, gender, whether the child had been abused or neglected, and placement in a special class.

In addition to looking at the impact of placement, we attempted to see if any other factors were related to changes in the children's well-being (i.e., improvement or deterioration). We looked at whether or not the child continued to be abused or neglected, the level of services to the child and family, and the number of placements for children in foster care. We found no statistically significant differences on any of these variables between those who improved and those who did not. However, our sample is very small, which makes it less likely that significant differences will be identified. Moreover, our measurement of services was relatively crude; we could not adequately evaluate the quality of the therapy received by parents and children. Perhaps a more fine-tuned measure would have told us more.

To summarize, most children did not show changes in socio-emotional status over the two years. Improvement in the foster group seemed to be a result of finding a good fit between the child and foster family. As for the home children, we cannot explain why some of them improved. The home children appeared to do slightly less well overall than did the foster children. The home children who were reabused were particularly at risk. Although the physical abuse itself often was not severe, there was a great deal of marital discord in most such cases, as well as parent-child conflict. This discord appeared to be at least as detrimental as the abuse.

Summary: Home Versus Foster Care

Despite the lack of change in ratings for most of the children over time, there were some differences in outcome between the home and foster groups. The foster children received somewhat better physical care; in particular, the children most at risk in terms of physical health seemed to benefit from foster care. The foster children also missed considerably less school. Whether because of fewer absences or more environmental support, there was some indication that foster care increased the chances that a child would perform adequately in school. Both foster placement and remaining at home were stressful for children, albeit for different reasons. Among the home children, the level of parent-child (or parent-parent) conflict remained high for half the children. Many children also had to cope with reabuse, continued neglect, or depressed parents. Although the majority of foster children also experienced conflict with at least one caregiver, by the end of two years two-thirds were in stable, nonhostile homes.

Surprisingly, despite the stress experienced by the majority of children, the average self-esteem and self-reported peer-relations scores rose for all groups. We cannot tell whether the children were truly more satisfied or their responses on these particular scales were affected by repeated administration. Still, nearly half the children, in both settings, continued to evidence emotional problems, and these seemed more severe among the home children. In addition, the home children seemed to have very poor social behavior at school—both with their teachers and peers—and their situations worsened over time. Although many foster children also experienced social problems at school, as a group they did not deteriorate.

In terms of overall socioemotional well-being, with respect to the aspects of development reported in this chapter, the foster children tended to be better off. However, the differences at the end of two years seem largely attributable to initial differences. There is a hint—no more—that foster care may have been beneficial (or less detrimental) than home placement to the overall well-being of slightly more children. A disheartening finding is that nearly half the children in both settings still seemed at substantial risk at the end of the two years. Moreover, as we shall see in Chapter 9, the loss of their parents was a significant issue for most of the foster children.

A final note of caution is in order. The conclusions we have come to must be considered only tentative, since the sample size was small and most of the changes were not substantial. Additional studies of larger groups with a wider age span are needed before firm conclusions can be drawn.

Nine

The Children's Emotional Relationship with Their Caretakers

SO FAR, OUR DATA indicate that the foster children fared at least as well as the home children, and probably better, in terms of self-esteem, school, and peer satisfaction. The majority of foster children also felt that they were "getting along" well with their new caretakers; by the end of two years, two-thirds were in homes that appeared to be their permanent new homes. Yet, the fact that these children had a co-operative relationship with their caretakers, or felt "satisfied" with themselves and their peer relations, does not fully answer one major concern about foster care. For most children, merely "getting along" with their caretakers does not ensure adequate emotional growth. We agree with Goldstein, Freud, and Solnit (1973), who argue that children need to feel that their caretakers are committed to them, emotionally involved with them, and loving of them.[1] These are feelings that one expects (but does not always find) in the parent-child relationship, inasmuch as biological and cultural factors push toward positive relations. Will these relations develop in a foster home? The question is especially important when we are talking about five-to-ten-year-old children who may have emotional problems, poor early attachment relations with their own parents, and a reluctance to trust or become committed to "new parents." Although there is ample evidence that foster and adoptive parents develop strong emotional commitments to infants and toddlers, and that these feelings are reciprocated, does this also happen with older children?

Although commentators have customarily focused on the problems of bonding in foster families, it must also be recognized that adequate bonding may not exist in families consisting of biological parents and their children. It is appropriate to be concerned if children who remain in foster care are not able to develop a strong sense of being wanted by their new caretakers, and secure with them, but any criticism of foster care on these grounds becomes mitigated if abused or neglected children living with biological parents also lack such bonds. If the home children do not see their parents as an adequate source of love and support, we might be more willing to accept foster care, even if totally satisfactory emotional relations do not emerge for many children.

In this chapter we focus on the nature of the attachment or emotional relationship between the children in our study and their caretakers. We begin by looking at the foster children.

The Foster Children

Unfortunately, measuring the foster children's emotional relationships with their caretakers was very complicated. We wanted to assess the relationship from both the adults' and the children's perspectives; we assumed that if the foster parent did not feel a commitment to keeping the child, it was unlikely that a secure, loving relationship would develop. On the other hand, the foster parent's commitment to keep a child cannot ensure that the child *feels* wanted or prefers the new family to the biological family. We also must take into account that most of the foster children had more than one caretaker during the two years; these children might have gotten along with one caretaker and not another. Although our main concern in the descriptions that follow is whether the children ultimately ended up in homes where they felt wanted, we hope also to capture the child's experience over time, as well as the nature of the particular relationship that existed at our last measurement.

Since for children in the age group of our study there are no direct measures of attachment or bonding from either the child's or the adult's perspective, we must rely on indirect measures and, to a degree, clinical judgment. First, we assume that where either the child or the caretaker had primarily negative feelings toward the other, it was unlikely that a sound attachment or commitment developed. On the other hand, the fact that in some other families the child and the caretaker liked each other and were getting along well does not necessarily mean that they felt committed to each other, in the sense in which Goldstein, Freud, and Solnit seem to use that term. To assess the children's feelings on this issue, we rely on our general clinical impression derived from their responses to all the questions pertaining to relations with their caretakers, especially their response to the question "Where would you like to live?"

THE ADULTS' PERSPECTIVES ON
THE RELATIONSHIP

We begin by reporting the caretakers' feelings; unless a caretaker was willing to keep a child, the child would not benefit from attachment to that parent. All the foster parents initially assumed custody willingly. However, they became caretakers under widely varying circumstances. At one end of the spectrum were "emergency foster homes," with foster parents who expected to care for the children for only a limited time, from a few days to a few months. Caretakers who view the placement as short-term are unlikely to develop a strong emotional commitment to the child. In contrast, some children were placed immediately with caretakers who expressed a willingness, even a desire, to provide a permanent home.

Because we expected involvement to evolve rather than blossom as soon as the child was planted in the home, we explored caretakers' feelings in different ways at different times. Shortly after a child was placed in a home, and every three months thereafter, we asked the caretakers how they were "getting along" with the child. We also asked them how long they expected to keep the child. After a child was in a home for at least six months, we asked the foster mother how "close" she felt to the child and if she wished she did not have the child to worry about. We assumed that six months was the minimum time for real closeness to develop. Finally, as reported earlier, we noted if ultimately the foster parents adopted or became legal guardians of the child, the clearest indication that the adults were committed to the child.

From all these measures, we developed a global picture of the caretakers' perspectives. As it turned out, there was substantial convergence between the "getting along" and "bonding" aspects of the relationship. By the end of two years nine of the thirteen white foster children were with caretakers who wanted to keep them permanently. These foster mothers reported that within their families all members were getting along well (but not necessarily very well) with the foster child, all felt close to the child, and almost all were highly involved in planning for the children, helping in school, and facilitating friendships.

Even though each of these nine children ended up in a home in which the caretaker wanted the relationship to be permanent, only two spent all two years in such a home—one with his grandparents, who were willing to raise him though they were not wholly enthusiastic about the prospect, and the second with foster parents who very much wanted to adopt him and had been committed to keeping him for almost the entire two-year period. The other seven spent at least six months, and in most cases a year, with foster parents who viewed the placement as temporary.[2] Typically, these children were placed in an emergency foster home, then a supposedly permanent foster home that was in fact not permanent, and finally in a home with foster parents who either adopted them or became their legal guardians. The patterns varied considerably. For example, one boy was in two short-term foster homes and then moved to another state to live with his grandparents, who immediately became his legal guardians. In contrast, one girl was rejected by several foster parents, but after twenty months was placed with a single woman who adopted her.

Finally, four of the thirteen foster children never lived with foster caretakers who made a total emotional commitment to them. One child was moved from foster home to foster home throughout the two years, never experiencing a sense of permanence or belonging. Although the other three lived in one home for a substantial period (two were in one home the entire time), they had difficulty getting along with these caretakers, who all indicated a lack of closeness to the child. Two of the children were with relatives who expected the biological mothers to resume custody. The third child was with foster parents who expected to raise the child until adulthood but were unwilling to become guardians or make a strong emotional commitment to him because of his behavioral problems.

To a large degree, it was a matter of luck for a child to end up in a home with strongly committed parents. The agencies did not attempt to match a child and a foster family. Even placement with a relative did not guarantee that the child would be loved and wanted. The only factor that seemed related to strong commitment was the child's behavioral adjustment. Not surprisingly, children who evidenced substantial behavioral problems were less likely to wind up in stable, committed placements than better-adjusted children, though there were some exceptions.

THE CHILDREN'S PERSPECTIVES

We turn now to the most difficult question. As just discussed, by the end of two years most of the foster children were in stable placements and most reported good relations with their caretakers. Yet the fact that a child was not having difficulty with the foster parents does not mean that the child felt wanted by them or was prepared to enter into a close relationship with new parents. Goldstein, Freud, and Solnit (1973) assert that after a child has been in a foster home for a relatively short time, the child's primary attachment shifts to the foster parents. Although these authors say that the timing of the shift will vary with the age of the child, the amount of contact with the biological parent, and the degree to which the foster parents assume the role of "psychological parent," they believe that in most cases allegiance will shift by eighteen months. However, there are no data, at least for children beyond infancy, on the time conditions under which a child comes to perceive a new caretaker as her "psychological parent." Not only must these children establish bonds with new caretakers, they must cope with the emotional loss of biological parents. Many clinicians claim that some children in foster care never come to accept separation from biological parents and either openly or secretly desire reunion with them. The child may have conflicting loyalties that prevent formation of stable emotional bonds.

We tried to examine the children's emotional relationship with both their foster parents and their biological parents. Because there are no measures of attachment for children of the ages in our study, we rely on the children's reports of how much they turned to their foster parents for emotional support and, most important, their preferences as to where they wanted to live, recognizing that neither is an ideal measure.

Foster parents as resources. We first look at whether a child perceived his or her caretaker as a resource capable of meeting the child's emotional needs. We asked each child whom he or she would talk to if troubled or worried, and if happy, and if wanting something; and to name the grownups who would stick up for her and who would help her "out a lot." The children could mention more than one person for each of the five questions; we counted the foster mother or father as a resource whenever that parent was mentioned as one, even if that foster parent was not the only or the first person mentioned. Although the questions are indirect measures of emotional bonds, it seems unlikely that children felt strong bonds to adults who did not meet their emotional and concrete needs.

We were surprised that even at the end of two years, many of the children did not mention their foster parents as major resources. Only six of the thirteen mentioned their foster parents on four or five items, compared with eleven of the eighteen home children and twenty-nine of the forty-two comparison children. Surprisingly, the nine children in "permanent" homes were no more likely to view the foster parents (in some cases adoptive parents) as resources than were the four children in "nonpermanent" homes. In fact, two boys in adoptive placements and one girl living with her older brother were among the children reporting the least use of the foster parents as a resource. There was no difference between children who had been in multiple placements and those who had lived in only one home. Nor did a child's age or a caretaker's attitudes toward the child show any consistent relationship with the child's responses. We were unable to discover any pattern in the children, adults, or interpersonal dynamics that made a placement more or less successful in this regard.

Children's desires about caretakers. Did the infrequent reliance on the foster parent as a resource indicate a lack of emotional ties? Were the children still primarily attached to their biological parents? From our interviews with the children it appears that approximately half still saw their biological parents as "psychological parents" and half looked to the foster parents, albeit ambivalently in some cases.

Virtually all the children expressed a continuing desire for visits by their biological parents, even if they had not been visited for a long period. Indeed, no matter how frequently or infrequently they were in fact visited, the children wanted more. Only two children did not want this—both had said they wanted visits whenever we asked about this until our last interviews, when they said they no longer felt this way. One had not seen her parents in nearly two years and was in an adoptive home at the time of the last interview. The other was living in a relative's home, and her mother joined her there; the child did not want to visit with her father, from whom she had been removed initially.[3] She had lived with the father for only eight months prior to the initial intervention, having spent most of her life with her mother. One child seemed ambivalent about visitation. He had not seen his mother in nearly two years. His ambivalence seemed to reflect insecurity caused by his foster parents' unwillingness to adopt him, rather than a real desire to see his mother.

Thus for most children contact with their biological parents was an important—or desirable—aspect of their lives, even though some reported the visits to be painful, confusing, or times in which they had to confront the parents' shortcomings. Their feelings were reflected by a boy who had not seen his mother in two years and who wished to remain in foster care, who nevertheless told us, "Every time the phone rings I think it's her because I love her"; and in the words of a six-year-old girl: "I feel like I'm born again when I am with my mom."

It does not, of course, necessarily follow that children who wish to see a parent would like to resume living with the parent. We tried to assess the children's preferences about caretakers in several ways. We asked the children directly, "Where would you like to live and with whom?" A substantial number of children responded to this question by indicating living preferences—most often saying, "living with my real mom." Others expressed a living preference when we asked them, "What would make you happiest in the world?" We also asked the foster parents for their assessments of the children's feelings. Although such assessments may have been based on inadequate information or subject to bias, many foster parents confirmed what we learned in talking to the children. In a few situations they provided a somewhat different picture, which led us to probe further with the child.

Based on what was conveyed by the child and the foster parents, we categorize the children's attitudes about return to the biological parents as shown in Table 9.1.

The majority of children still had clear ties to their parents. Over half (seven) did not want to remain with their caretakers, but wanted reunion with a biological parent. Two children wanted to live with both their biological parents and their foster parents. These two children lived with their grandparents; they wanted to return to their parents and to have their grandparents come with them. Only two children definitely wanted to remain exclusively with their foster parents, but two others were ambivalent.[4] One girl said, "I like my mom and I wish she could take me, but sometimes I don't want to go home with her. I don't like the way she acts when she is drunk. She always tells me that she won't drink again. I don't believe her anymore."

We looked at a number of factors in an attempt to distinguish those who wanted to return to biological parents from those who wanted to

TABLE 9.1

Foster Children's Preferred Caretaker, at Two Years

Child's preference	Number of children (N = 13)
Return to biological parent	6
Live with previously non-custodial parent	1
Stay solely with foster parent	2
Live with both foster parent and biological parent	2
Ambivalent	2

stay with foster parents. Not surprisingly, the four children who were in nonpermanent placements all wanted reunification; among the other nine children, only three wanted this. Thus, to feel wanted may be a necessary but not sufficient condition for a child to become emotionally attached to a new caretaker. However, among the nine children in permanent placements, there were no apparent differences between the three who wanted reunion and the other six. We looked at the child's age, sex, number of moves (to new foster placements), school satisfaction, number of children in the foster home, and the foster parents' involvement score. We were of course dealing with very small numbers, so finding relationships was highly unlikely. Still, we were surprised that the length of time in the current home did not distinguish the groups. One of the three children who wanted reunion had been in a single foster family the entire time. The other two had been in long-term placements. All three placements were stable and likely to remain so, yet returning to their biological parents was central to these children. One six-year-old boy showed extreme commitment to his biological parents. He refused to be adopted by the foster parents who had become his guardians, even though he had chosen to live with this family (he had been in another foster home and asked to be moved to that of a schoolmate, whose parents agreed to take him). He very much liked the foster parents. Yet when asked if he was ever "scared," he said, "Yes, that maybe I'll get adopted. I don't want to get adopted. I want my real mommy." He had not seen his mother in two years. Interestingly, this boy's five-year-old brother was eager to be adopted, a major source of conflict between the two boys.

We examined the relationship between the amount of visiting by the biological parent and the child's desire to return home. However, be-

TABLE 9.2

Foster Children's Preferred Caretaker, Related to Parental Visiting, at Two Years

Child's preference	Children who visited with biological parent frequently	Children who visited with biological parent infrequently
Return to original parent or other parent	3[a]	4
Remain solely with foster parent	0	2
Stay with both foster parent and original parent	0	4

[a]Includes one child who wanted to live with her previously noncustodial mother. The mother was living with the child at an aunt's house for the last three months of the study.

cause all three children whose parents visited regularly also lived in nonpermanent foster homes, it is impossible to separate out the effect of visitation from the lack of a permanent alternative. Undoubtedly the actions of the biological parents influenced the attitude of the foster parents. If the biological parent stayed involved and the children seemed to retain attachments to them, the foster parents assumed that the children would return to the parent. Therefore, the foster parents may have developed less of an emotional tie. In contrast, where the biological parents were not involved, the children became more and more integrated into the foster family and the foster parents more attached to the child.[5]

Infrequent visitation, however, did not necessarily mean that the child wanted to remain with the foster parents. Three children stated that they wanted to return home despite the fact that their parents visited infrequently and that they were in permanent placements in which they *expected to remain*. See Table 9.2.

The expressed desire of the children to live with their parents may not indicate an unsatisfactory relationship with a foster parent, or even a "real" desire to restore the biological family. Many children clearly fantasize about absent parents. This is true of adopted children and children in divorced families. The child may just want to have contact with the absent parent. Some children also may feel that they have abandoned the absent parent unless they express the desire for reconciliation through return. Still, despite the children's generally positive attitude toward their foster parents, there is reason to think that foster parenting may not have substituted for the child's emotional ties to the biological parents for at least half the children.

The Home Children

The fact that half the foster children expressed the desire to return "home" gives us pause about the desirability of foster care, though, as we discuss in Chapter 11, this factor should not necessarily dominate our policy judgments. Most of the children were doing well in foster care. Moreover, their attachment to their biological parents often seemed harmful (one girl felt guilty about leaving her mother when she was drunk and needed help). In any case, it was not only the foster children who expressed problems with the parent-child emotional relationship. Many of the home children also felt unwanted or emotionally rejected by their parents.

In the case of the foster children, we wanted to see whether, in the relatively short time most of the children had been in their new homes, they were able to develop some emotional attachment to their new caretakers. For the home children we have no doubt, both as a theoretical matter and from our interview data, that there was some type of emotional relationship between the children and their parents (mothers and/or fathers). Most child development experts believe that the vast majority of children are "attached" to biological parents with whom they have lived. The issue is the quality or nature of the attachment, not its existence (Bowlby 1982; Sroufe 1983). Thus, for the home children we tried to evaluate the quality of the emotional relationship. Did the child feel wanted and secure, or rejected? Was the parent a source of emotional support?

Again, we faced a difficult measurement problem. We had no direct measures of the relationship; nor did we have regular assessments by a mental health professional. Therefore, we will present a more clinical picture, drawing inferences from the mother's statements about her feelings toward the child, and these data: the children's response to the question "How are you getting along with your parent?"; the children's use of their parents as a resource; statements by the children in response to the question "With whom do you want to live?"; negative responses by the children when we asked if their parents felt proud of them; and any statements the children made in response to open-ended questions about how they were doing (for example, one child expressed the wish that she could go "up in the clouds, with no people, just me").

We do not believe the responses to any, or even all, of these questions provides a totally adequate assessment of a child's attachment to, or feelings about, a parent. In particular, positive answers are not a clear indication of a good relationship; we believe negative responses carry more weight. We would expect that children are prone to answer the questions in a positive direction, since they may not want to admit to outsiders (or themselves) that they have trouble with their parents. As one boy said to the interviewer: "It's hard to say things about someone you like—it hurts." Thus negative responses, especially those maintained over several interview periods, probably reflect real problems.

In light of the clinical basis of our judgment, we do not attempt to develop any precise rating of the nature of the attachment or the degree of emotional support each child felt. Instead, we divide the children into three groups; those who had consistently good relations; those who clearly appeared to lack emotional support and who felt rejected and abandoned; and all others. The children in the "all others" group derived some support from their parents, but many of them lived in fear of physical punishment or emotional rejection, and others bore the burden of feeling responsible for their parents, rather than feeling protected by them.[6] In this "all others" group, we could not tell whether the good outweighed the bad.

In three of the nineteen white home group families, there appeared to be a warm, secure, supportive parent-child relationship, from which the child clearly benefited. Thirteen other children obviously had a strong emotional investment in the relationship and felt dependent on their parents, but the emotional relationship was mixed. For example, four of these children reported, on at least one occasion, that they rarely used their parents as a resource; and several indicated feelings of rejection. Eight stated, at some point, that they were getting along poorly with their parents. Ten children also stated at least once (five children twice) that they would like to live somewhere without their parents, usually "by myself." Our interviewers felt that the majority of these children's mothers were either hostile and abusive toward the children, or concerned with but psychologically unavailable to them. Several children's statements revealed the impact of such behaviors. One child told us: "My mother calls me bad names—'jerk,' 'stupid.' It feels bad and hurts and I feel sad inside. Sometimes I need more love than she can give me. She is like an antibody—she attacks." Another child said: "I wish I was dead because I get hit a lot."

Not surprisingly, this group of children often expressed ambivalent feelings toward their parents. For example, one boy said he worried that "Mother is always sad and always yelling at me," and that he was afraid of "mom or dad hitting me." However, he indicated that he also worried that "mom and dad will get a divorce, because I love my mom." Another boy said that what would make him happiest in the world would be "if my father was here—even though he gets drunk and tries to kill us, we still love him." This boy later indicated he was frightened "when I have a nightmare—I dreamed my mom was trying to kill my dad and then he tried to kill her." A third boy, in answering the question "who sticks up for you?," said "My mom and dad—I just love them. [A pause.] When they punch me a lot I don't like them—on Saturday and Sunday when I'm not being good." And one girl who said that she would like to live with "nobody, not with my mom," also responded that she got along pretty well with her mother: "She shows me that she loves me—hugs and kisses me." Thus, while the children often expressed their love for their parents and their desire to remain with them, they certainly did not seem to feel secure and wanted.

There were at least three children who seemed to have an especially limited relationship, from which they were deriving almost no emotional support.

At the time of intervention, Michael was hated by his mother; his sister, an infant, was emaciated and starving. When asked what would make her happiest in the world, the mother answered "foster care for all the kids—I want to get rid of the two assholes." The father was completely detached from the children, rarely interacting with them. Michael said his parents weren't proud of him, he did not use them as a resource, and he wanted to live "someplace else" with "anybody." Throughout the two years, he had very low self-esteem, though he did well with peers and was liked by his teacher.

Elizabeth's parents had been in conflict for a number of years. Elizabeth had major behavioral problems at home and at school. She was seen by her mother as unmanageable. When asked where she wanted to live, Elizabeth was emphatic that it should be a place with no parents. She felt that her parents were not proud of her and that she could not bring her troubles to them because she "would be embarrassed." When asked "Who takes care of you?," she said "Nobody." She reported that her mother "tells me that she hates me." Over the two years family relations improved through counseling, but there never was a time when Elizabeth saw her parents as a positive help in her life.

James came to the attention of child protective services when a teacher saw his mother kick him in the stomach after he had fallen. He was in a school program for emotionally disturbed abused children. He was viewed as hyperactive and unskilled with language. His mother sought out counseling. She said she felt very close to him, but never demonstrated any closeness. She never hugged or kissed him and constantly yelled at both James and his brother. She often talked of placing the children in foster care. James reported that he did not get along with his parents, that he did not use them as a resource, and that he wanted to live at his special school "with someone who likes me." He needed a great deal of attention from the teachers and formed intense relationships with them. His strongest wish was that he would be "a good boy."

Overall, we sensed a very mixed picture for most of the home children. Many were often afraid, insecure, and depressed. They longed for better relations with their mothers. Yet most derived some sustenance from the relationships; few if any of the children would have chosen to live elsewhere. Perhaps this is not a meaningful test. Few children are in such bad situations that they will openly accept separation and rejection. Except in the worst of circumstances, children prefer the known to the unknown. To abandon one's parents and be abandoned by them is not accepted as an option by children as young as the ones we studied. Thus, we must ask who were worse off—the foster children who longed to return to their original homes, or the home children who longed for a loving relationship, free of pain, fear, and insecurity.

Ten

Two Children

In the previous chapters, we looked at the average impact of intervention on each group of children. We examined changes in various facets of the children's development, looking separately at each domain. This type of analysis necessarily has a somewhat abstract quality. In this chapter, we will present case studies of two children, one at home and one in foster care. We hope to convey, through these studies, a more concrete and complete picture of the impact and meaning of intervention.

Case studies have both advantages and disadvantages as a way of providing policy-relevant data. Through a case study it is easy to convey the multitude of factors that may affect a given child's development over time. A case study also allows us to capture the complexity of a child's situation; for example, we can show how a given child's deficits in one area are balanced by strengths in another, or how the child's internal and external situations change almost constantly.

However, case studies can be misleading for the same reasons they are revealing. There are no *truly* representative cases. Our singling out one case and reporting specific factors about it may encourage unwarranted generalizations, when in fact its significance can be understood only in terms of its unique configuration of factors. In our presentation of these cases, we will try to provide a portrait of the child in his or her specific world, one that changed over time. We chose cases with themes that recurred throughout our study. We discuss these themes at the end of the chapter. Still, we believe that the outcome for each child depended on the unique characteristics of the child, parents, and other caretakers, as well as on external factors that came into play in the course of intervention.

A Home Case

Tommy R, an eight-year-old Caucasian boy, came to the attention of authorities when a baby-sitter noticed extensive bruises on his arm, hip, and buttocks. Tommy's nine-year-old brother also was bruised. Tommy lived with his mother, father, and older brother, in a two-bedroom apartment in a motel. The baby-sitter informed the motel manager about the children's bruises and the manager called the police. Tommy and his brother told the police that they had been beaten by their mother with a heavily buckled belt. Tommy also reported that he had been kicked while lying on the floor and choked so hard by his father that Tommy feared death. The children reported previous instances of being kicked, choked, and beaten. They were taken by the police to the county children's shelter. The parents were arrested and charged with criminal child abuse.

Tommy's parents both worked at a military installation near the motel. Mr. R, twenty-eight years old, had been a serviceman for six years; Mrs. R, twenty-nine, was a civilian working on the base. The family had moved several times in the past five years because Mr. R was reassigned to different military installations. There was evidence that Mr. R drank a great deal, that Mrs. R had a history of emotional problems, and that the family seemed to be struggling financially.

Mr. and Mrs. R both admitted spanking their children excessively. They explained they hit the boys because the boys had left the apartment "in chaos" while the R's were out shopping. (The boys admitted to having had a water balloon fight, which messed up the motel apartment.)

Initially, neither boy wanted to return home. Tommy indicated that he liked the children's shelter because he got lots of food and was not spanked. Mrs. R felt that the boys would be better off in foster care (Mr. R was still in jail at this time). She indicated that she was having severe problems controlling Tommy, who had been diagnosed as hyperactive. Even before this current incident, Tommy was being seen by a family therapist, who supported Mrs. R's desire to arrange foster care for the children.

When Mr. R was released from jail, however, he strongly opposed foster placement and Mrs. R then changed her mind. The parents expressed willingness to undertake further family therapy if this would enable them to regain the boys. Both boys also changed their minds and asked to be allowed to return to their home, Tommy stating that he missed his parents, and his brother saying that he was tired of the shelter and did not want to make his mother sad by not going home. Despite the reservations of the therapist, the boys rejoined their parents after three weeks in the children's shelter. The juvenile court ordered that the parents continue family therapy under the supervision of the Department of Social Services; Mr. R entered an alcohol treatment program. The parents pleaded guilty to misdemeanor abuse charges and were placed on probation.

When we assessed Tommy, the picture of a problem child with a number of emotional problems emerged clearly. He scored in the lowest quartile of our sample in self-esteem, answering almost all questions in negative terms, and admitting that he wished he were a girl because "girls do better things." He reported not getting along with other children at school, and this was confirmed by his teacher. He was doing poorly academically despite an average IQ. Mrs. R described him as high-strung, with a strong temper and a short fuse. She cited as serious problems his disobedience, screaming, tantrums, lying, and his arguing with and hitting other children. In the past few months, Tommy had regularly engaged in vandalism and stealing, had been setting papers on fire and hoarding food. For Mrs. R, Tommy was a child too difficult to handle most of the time. She clearly was ambivalent about continuing to care for him and acknowledged that this ambivalence began before Tommy was born, when Mrs. R had not wanted another child.

Tommy's life had its positive aspects. He was healthy physically. He loved school. His teacher did not find his behaviors particularly problematic; she indicated that he was easy to be around. Tommy felt he was getting along well with neighborhood kids, though not the children at school, and he appeared to have a close relationship with an elderly couple who took care of him while his parents were at work. Still, his overall responses in our interviews indicated a great deal of fear and anxiety about his relationship with his parents.

For a three-month period following intervention, the situation appeared to have improved. The family moved onto the military base, into a two-bedroom townhouse. Tommy continued seeing the therapist, who often came to the house if the parents failed to bring Tommy in. The parents also began sessions with this therapist. In addition, a social work intern, assigned by the court, visited Tommy once a week and took him on various outings. Toward the end of the three months, Mr. R, who was a source of major anxiety for Tommy, was given a temporary military assignment far away from home.

Mrs. R saw Tommy's behaviors as much improved at our interview three months after intervention. She felt the family therapist was teaching her more positive ways of dealing with Tommy. As a result there were no incidents of severe spankings. However, Tommy continued to be disruptive in school, regularly getting into fights. He did not like the children at school, though he did think of himself as a good student.

By six months after intervention, the situation had begun to deteriorate again. Mr. R had returned, and this seemed to create additional stress in the family. Spanking was again being used to control Tommy's disruptive behavior. Still, Mrs. R reported fewer extreme behaviors; there were no incidents of vandalism or fire-setting. Moreover, Tommy's self-esteem, though still low, was no longer at the bottom of our scale; he no longer wanted to be a girl. His school satisfaction remained high and he showed less fear of his father. However, he still had problems with other children, saying, "This is not a good place to live—a lot of kids are after you."

During the next twelve months the parents' situation, their relations with Tommy, and Tommy's emotional well-being continued to fluctuate. The mother quit her job for a period, which put the family in financial trouble. There was a great deal of marital conflict, related in part to the father's alcoholism, in part to his seeing other women. Tommy was aware of this conflict and afraid that his parents would separate. The father's drinking continued to be a major problem. For a time he was sent to an alcohol rehabilitation program in another state, and then joined Alcoholics Anonymous upon his return. Neither program had a major impact, though Mrs. R found attending Alanon meetings very helpful to her. Mr. R had other temporary assignments, in Alaska and Kentucky. During the periods of his absence there was reduced tension, yet mother and children seemed to miss him.

Tommy's behaviors also varied widely during the next year. From his mother's perspective, one day he would be very cooperative, the next day a real terror. The most distressing problem to her was his frequent lying, especially if she confronted him with this misbehavior. She reported that he had terrible tantrums, fought regularly with his brother, and had difficulty getting along with other children. Toward the end of this period, Mrs. R indicated that Tommy often left home without telling her where he was going, and stayed away for long periods.

Because of this behavior she had again resorted to hitting him with a belt.

However, Mrs. R also said that Tommy could be cooperative and lovable and that he had become much better at helping around the house. For a six-month period she reported a significant decline in "extreme" behaviors—there were now no instances of vandalism, fire-setting, stealing, or food hoarding, though this last behavior resumed after the father left for Alaska. Most positively, Tommy was doing better academically; he had been transferred from a special reading class into a regular class and his grades were improving.

Tommy's self-reports also evidenced fluctuating periods of relative happiness and great stress and tension. He always reported major difficulties in getting along with other children. He had constant fights at school; he told us that he had to be "tough" or would be attacked by other children. His self-esteem scores varied from low to extremely low. At one point he told our interviewer, "I've got something wrong with me. I'm hyperactive. This is making me sad because I hurt people." Even though he was doing better academically, his school satisfaction declined over time.

Tommy's feelings about his parents were extremely ambivalent. He clearly looked to his mother for love and support and turned to her when he had problems. Tommy said he missed his father when Mr. R was away from the family; nevertheless he felt that he got along "okay" with his mother but badly with his father. When asked "What makes your parents special or nice?" he answered, "Nothing." He reported being afraid of his father and expressed concern over his father's drinking. Still, he was very worried that his parents might separate; at all times after returning from the shelter, Tommy wanted to live only with *both* his parents. Tommy continued to visit with an individual therapist throughout the two years. Both his mother and Tommy saw benefits from the therapist's involvement, though there was only marginal change in Tommy's behavior.

The court-ordered services, including therapy for the parents, parenting classes, the social work intern, and social work supervision of the family, continued for a year following intervention, at which time court jurisdiction over the family was dismissed. The mother had mixed but mostly negative feelings about these services. The parents often failed to attend family therapy sessions—and therapy continued largely because the therapist came to the home when the parents did not show up. Although Mrs. R liked the therapist, she disliked the social worker, who was, she said, "always canceling appointments and telling me to do the opposite of what the therapist says." Mrs. R particularly resented the social worker's restrictions on her use of spankings and other punishments, which Mrs. R said were supported by the therapist. She commented that at the time court supervision ended, Tommy told her, "Now you can beat me up again." According to Mrs. R nothing good resulted from court supervision. Mrs. R also felt that the parenting classes were not helpful: "They are for parents with different types of children." She did think that the social work intern had been helpful to Tommy, though it had been quite hard for Tommy to end this relationship at the end of the year.

There was no evidence that the court-ordered services positively affected the marital situation, the father's drinking problems, or the mother's ambivalent feelings toward the children. The family therapist did provide Mrs. R with some ways of dealing with Tommy's behavior, though we saw no evidence that she gained insight into Tommy's needs or the relationship of the parents' behavior to his problems.

At our last set of interviews, two years after the initial intervention, it appeared that even though the court intervention seemed to have had some positive impact, to a large degree little had changed during our study. On the positive side, neither Tommy nor his brother had been seriously injured during the two years by their parents, who, in fact now used physical punishment quite infrequently. Mrs. R also saw more positive aspects in her relationship with Tommy. There were periods when she felt close to him and found him very helpful. She was pleased that his school work had improved, that he was actively involved in Cub Scouts, and that Mr. R was participating in some projects with Tommy.

At the final interview Tommy, now ten years old, appeared friendly and somewhat eager to talk. He was significantly less angry than at some earlier interviews. His view of his neighborhood had improved. He talked about being part of a group of kids that "hung out" together. When asked what had brought about this change, Tommy candidly explained that he had begun to act nicer. He felt that most of the children there did not like him. He described the boys in his class as forming a gang that was very tough and loved to fight. Despite these problems, he loved school. He liked having books available and doing book reports.

Tommy also related that he was getting along better with his mother.

He saw himself as being helpful and his mother as being proud of him. His relationship with his father, too, had improved. He talked about being involved in projects for Cub Scouts with his dad. He also felt that if he were worried or troubled he could go to his father for assistance. Finally, for the first time in the two years, Tommy scored high on our self-esteem measure. He gave positive responses to every question except one about "feeling lucky."

Yet despite these optimistic signs, Tommy's situation was far from stable, and there were areas of development that were still highly problematic. Mr. and Mrs. R continued to have marital difficulties; Mr. R continued to drink heavily. The day-to-day life at home appeared somewhat chaotic; meals were not regular, the children were more often than not wearing dirty, ill-fitting clothing, and Tommy's personal hygiene was not good. Although Mrs. R could describe her life and her children's personalities in some detail, she did not seem able to organize her life or to give Tommy adequate structure and consistent, good-quality care. Mrs. R said that the children made her nervous and that she felt better when they were cared for by others. She felt less close to Tommy than at the beginning of the study.

There were other signs of difficulty. During the study it was observed that Tommy would eat sugar by the handful, which his mother felt contributed to his hyperactivity, and this eating behavior continued. His mother reported that lying and food hoarding continued, and that Tommy destroyed toys; Tommy also had begun pounding his head against the wall. Tommy still ranked his school peer relations as very bad; so did his teacher. Moreover, his teacher, though rating him average in likableness and attractiveness, had trouble dealing with him. She pictured him as needing to have his own way, socially insensitive, and unable to get along with other children. She reported that Tommy "will go to *anyone* for companionship" regardless of appropriateness, and that "he has no friends . . . he needs a new image . . . he has tried very hard to control his temper, but is strung up higher than a kite. Basically, he is a little boy who is in dire need of tender loving care."

In summary, Tommy was a child from a family with substantial social and behavioral pathology in both parents and children—an emotionally impoverished family. After the provision of services, there was no evidence of further physical abuse. Although there were some indications of improvement in Tommy's self-esteem and social behavior, at the end of two years he still exhibited significant emotional problems, as reported by his mother and teachers. He had major difficulties in getting along with his peers. Since there was little likelihood of a major change in family dynamics, it seemed probable that Tommy would experience major problems in the future.

A Foster Case

George S, a nine-year-old Caucasian boy, and Harry, his ten-year-old brother, were taken into protective custody by the police, who responded to a telephone report that the children were not being cared for adequately. The boys were living with their father in a pickup-truck camper, kept in a parking lot. The father was in the camper when the police arrived, but the officers decided that the camper was an inadequate living environment because it "smelled bad and was jammed full of beds and junk."

The father and the two boys had been living in the camper for four months, since Mr. S had been fired from his job as an apartment manager. Mr. S had a long history of alcohol problems; at the time the boys were taken by the police, he stated that he "drank a lot" and that he realized he was "not caring for the boys very good." He said he had not been able to obtain welfare assistance after losing his job.

Mr. S had been the sole custodian of the boys for a year, following his separation from his wife. Mrs. S, who was living "somewhere in the area," was a drug addict. She had provided only minimal care to the children for several years prior to the separation. Mr. S told our interviewer that his wife had constantly abused the children, both verbally and physically. This was one reason for their divorce. Mr. S, who had only seven years of formal education, had supported the family until he lost his job. His alcohol problem appeared to worsen following the separation. Several months before the boys were taken into custody, Mr. S had earlier been in a detoxification center, but he felt that such programs were "a waste of time."

Following removal from their camper home, George and Harry spent five weeks at the county children's shelter, while court proceedings were pending. George's adjustment was described as quite good; his brother had numerous difficulties with both other shelter children and the staff. From the moment they were taken into custody, both George and Harry were adamant about wanting to live with their father. Mr. S was also desirous of having the children returned to him. However, perhaps under some pressure, he consented to their placement in foster care "for two or three months," until he could find housing and the means to provide for them properly.

Following court disposition, George and Harry were placed in a "temporary" foster home. From the day he arrived, George's foster mother thought him wonderful; she described him as lovable and well behaved, though occasionally moody. She said George had no trouble adjusting to the foster home, no problem behaviors, and no transitional difficulties such as bed-wetting or nightmares. She reported that George got along well with other children.

Her description matched that of Mr. S, who said that George had always been a totally lovable child. (At one point in our interview, Mr. S said he thought that there had been a conspiracy to separate his children from him because they were so wonderful that someone else wanted to have them.) Mr. S said that George had never been unmanageable while living with him, though George was extremely active and easily distracted, which sometimes caused him difficulty at school. In fact, school was the one area in which George showed problems. He had been retained in kindergarten and was still doing poorly academically at the time he was placed in foster care. He had missed a great deal of school, which contributed to his academic difficulties; but he also scored only 77 on our IQ test.

George's teacher found him extremely attractive and easy to be around. She rated him average on social competence; she noted that he had some difficulties with peer relations, though his score was average compared to the entire abused/neglected group. She thought George seemed to have a high sense of self-worth.

At our initial interview, George was friendly and seemed very interested in answering our questions. He remarked that he liked living with his emergency foster mother, whom he called "Aunt Nanni," and her husband, his foster father, because the family always engaged in fun activities. All George's comments about himself, his father, and his foster parents were positive. He described himself as being well-liked, both at school and in the neighborhood. On our self-esteem measure, George gave no negative response. His answers to those questions were given rapidly, suggesting that he had few doubts about himself. George viewed a large network of people as supportive, including his father, older foster brother, foster parents, and his biological brother.

The most pressing issue for George was returning to his father. He talked often about how much fun the weekly visits with his father were, and seemed eager to relate in detail the activities they shared. He viewed the foster home as temporary, stating with certainty that he would be returned home as soon as his father found a house.

After George had been in the foster home for three and a half months, his father still had not obtained housing, though he now had a job and paid the county $104 a month toward support of the children. Because the foster parents had agreed to take the children only on a temporary basis—she did not want to become too attached to them—a more permanent foster home now had to be found. The new home was with a Hispanic family who lived approximately thirty miles from the father's place of employment. The family had one child of their own, an eight-year-old boy who was in the same grade as George.

George's transition to the new home appeared to go very smoothly, even though, including the children's shelter, this was his third placement in less than six months. The new foster mother, like the previous one, described George in glowing terms. She said, "George is very lovable. He likes to be hugged and kissed." Her only negative observation was that when George misbehaved, which was seldom, he became moody. She indicated that he had great difficulty with reading and math. George would react to comments about these difficulties by becoming moody and somewhat withdrawn. She was concerned about George's slowness with homework; it took him hours to complete a simple assignment.

George's own picture of his new home was positive, though he was somewhat less enthusiastic about it than about the previous home. He thought his new foster parents were nice, and he said he never argued with them; he did fight with his foster brother quite often, however. George indicated that he was having some problems in school, mostly with homework. He did not see himself as being as good a student as his foster parents wanted him to be, but neither did he consider this a problem. His self-esteem was still quite high, though he now gave some negative answers to questions on the self-esteem scale.

Despite his general contentment with the foster home, George's major desire was to return to his father. Mr. S now was visiting every other week, rather than weekly. The visits were quite regular, despite the distance and conflicts Mr. S was having with his social worker. The father continued to tell his sons that he would soon have housing in which they would be able to reunite. George reported that the visits with his father were very satisfactory, and would explain in very serious tones that it was a long trip for his father to make, that his father had only a motorcycle, and that if it was too cold he was not able to visit. George was asked about visits from his mother, who had begun accompanying the father a few months earlier. George said that she had not visited him for a while and that he missed both parents very much.

George seemed very aware of his father's conflicts with the social worker, and gave a lengthy explanation of the unfairness of the social worker toward his father. He believed his father would ultimately show the judge how stupid the social worker was. At this time, George also began to express fears for his father's well-being, worrying that his father might be kidnapped or killed in a motorcycle accident.

A year after intervention, George was still living in the second foster home. His brother Harry had been placed in a camp for problem children because of misbehaviors at school and home. Mr. S had not been told about the removal before it occurred, and was very angered by it. Our interviewer telephoned the social worker to learn more about the situation. The social worker said that Mr. S had not been notified because he did not return the social worker's calls. Our interviewer was surprised that it was difficult for the social worker to reach Mr. S, whose job it was to answer the telephone where he worked; our interviewer never encountered difficulty reaching Mr. S by phone. Although the foster mother indicated that Harry could rejoin the foster family if his behavior improved, George worried that the banishment accorded his brother might also happen to him.

Despite the experience of his brother, George continued to have few difficulties or developmental delays. Although the foster mother was a bit worried that George might copy his brother's misbehavior, she still described him as a warm, lovable, and loving boy. She reported no behavioral problems and no family conflicts and said her own son liked George. Our interviewer observed that the foster father clearly was very involved in George's care and appeared to have a warm, supportive relationship with him. As in the past, the parents' only concern was with George's school performance. With George listening, the foster mother recounted a conversation with his teacher, who felt that George would always be very slow in learning and would always need special help.

The teacher's report was highly favorable, however. Despite his low IQ George was in a regular class. Since the class was a combined third and fourth grade, he had the same teacher for two years. She saw him as socially competent and likable, and thought he got along well with other children; however, she now reported that he seemed to show less of a sense of self-respect and self-worth (perhaps this was related to his poor academic performance).

During his interviews George was warm and friendly. He reported that he really liked his foster mother. He saw nothing negative about the foster home and felt that the foster parents loved him, were proud of him, and cared for his needs. He did not say he missed his brother. His self-esteem remained very high and though his enthusiasm for school was clearly waning, he still pictured school and his peer relations quite positively. We could find no evidence of significant emotional problems in our talks with him.

George was clearly concerned, however, with the declining number of visits from his father. Mr. S, still living in his camper, now had two jobs and missed many scheduled visits. George looked forward to every visit and talked at length about the fun they had on each occasion. He stated that living with his father was what would make him the "happiest in the world," and that he had asked his foster mother to say a prayer at church that his father would find a house.

During the entire first year Mr. S perceived George as adjusting very well to the foster home. He had not noticed behavioral problems and believed George to be the same lovable child he had always been. Although continually telling George he was trying to regain custody of him, Mr. S seemed to us to be ambivalent about this. He complained that even though working at an extra job at a gas station nights and weekends, he still could not raise enough money for an apartment. He stated that George might be better off with the foster family, who had a "nice house" and could give him things. He also observed what George had reported, that George was now involved in sports, a source of great satisfaction and accomplishment for George.

Mr. S did express complaints about the foster family, one of them being that the church service George attended with them was in Spanish (though the foster mother said the service was in English); he was concerned that George might lose his "Anglo culture."

During the second twelve months, the pattern that began toward the end of the first year continued. Mr. S's visits decreased dramatically. At one point he did not visit George for more than three months; when George tried to call him on Father's Day, he could not be found. Mr. S also failed to obtain housing and always had another excuse for this failure. The conflict between the social worker and father continued. The social worker would not allow visitation until the father contacted him. Mr. S refused to do this. During our interview with

Mr. S, he was in tears as he described how, when he began to realize he would never solve his problems, he spoke to the foster family about keeping the boys permanently despite his concern about the family's ethnicity. The foster parents indicated their willingness to assume permanent custody and now expected this to happen.

Two other major changes also occurred during the second year. George's brother returned to live with the foster family and a new foster child, a twelve-year-old boy, was placed in the home. The foster mother thought that all the boys were getting along well.

Despite the trauma the absence of his father caused George, his foster mother felt that George was still doing quite well; however, she described George as more moody, which she attributed to the father's absence. She also seemed somewhat exasperated by George's "forgetfulness and losing things." She reported one incident of a behavior problem at school, for which George had lost privileges at home. None of these criticisms indicated a feeling on her part that George was a problem or that he had emotional problems. Rather, her willingness to report problems appeared to us to be related to her beginning to view George as her own child, also to her greater familiarity with our interviewer.

Our interview with George revealed signs that he was under stress. At our eighteen-month interview his self-esteem score dropped significantly, which might have been related to his school failures. Although he said he was pleased with his brother's return, he was much less happy with his peer relations. School was a particular problem. He described the work as both hard and boring and insisted he "hated" school. He had the same teacher as in the previous year but felt that while she was "okay," she had become more strict. George's perception of school was quite different from that of his foster mother, who had said he was doing well academically. He thought he wasn't doing well at all.

George continued to express positive feelings about his foster parents. Yet when he was asked where he most wanted to live, he now named his previous foster home. Above all he missed his father, and attributed Mr. S's absence primarily to his conflicts with the social worker. For the first time, however, he was somewhat critical of his father, saying that his father would be able to find a house and visit more often if he didn't drink and smoke so much. When asked why he thought this, George answered, "You know drinking and smoking cost a lot of money." He also reported missing his biological mother and told us he believed it was not possible for her to visit because she had a terrible allergy that required her to stay in a glass-enclosed room until she got better. George added that his father had told him this and that he was praying his mother would be well soon. George now expected to remain in foster care for two years or more.

At our last set of interviews, Mr. S had not visited George for more than six months. He had telephoned just before Christmas and promised to visit, but did not do so. In fact, neither George nor Harry had spoken to him at all since our previous interview. We attempted to contact Mr. S where he had been employed. We learned that he no longer worked there; nor had he said where he could be located.

The foster parents now assumed they would raise George and his brother to adulthood. Clearly very committed, they saw George as part of their family. The foster mother reported that he was well adjusted and very loving. However, she complained that he fought on the playground, was lax about doing his homework, and that he complained about chores at home. However, she did not consider these problems serious. Instead, she seemed to view them as normal stages in childhood.

The foster mother's impressions were consistent with those of George's teacher. Her rating of his social competence, classroom behaviors, peer relations, and general likability were quite similar at each of our three interviews.

At our last interview with George, he also portrayed himself as happy with most aspects of his life. He felt well cared for by the foster parents and liked his neighborhood and friends, though he was less positive about his peer relations than he had been in the first year of placement. He described some difficulties with two new foster children who had recently been placed in the home. George was very open about his dislike of school, still finding it boring and difficult, which he handled by "fooling around" in the classroom. During our school observations of George on the playground, he was often involved in fights, yet he denied these incidents when asked about them.

Throughout the two years George had struggled to make some sense out of his father's situation. Initially, he made excuses for Mr. S's failure to visit. Later he showed some anger at his father for not visiting. Finally, at our last interview, he preferred not to talk about the subject at all. When asked, "Why doesn't your father visit?", he answered that he really didn't know. He continued to worry about his father, though, and revealed that when it was rainy or windy he feared that, wherever his father's camper was, it might blow over. Despite his obvious happiness with his foster parents, he still insisted that "going to live with dad" would make him "happiest in the world." He continued to believe that this would happen—no one had told him anything different—but he had no idea when.

Generalizations and Reservations

Tommy's and George's cases were typical of many in our study but also unique. The real world of abused and neglected children does not provide researchers or policymakers with homogeneous groups of children in home or foster care. Some of our cases began with situations similar to George's and Tommy's but yielded different outcomes. In fact, though we had only limited data regarding the siblings of Tommy and George, it seems reasonably clear that even they fared differently than their brothers.

Tommy typified a number of characteristics shared by the home children. His well-being fluctuated over time. Although he clearly did poorly in many aspects of development, he did adequately in others. Although he came under court jurisdiction because of physical abuse, he seemed to be more at risk with respect to social development, especially peer relations. The emotional rejection by his parents seemed a greater threat to his well-being than the physical abuse. His family experienced multiple problems, including marital conflict, alcohol abuse, mental illness, and social isolation; as with most of the study children it was impossible to single out abuse as *the* cause of the child's problems when so many other factors placed the child at risk.

Tommy's situation also differed from the "norm" in significant ways. Not only did he have more behavioral problems, so did his family. The combination of emotional rejection, parental conflict, and alcohol abuse, together with the fact that his father regularly spent lengthy periods away from the family, may have put unique pressures on Tommy. In addition, Mrs. R was ambivalent about keeping her children. On the other hand, only a few other families received as many services as the R family did, especially the type of individual therapy Tommy received. Despite these services, the R family's problems seemed somewhat more intractable than those of a number of other study families.

George, too, was both typical and unique. Like many of the foster children, he exhibited relatively few problems when we first saw him and changed relatively little over time. His situation indicates why we

had such difficulty deciding whether the initial status of the foster children reflected a positive impact of foster care or a continuation of past
behavior. George's father described George as lovable and well-behaved
at home, much as he was in foster care. Yet if this was so, why had the
abuse, neglect, and family conflict to which he had been exposed had
so little effect on his development? George also typified the foster children in his general satisfaction with his foster homes. Despite multiple
placements, other children moving in and out of the foster home, and
substantial uncertainty about when or if they would again live with or
even see their biological parents, the majority of foster children appeared quite resilient.

Finally, George typifies the majority of foster children in his ongoing allegiance to his biological parents. Resolving the loss of these parents was perhaps the major emotional task for most of the children in
foster care. For each child this was a unique task, however. They had
experienced quite different relationships with their parents before and
during placement. They were in quite different types of placements—
some with relatives, some with family friends, and some with people
who had been total strangers. Their new caretakers had differing attitudes toward keeping the children and toward the biological families.
For example, George had two stable placements, each with very caring
foster parents. He had only one school teacher in two years. In these
and many other ways, George's life differed from that of other foster
children.

From a research perspective, the cases of Tommy and George are il-
lustrative of the difficulty faced in trying to assess whether an alternative
intervention would have been better for the child. Would Tommy's development have differed for the better had he been placed in foster
care? Among the questions that might be relevant are: How would a
foster family have responded to his behavioral problems? Would his
biological parents have relinquished contact with him, as did George's,
or would he have been subject to placement and then reunion with his
biological parents? Would Tommy, who was in many ways very close
to his mother, have formed new bonds to foster parents? Even if
he did not form new bonds, were his emotional problems so severe
that he would have benefited from whatever type of foster care was
provided?

For George, we can only speculate on how he might have done if
left with his father. It seems likely that his school problems would have
continued or worsened. But would his general emotional well-being,

which seemed quite good at the time of intervention, have worsened? What would have been the impact of Mr. S's continued drinking and marginal provision of physical care on George's self-esteem, peer relations, and general satisfaction? If George received only marginal care, would that have been worse for him than the loss of his parents?

As these cases illustrate, courts and social service agencies might consider a large number of factors in deciding between home placement and foster care. It is unlikely that research will be able to identify even the most significant factors that a court or social work agency should take into account in making *individual* case decisions. As we discuss in Chapter 12, the problems in obtaining adequate sample sizes and accurate data may make it impossible to obtain conclusive data for deciding how to balance the various factors in individual cases. Moreover, even if a number of important factors could be isolated, the decision maker often does not have crucial information at the time the decision has to be made. For example, it is usually not possible to assess very accurately at the time of intervention the way parents will respond to services, or whether a "good" foster home will be available, both of which may be very important to the outcome in a given case. Therefore, decisions will have to be made on the basis of limited knowledge. We discuss the policy implications of this problem in Chapter 12.

Eleven

The Black and Hispanic Children

FOR THE REASONS DISCUSSED in Chapter 3, our report has focused primarily on the development of thirty-two white children over a two-year period. We compiled data on sixteen black children and eight Hispanic children, but their unequal division between home and foster care limited our ability to assess the impact of alternative placements for these children. Moreover, since most of the black foster children were placed with previously noncustodial fathers or with relatives well known to them, their foster care experience was considerably different from that of the white children. Our data for black and Hispanic children provide a picture of the impact of intervention and the effect of abuse and neglect on development that is somewhat different for these children than for white children. Most significant, the abused and neglected black children showed higher levels of well-being than the abused and neglected white children in all areas, except their academic performance and history of emotional problems. In fact, there were no significant differences between the black abused/neglected and comparison children on most measures, despite the fact that the physical abuse noted in the black cases was more serious than for whites. We have too few Hispanic children to make statistical comparisons with the other children, unfortunately. Based on the little information we have, it appears that the Hispanic children differed from black and white children both in terms of the nature of the abuse or neglect and in their development.

Although our findings must be considered tentative, we were able to do a limited analysis of the impact of intervention on the black and Hispanic children. Originally there were five black children in the home group and eleven in the foster group. Three of the foster children were returned to their mothers within six months of placement, leaving eight children in foster care for two years. By looking at the three children returned to their parents and the five children originally at home, we are able to compare the development of eight "home" and eight foster children. We also examined the development of the six Hispanic children who remained at home the entire two years, which increased our understanding of the effects of leaving children at home.

The Black Children

REASONS FOR INTERVENTION

Eleven of the sixteen black children came to agency attention as a result of physical abuse. Eight were quite seriously abused; six had been hit or whipped with objects (usually an extension cord) and had suffered severe injuries, including broken teeth and eye wounds; another child had been hit in the face with a belt and burned with an iron; another had also been severely burned and required weeks of hospitalization. All eight children had been abused previously, many seriously, and most did not want to remain with their parents because of fear of repeated abuse. We consider three of the eleven abuse cases moderate compared to the others. One child suffered a broken arm and another had been hit with a fishing pole; however, each case involved a one-time episode, where a caring parent overreacted to misbehavior by the child, and in neither case was there much likelihood of future physical punishment. The final abuse case involved a severe spanking by hand, by a parent with no history of prior abuse.

Four of the five neglect cases also were at the most serious end of the spectrum. One child was suffering from severe malnutrition because his severely depressed mother did not provide any food for long periods of time; one child (eight years old) had a history of delinquent behavior and fire-setting, and his mother provided no supervision; and two children lived in extremely disorganized homes with parents who clearly provided no physical or emotional care. The fifth child lived in an abandoned shed with no electricity or water, and her parents provided little supervision; however, they seemed concerned with her well-being, so we consider the neglect moderate.

MATERNAL BACKGROUND

Although the reasons for intervention were more serious than those involving the white children, in terms of the extent of the present injury and the potential for future injury, there was little difference in the background characteristics of the black and white mothers. The majority of the sixteen black mothers were divorced or never married, half had incomes of less than $500 a month. They were relatively well-educated: a third had had some college. Most had high self-esteem scores, but half the mothers were quite isolated. The background characteristics of mothers of the black abused/neglected and comparison children are summarized in Table 11.1.

Although the mothers of the comparison sample resembled the abusing and neglecting mothers in terms of income, marital status, education, self-esteem, and social embeddedness, there were significant differences in other aspects of their backgrounds. Half the abusing and neglecting mothers had long histories of drug abuse, mental illness, and physical violence. Four mothers had been sixteen or younger at the time of the study child's birth. Four of the children had been raised primarily by relatives because the mothers had been unable or unwilling to care for the child. Many of the mothers had been battered by spouses or boyfriends. Thus, for at least half the group, the mother's backgrounds were indicative of very poor child-rearing skills.

THE INITIAL STATUS OF THE CHILDREN

Although the backgrounds of the black and white mothers of the abused and neglected children were relatively similar, their children's development was quite different. The picture was complex. Like the white children, the black children evidenced substantial academic and emotional problems. However, there were few differences between the black abused/neglected sample and the black comparison children in teachers' ratings and in the child's personal satisfaction. In both domains, all the black children did considerably better than the white abused and neglected children. We speculate on the reasons for these differences later.

There were eight boys and girls in the sample. Their ages ranged from five to nine, with almost equal numbers of each age. In presenting the data we will combine the five home and eleven foster children because, as contrasted with the white children, the two groups showed no significant differences. In addition, because of missing data, we have information on only three or four home children for many variables, too small a number for meaningful statistics.

Physical health. The children tended to be above-average in both height and weight. The median percentiles were 65 for height and 66

TABLE II.I

Demographic and Personal Characteristics of Black Mothers of Abused/Neglected and Comparison Children

Characteristic of mother	Abused/neglected (N = 16)	Comparison (N = 24)
Age at birth of child (years)		
Range	14–25	15–34
Median	20	21
Marital status		
Presently married	6%	25%
Divorced or separated	56%	58%
Single, never married	31%	13%
Widowed	6%	4%
Education		
Did not complete high school	38%	33%
Graduated from high school	25%	38%
Attended college	38%	29%
Employment		
Full-time	31%	38%
Part-time	31%	0%
Not working	38%	62%
Monthly income		
<$500	50%	42%
$500–$1,000	38%	50%
$1,001–$1,500	6%	4%
>$1,500	6%	4%
Time in residence		
1–3 months	38%	17%
4–12 months	12%	21%
13–24 months	50%	62%
Self-esteem		
Low (0–3)	19%	21%
High (4–6)	81%	79%
Embeddedness		
Low (−9 to −1)	13%	17%
Moderate (0 to 3)	44%	29%
High (4 to 10)	44%	54%

for weight. One child, who was suffering from severe malnutrition, was below the 10th percentile on both measures. The children's health also was generally good, though a relatively large number of children (six of sixteen) had uncorrected problems with their vision and one child showed evidence of neurological damage. Approximately 70 percent (eleven) of the mothers reported that their children's health was very good or excellent, the same percentage as for the white children. However, five children, all of whom had been whipped with extension cords on many occasions, had multiple scars.

IQ scores. The average score of the children on the WISC test was similar to those reported for the national samples of black children. The scores ranged from 42 to 113. The child who scored 42 had the lowest score of any child in the study. Two other children had total scores below 70.

Academic performance. Unlike the white children, the black abused and neglected and comparison children did not differ very much in how often they attended school. Of the fourteen abused and neglected children who were in school, three (21 percent) were absent more than 10 percent of the school year. Four (18 percent) of the twenty-two comparison children also were absent this often.

As teachers of the white children had done, teachers of black abused and neglected children ranked them lower in academic performance than their comparison group. Fifty percent (six of twelve) of the abused and neglected children received scores of 4 or 5 on our five-point scale; in contrast only thirty-two percent (seven of twenty-two) of the comparison children were ranked that low. The abused and neglected children were much more likely to be ranked at the very bottom of the class than were the comparison children. Again in contrast to the white sample, all the lowest-rated black children also had low IQ's. The three children with the highest IQ's were rated average or at the top of their class. Even more striking than the teachers' rankings were the retention and special class statistics. Among the abused and neglected group, five children were retained and three were in special education classes. Only one of the twenty-four children in the comparison sample was retained; one was considered gifted. The fact that so many of the abused and neglected children were retained or in special classes makes the low teacher ratings even more dramatic.

Behavioral and emotional problems. Eight of the sixteen children seemed to have serious emotional problems, though only three were in therapy or had been advised to seek therapy before intervention. (Three children received regular mental health counseling after intervention.) The most prevalent problems were fighting with other children at school or stealing. Five children had a history of theft; three of the five also were very aggressive toward their peers. One boy had been expelled from school on several occasions because of fighting. Most of the parents who reported stealing also indicated that they were having difficulty with the child's lying.

Three other children were quite depressed and withdrawn. All three had mentally disturbed mothers, who provided their children with very little emotional support. One of these children, upon placement in foster care, became very destructive, tearing up her clothes and destroying toys and furniture in the foster home.

Although the other eight children did not have major emotional problems, three of them exhibited behavioral problems that seemed to be related to their parents' divorces, not to abuse or neglect. All three children were very unhappy about the divorce and ambivalent about where they wanted to live. These children were seen by their parents as defiant and unruly.

Five of the eleven children initially in foster care manifested short-term emotional problems associated with placement. Three children began bed-wetting, one child began stuttering, and one child became very withdrawn. Several of these children also continued to exhibit behavioral problems they had exhibited at home, including stealing, lying, and fighting.

Social behavior at home and parent-child relations. Because many of the children had academic and emotional problems, we expected them to experience problems in social behavior at home and school. We were wrong. There were no differences in the parent ratings of the abused and neglected and comparison children. Although the comparison children were rated slightly higher by the teachers, most of the abused and neglected children received positive assessments, far more so than for the equivalent white children.

In light of the fact that many of the black children had been severely and repeatedly physically abused, the mothers' assessments of the children were puzzling, perhaps unbelievable. On the child behavior scale (CBS), the mothers of the abused and neglected children reported fewer problem behaviors than did the mothers of the comparison children. (Perhaps the mistreated children were afraid to complain.) The following tabulation shows the percentage of biological mothers reporting one or more of seven behaviors (crying, whining, pouting, complaining, yelling, disobeying, and lying) as "occurring a lot" and "being a problem":

Number of behaviors	Abuse/neglect ($N = 14$)	Comparison ($N = 24$)
0–1	79	67
2–3	21	16
4–7	0	16

The group means on the social competence scale were virtually identical, 3.7 and 3.6 (respectively for the abused/neglected and comparison groups). These scores were the same as those for the white abused/neglected children and higher than those for the white comparison group.

The mothers' responses on both the CBS and social competence scales were quite at odds with many statements they made in the course of the interviews. In talking about the abuse incidents, they usually justified having hit the child on the basis of the child's behavior. They also told us that the children were difficult to deal with (as previously indicated, five of the mothers reported that the child had a history of stealing or lying). There clearly was substantial parent-child conflict in most of the abuse cases. Many of the children reported difficulty in getting along with their parents. Therefore, we do not believe that the CBS and social competence scales are accurate measures of conflict in the home.

Social behavior at school and teacher ratings. In general, the teachers rated both the abused/neglected and comparison children similarly, though the means of the comparison sample were higher on likability and peer relations. See Table 11.2. The group means of the black children were similar to those of the white comparison and foster children. However, there were four children who exhibited substantial behavioral problems at school, either by fighting or by withdrawing from all social interaction.

Children's personal satisfaction. Probably our most puzzling finding relates to the children's personal satisfaction, as measured by the self-esteem, peer relations, and school satisfaction indices. The abused and neglected black children had even higher scores than their comparison group, in fact, the highest scores of any group we studied. Very few reported dissatisfaction. We thought the high scores might be accounted for by the foster children, who generally indicated that they were happy to be away from homes in which they had been regularly beaten (remember that most of these children were fostered by grandparents or previously noncustodial fathers, so the change of caretaker

TABLE II.2

*Teachers' Ratings of Social Behavior, Likability, and
Peer Relations of Black Children*

Measure	Abused/ neglected (N = 12)	Comparison (N = 23)
Social behavior		
Mean[a]	3.6	3.6
SD	7.6	5.5
Range	2.5–4.6	2.3–4.5
Likability		
Mean[b]	3.5	4.1
SD	5.0	3.0
Range	−6–+10	−1–+10
Peer relations		
Mean[b]	.9	1.4
SD	3.7	3.5
Range	−4–+6	−3–+9

[a] On 1–5 scale, 1 = low.
[b] On −10–+10 scale.

was not dramatic). However, there were no differences between the home and foster children. See Table 11.3.

Summary. Except for their academic performance, the black abused and neglected children on average seemed to show no development deficits, as measured by the development status of the comparison children. They clearly seemed better off than the white abused and neglected children; their teachers saw them as having better social skills, their parents thought they were better behaved, and they reported higher general satisfaction and better relations with their parents. Except for school work, they were indistinguishable from the white comparison children. Yet the majority of them were in great danger of suffering continuing severe injuries from physical punishment or neglect. Thus, it was not irrational or inappropriate that they had been removed from their parents.

We cannot explain the apparent lack of negative effect of the abuse. Perhaps some of the mothers were providing emotional support even though they used severe physical punishment—this was clearly the case in three of the five home cases. The situation was less clear in most of the foster cases. Perhaps these children derived support from their extended families; many of the children had spent much time with

TABLE 11.3
Black Children's Initial Self-Esteem, Peer Relations,
and School Satisfaction Scores

Rating	Home	Foster	Comparison
Self-esteem			
Mean[a]	5.0	6.0	4.9
SD	3.8	4.5	3.6
Range	2–10	−2–+12	−4–+10
N	*4*	*10*	*24*
Peer satisfaction			
Mean[b]	5.7	4.2	3.9
SD	3.3	3.6	3.0
Range	2–10	−2–+9	−5–+9
N	*4*	*10*	*24*
School satisfaction			
Mean[c]	5.0	5.0	4.0
SD	1.0	1.3	2.2
Range	4–6	4–7	−3–+6
N	*3*	*8*	*24*

[a]On −12–+12 scale.
[b]On −10–+10 scale.
[c]On −8–+8 scale.

grandparents or other relatives or perhaps the foster children were just happy to be away from their abusing parents. Whatever the reason, the task of the social agencies was to protect the children's physical well-being while not jeopardizing their emotional functioning.

Change over Time Among the Black Children

Because only eight children remained in continuous foster care, and only four in continuous home placement, we believe that a statistical comparison of change over time is inappropriate. Moreover, in a number of cases, special factors seem to account for the outcome for particular children. Therefore, we will utilize a clinical approach, describing each individual case.

THE HOME CHILDREN

There were five children at home initially. Three others were initially placed in foster care and then returned to their mothers within six months of the placement: one had been placed with the father; one with his grandmother; and one with an unrelated foster family. All three biological mothers had remained involved in the care of the child. Since the three children spent eighteen months of our study at home, we will look at changes in their well-being from the time they returned home until the end of the study as part of our assessment of "home" placements. Thus, we can explore the outcome at home for eight children.

Of the five children left at home initially, two fared very badly. One, an eight-year-old boy, was initially one of the most severely deprived and disturbed children in our study. He continued to function poorly throughout the two years.[1] During that time he spent six months away from his home, three in a juvenile detention facility following his arrest for burglary, and three at a grandmother's in another state, where he was sent by his mother to avoid his being removed from her custody. At no time did his mother provide adequate care or supervision. He seemed destined to join his two older brothers, who had spent much of their lives in juvenile correctional facilities.

The second child, a girl of five, had been severely neglected by a mentally disturbed mother. At the time of intervention, the mother and her four children moved to a home for battered women, where they remained for two months. While there the mother provided very deficient care for her children, and on leaving the shelter she could not provide even that; therefore, for three months the children were placed in a foster home. The mother then resumed custody, but two months later the children were again separated from her because of inadequate care. They remained in foster care for the rest of the two years. While with her mother, the study child was depressed and withdrawn. She seemed unable to cope with her mother's transient life-style and with the beatings her mother continued to receive from the father. Upon entering permanent foster care, she exhibited a number of behavioral problems. She was extremely troubled by her mother's failure to visit. She began mental health therapy, however, and her foster parents were very committed to her. By the end of the two years she seemed to be functioning normally. She wanted to remain with the foster parents.

The three other home children provide a very different picture. Each case had special aspects. Two involved serious but one-time incidents of abuse. The third involved relatively minor physical abuse, but the mother was well-known by workers in child protective services. Removal was possible in all three cases; in one the social worker recommended removal but the judge ordered the child to be left at home; nevertheless, in our judgment all three children lived with competent, caring parents, and removal would have been inappropriate. Two of these three children had been functioning well in most domains initially and generally continued to do well, though they had low scores in at least one domain. The third child had relatively low teacher ratings and personal satisfaction scores initially but, at the end of two years, was in the highest range on virtually every measure. Thus, the outcomes for all three children were positive.

For the three children who were returned from foster care to their mothers, circumstances ranged from mixed to horrendous.[2] The horrendous case was a child removed just before her fifth birthday because of the very poor care given by a mother with a drug addiction. The home was without any food and the child was left unattended for long periods. There was evidence of past physical abuse. However, the child was extremely unhappy in her foster family and was returned to her biological parent after five months. During the following eighteen months, her arm was broken by her mother, and evidence seemed to indicate that the child had been raped by her non-custodial father (in each instance the social worker decided that the evidence of abuse was insufficient to justify removal). Her personal happiness had increased upon reunion with her mother, yet she became less happy again toward the end of two years. She was retained in school because of academic problems. She did show improvement in classroom behavior in school, however, though her teacher felt that she had poor peer relations. She was extremely withdrawn both at home and in school.

A second child, six years old, also deteriorated following return to his mother, though there was no indication that he was reabused. He had originally been placed with his grandmother, after being hit in the face with a shoe by his mother. For the next six months, his mother and grandmother fought to establish custody. When the court ordered him returned to his mother, he told us, "My mommy won me back." Following return, his development deteriorated in all domains except for his relations with his mother, which improved somewhat. The decline was especially dramatic in school, where his social and academic ratings went from low to extremely low. He also reported that he had fewer friends. Although his self-esteem scores increased following his return, these were relatively low among the black children. He also told us during our last interview that he sometimes worried about his grandmother, "because they are my best family."

The third child, also six, had a more mixed outcome. She had been removed from her mother because of physical abuse. She lived for six months with her father and stepmother. She was unhappy about living with her father and anxious to return to her mother. She evidenced general improvement following her return. She was performing adequately in a special education class (she had a 75 IQ), her self-esteem and peer satisfaction increased substantially, and she received average scores on social behavior at school. Her mother reported fewer problem behaviors over time, but there were still problems with lying and stealing. More significantly, the mother remained ambivalent in her desire to keep her children and inconsistent in her discipline. On one occasion, she again whipped the child with an extension cord, which led to the resumption of court supervision. This child remained in a high-risk situation and it seemed to us likely that she would continue to have behavior problems.

In sum, the picture for the home group of black children was mixed. Three children, whose parents were the least abusive and least disorganized, did well at home. Four of the other five did poorly. Two of these children were in great difficulty right from the start; two others deteriorated during our two-year study. The mother of each of these children also functioned poorly in terms of providing adequate care for, and supervision of, her child. The situation of the fifth child also was problematic because of the threat of future abuse.

Thus, for the black children, as for the white, remaining at home entailed significant risks. Unfortunately, as we shall see next, foster care was not clearly the answer, at least for half the black children.

THE FOSTER CHILDREN

Eight black children remained in foster care throughout the two years. Four were in quite stable placements, spending virtually the entire two years in the home of a relative—three with their grandmothers and the fourth with her father; at the end of the two years each placement appeared to be permanent.[3] The other four foster children experienced multiple placements. Two ended up in stable placements, one with his grandmother, one with her father; and a third child moved from relative to relative during the two years. The fourth was placed in several foster homes and then, at the end of the second year, in a residential treatment facility. She was the only black child who did not spend any of the two years in the home of a relative.

The outcomes for these eight children were quite varied. For three, the foster care experience definitely was positive. Two showed no developmental problems initially and continued to do well, in most respects, throughout the two years. The third showed marked improvement during the two years and was doing extremely well in every domain at the end. For example, he went from the lowest academic rank to the highest and from low teacher ratings in the social area to very positive ratings. This child had been severely and repeatedly abused by his mother. He went to live with a highly committed and caring grandmother where, from the first day, he indicated his happiness to be away from his mother and constantly asserted that he wished to remain with his grandmother forever. The other two children were happy in foster care, though they did not want to remain with their foster parents permanently. One decided to resume living with her mother after having spent two years with her father; the other had lived with various relatives in the Bay Area but saw her parents regularly. She desperately wanted to resume living with them, but this was unrealistic since they both had severe problems with alcohol, which totally disabled them.

Three other children did not do at all well in foster care. Two were boys living with grandmothers; the third was a girl living with a nonrelative. All three had been functioning poorly initially; two of the three were doing worse at the end of two years. All recorded diminished personal satisfaction, received low social behavior ratings throughout the two years, and were doing poorly academically. The worst outcome was for the girl, an eight-year-old, whose emotional problems increased over time and eventually resulted in her being placed in a residential treatment program.

The remaining two children are hard to categorize. They showed improvement in some aspects of development but decline in others. They both spent a year in non-relative placements, during which they made good progress. Then each was placed with a relative (one with her father, one with his grandmother, both in other states), and their progress seemed to deteriorate. Their biological mothers continued to have substantial problems, and it is doubtful if these two children would have been better off remaining at home. Foster care may have been preferable, but this is not an easy conclusion to draw.

OVERVIEW

The outcome for the black foster children, as a group, parallels the outcome of the black home children. The children doing the best initially continued to do well in both settings. Those doing poorly initially continued doing poorly, except for one foster child. The quality of care—both at home and in foster care—was an important factor. But, as was the case for the white children, intervention did not significantly improve the well-being of the most damaged children, even those with good caretakers.

The fact that most of the black children were with relatives seemed to be a mixed blessing, at best. Placement with relatives made the transition to foster care easier, especially for those children who had lived previously with the relative; in three cases, however, the transition created substantial conflict between the new custodian (a grandmother) and the mother. None of the grandmothers wanted to return the children to the mothers and fought hard to retain custody. The three previously noncustodial fathers who were entrusted with their children's care were ambivalent about custody, and the status of their children remained uncertain. Two of these children encountered conflict with their stepmothers. Thus, all the children were troubled by conflicting loyalties.

It must be stressed, however, even though the outcome in the foster cases was problematic, that there is little reason to think the children would have done better if left at home. In light of the long histories of abuse, the limited affection many mothers showed their children, and the scope of the problems the mothers continued to experience even after responsibility for the child was lessened through foster placement, we believe that the majority of the eight children in foster care would have fared badly if left at home.

The Hispanic Children

INITIAL STATUS

The sample. There were eight Hispanic children in our sample initially. Six were placed at home, two in foster care. The home group included three children selected somewhat differently than the other children in the study. These children lived in Santa Clara County, not San Mateo, and thus were not left at home as a result of the special legislation in effect in San Mateo County, which is adjacent to it.[4] We included them because they were very similar to cases we studied in San Mateo County, in terms of the seriousness of the incident leading to intervention and the mothers' backgrounds. In fact, in two of the three cases, social workers in Santa Clara County placed the children in foster care but after a month returned them to their biological parents because of lack of a permanent foster home. Thus, it seems highly likely that these children met our comparability standard.

All six children in the Hispanic home group remained at home for two years. Of the two children in foster care, one returned home and one stayed in foster care. We will describe only the six home children, since a home-foster comparison is obviously impossible.[5]

Incidents leading to intervention. Three of the children had been abused; three neglected. Although each incident of abuse was moderately serious (the children had been hit with objects, and there was a history of abuse), the children's well-being seemed more threatened by emotional rejection than by physical punishment. Each of the mothers saw the child as willfully disobedient and extremely difficult to live with. They regularly made these feelings known to the children.

The three incidents of neglect were serious. One girl, eight years old, for several weeks had been begging for food at a shopping center with her youngest siblings. The family lived in a motel room nearby. A second girl, also eight, had not attended school for two months. Her mother did not want her to go to school. On several occasions when her father had taken her to school he remained in the classroom and masturbated. The third child, nine years old, also had missed a lot of school because his mother kept him at home to care for his younger siblings. She would sometimes disappear for several days. Two of these three mothers also seemed to reject the child emotionally.

The emotional rejection in the Hispanic cases stands out clearly. The six mothers had very little involvement with their children, less than in the other groups we studied. As we discuss below, they reported very negative feelings toward the children. This attitude stood out particularly because the five comparison Hispanic mothers were very highly involved with their children.

Maternal background. The families of the Hispanic children experienced the worst circumstances of any group. All the parents were poor, out of work, and lacking in education. Four of the six families had incomes of less than $500 a month; none had incomes greater than $1,000. Only one of the parents was employed full time. None had more than a high school education. Four of the six had no social support systems. Three of the mothers had a history of mental illness. Thus, based both on the precipitative incidents and the maternal backgrounds, all the children were at high risk of future abuse or neglect.

The children. In many respects the picture that emerged of the Hispanic children's development was as unusual, and surprising, as that of the blacks. The overriding feature was the disparity between the parents' assessments and the teachers' ratings. All the mothers viewed their children as having major behavioral problems. They rated them low in social competence, high in problem behaviors, and high in terms of psychological problems. In marked contrast, the teachers seemed to love the children, giving them the highest scores of any group on social behavior and likability. Except for those with high absentee rates, they also were seen as average or above-average students. The only problem the teachers perceived was with peer relations; half the children were reported as experiencing peer problems.

In contrast to the comparison Hispanic children, all of whom scored very high on virtually all measures, the abused and neglected children presented a mixed picture. All of them indicated they had trouble getting along with their caretakers; four reported extremely bad relations. For example, one child, whose father was black, was constantly called "a nigger" by her mother, who told her that she was ugly and that no one liked her. Only two of the children made use of their parents as a resource. The conflict and emotional rejection seemed to take a particularly heavy toll on three of these children. For example, one girl in responding to an item on the self-esteem scale said, "I don't want to be anything. I would rather be a paper thrown in the garbage dump— torn up and dead." A second child said, "I wish I was dead because I get hit a lot." This child and a third one both indicated they would like to live with someone other than their mother. However, though three children had very low self-esteem scores, three others had high scores and half reported good peer relations.

Thus, the major threat to the children seemed to be the poor quality of their emotional relationship with their parents. Although the lack of parental involvement and supervision and intense parent-child conflict did not seem to impair the children's school functioning, it appeared to greatly affect the self-esteem and social skills of at least three of the six children.

CHANGES DURING THE TWO YEARS

The children's home situations. All six children remained with their parents for the entire two years. Although five of the six parents received some support from a social work agency, generally this had little effect: in only one home environment was there substantial change; the mother responded favorably to counseling, obtained a job, and became much more involved with her child. The other five parents had periods of adequate functioning but often were depressed and experienced periods of total disorganization. Frequently their problems were related to their extremely bad economic situations (perhaps their personal problems influenced their economic situations as well). Three of the six families moved frequently and generally occupied inadequate housing, including cars, garages, and the homes of relatives with whom they did not get along. Because they were consumed with their own problems, they had little time for their children.

The children's well-being. Like their parents' well-being, the children's tended to fluctuate during the two years. Only one child was clearly better off at the end of the two years; one child was clearly worse off. For the rest, the picture was mixed.

The best outcome occurred for Tony, ten years old. He had been beaten with a paddle, in part because of encopresis (an inability to control bowel movements). Following intervention, he received medical treatment that eliminated the problem. At the time of intervention, he had been emotionally rejected by his mother, who said she wished he lived with his father. During the two years, the relationship between mother and son improved substantially, though she still provided only minimal academic help to Tony and had mixed feelings about keeping him. Tony's self-esteem and peer relation scores increased considerably. He had more positive feelings about his mother. Although his situation was not ideal, he seemed to be doing adequately.

On the other hand, for Christina, also ten, the problems between her and her mother increased over time. By the end of the two years the situation had gotten so bad that her mother let Christina permanently join her grandparents, who lived in the state of Washington. Christina had wanted this for years, so she was happy. Prior to the move she had run away from home, and been caught stealing from her teacher and her friends' parents. Interestingly, despite these problems, Christina received very high social ratings from the teacher and was doing well academically. Her self-esteem scores went from low to high and she reported good peer relations. Yet she clearly was a very troubled child, largely because of the poor relationship with her mother. Since her mother's own emotional problems were severe, the move to her grandparents probably was the best possible outcome.

The outcomes for the other four children are very hard to categorize. Each child definitely experienced improvement in some aspects of development. However, each child also remained at substantial risk.

For example, one eight-year-old child missed an entire year of school because her mother did not keep a permanent residence and did not want to send her to school. A second child received no medical care during the two years, though she had several major illnesses and regularly ate spoonsful of salt and butter. A third child was constantly ridiculed and called derogatory names by her mother, who, on one occasion finding her and her sister playing "doctor" with a boy their age, called the girl obscene names, accused her of liking to be fondled, and told her she would probably grow up to be a "whore."[6] The fourth child, nine years old, continued to have primary responsibility for the care of his younger siblings and to miss many school sessions. Three of the four cases were troubled by parent-child conflict, though the conflict generally decreased during the two years.

Nevertheless, each of the four children also showed signs of positive growth in one or more aspects of development. They all were well liked by their teachers and all but one of them seemed to find school a major source of emotional support. They generally scored high on the self-esteem scale and had adequate peer relations.

In sum, intervention improved the well-being of most of the children, but it had a major impact on only one case. In light of the poor emotional relationship between the parents and children, largely stemming from the parents' own emotional problems, all the children remained at risk.

Summary

The outcomes for the black and Hispanic children provide further evidence that unless intervention significantly improves parental functioning, children left at home remain at substantial risk. As was the case with the white children, the greatest threat was to the child's emotional, not physical, development. Although reabuse did occur and in one instance was quite serious, the children were not in danger of suffering severe injuries.

The experiences of these children also indicate that some children do well, others poorly, both at home and in foster care. No single feature predicted a successful outcome at home or in foster care, though, as one would expect, the presence of a competent, caring adult seemed to be the most important factor.

Although we would not draw definitive conclusions from such small samples, we found some indications that the patterns of interaction varied in the families from different ethnic groups, and as a result different aspects of a child's development were affected. The white children had poor social skills and showed the most emotional disturbance. The Hispanic children showed the effects of emotional rejection: they had low self-esteem and reported poor relations with their parents. The black children had academic and emotional problems but developed adequately in other areas.

Finally, the fact that a number of the children were doing adequately overall or in a particular aspect of development (for example, the Hispanic children at school) should make us cautious in assuming an invariable or consistent impact from abuse or neglect. As a number of recent studies show (Garmezy 1981), some children have a resilience or adaptability that enables them to perform adequately despite tremendous environmental stress. An interesting aspect of our findings is that abused and neglected children of different ethnicities may develop special strengths in particular developmental areas. The differences may reflect different demands and stresses experienced by the children of each ethnic group. They may have developed different strategies to cope with differing stresses. However, given the small sample, this finding merely suggests an avenue that others may wish to explore further.

Twelve

Policy Implications

WE UNDERTOOK THIS STUDY because of our belief that public policy regarding the protection of abused and neglected children ought to be based on more than ideology and fiscal considerations. Although policy decisions must ultimately rest on value preferences, evidence about the costs and benefits of alternative policies are critical in making value choices. We retain the belief that research is essential. However, we have learned a great deal about the limits as well as the benefits of research in developing public policy in this area. Before addressing the policy implications of our study, we will identify some of the study's limitations.

Our study provides a substantial amount of information about a small number of children. Looking intensely at these children proved to be very revealing. We found that many children functioned well in one domain and poorly in another, and that intervention had a differing impact on each domain. Therefore, the question "Is home or foster care better?" must be refined by asking further, "In terms of which aspects of development?" and "For which children, under what conditions?"

Unfortunately, intensive evaluation usually requires sacrificing sample size. Rarely will the money be available to study large numbers of children intensively.[1] Small samples often mean that important questions cannot be answered. The small sample size limited our ability to determine which factors were associated with the initial status of the abused and neglected children and which factors accounted for change in individual children. Moreover, we do not feel comfortable generalizing our findings to the nationwide population of children in foster care. Obviously, our findings about the impact of foster care are limited to children in the five-to-ten-years-old age group. We doubt that our findings are applicable to younger children, who might benefit more if permanently separated from inadequate parents. Even for children in the age group we studied, some of our findings might not be replicated if the study were conducted with another sample. Some of our findings may have been influenced by chance. In addition, it is likely that some of the factors that may have accounted for the outcomes in our cases would not be present in other states, or even other counties within California. For example, the outcomes for both home and foster children probably were influenced by both the quality of services to the home families and the quality of the foster homes. There is substantial variation in the quality of services and foster homes in different areas of the country and within each state.

Our analysis also was complicated by the fact that the developmental status of the home and foster children differed somewhat at the time of our initial interviews, which took place after the children had been in foster care for several months. Since there was relatively little change in the overall well-being of the majority of children during the two-year period, the reasons for the initial differences are crucial for policy analysis. As we discussed in Chapter 5, we cannot know whether they were attributable to random variation, to differences in the children prior to intervention, or to an initial positive impact of foster care. Thus our study, which required an enormous investment of time and more money than is often available for policy-oriented social science research, became more exploratory than we had hoped or envisioned. As Lee Cronbach has written, "The hope that an evaluation will provide unequivocal answers, convincing enough to extinguish controversy about the merits of a social program, is certain to be disappointed" (Cronbach 1982, p. 3).

Despite these limitations, we were able to address several important policy issues. We began with two central research questions: (a) Should a legislature, in enacting laws regarding alternative interventions, adopt a general preference for home supervision or foster placement? (b) What factors should a social worker or judge consider in deciding whether to use foster care for an individual child? Although we cannot provide definitive answers to these questions, we are able to delineate some of the benefits, and some of the costs, of alternative placement decisions. Our findings are most relevant at the legislative level; we have less to say to those deciding individual cases. In addition, we have identified some developmental areas in which abused and neglected children seem to be at particular risk. Our findings clearly indicate that major changes are needed in the types of interventions intended to protect abused and neglected children. In the following sections we suggest some general policies that might promote the children's well-being, regardless of whether they are living with biological parents or are in foster care. Our data also raise questions about some general theories of child development. Therefore, we end by exploring several issues relevant to those interested in research in child development.

Benefits and Costs of Alternative Placements

INFERENCES FROM THE DATA

We look first at the question "Should a legislature prefer, in general, home supervision or foster care, *for the type of cases evaluated in this study*?" Our data do not provide a clear-cut answer. Rather they illustrate the complexity of the choices, or trade-offs, that must be made. We first review the data, then discuss their implications.

Looking only at what happened to the children from the time we first saw them until the end of the study, two years later, there was not a great deal of difference between home and foster care. On *average*, there was little change in the relative well-being of each group of children. However, those changes that did occur favored foster care. Initially twenty-three white children, five black children, and six Hispanic children were left at home. During the two years, four white children and one black child (15 percent) had to be removed from their parents' custody because of continued abuse and neglect. As a result of the policy favoring leaving children at home, these children were left in an inadequate home for a longer period of time than they might otherwise have been. Trying to forestall removal is clearly costly in human terms, though only one of the children we studied seemed to show deterioration as a result of this. Looked at from the other perspective, however, 85 percent of the home group of children—considered to be in high-risk situations—were able to remain at home without being abused or neglected to a degree requiring removal.

The outcomes for those children who remained at home throughout the two years were mixed, at best. Nearly half the children were subjected to some degree of reabuse or continued neglect, though none of the children suffered serious physical harm. Yet despite the fact that many of the home environments remained only marginally adequate, there was, on average, no deterioration in the well-being of the home children in most areas of development. The only clear area of decline was in social behavior at school. In fact, with regard to the children's personal satisfaction, the home children had higher self-esteem scores and reported better peer relations over the course of the two years, though they were still the least satisfied group on these measures.

The relative stability of the home group must be viewed in light of the many problems initially exhibited by the children and noted throughout the two years. The academic performance of most home children remained below what would be expected based on their IQ scores. Nearly half the children continued to miss substantial amounts of school. Their relations with their parents remained poor; approximately half the children continued to have significant emotional problems. Thus home placement, even with services to the family, did not help the children overcome their academic, emotional, and social problems.

The outcomes for the foster children were somewhat more favorable, at least for the white children. It seems clear from our data, which are consistent with the findings of Fanshel and Shinn (1978), Festinger (1983), and others, that foster care was not detrimental to most children. All but two children were protected from further abuse or physical neglect. There was no area of development (except teachers' ratings of peer relations, in which all children—home, foster, and comparison groups alike—were rated lower over time) where the white foster children, as a group, appeared worse off at the end than initially.

In most aspects of development, the white foster children were better off at the end than at the beginning. The black foster children were not. There was some improvement in both the physical health and the academic performance of the white foster children, though few children either at home or in foster care had health problems, and most children in both settings continued to experience academic difficulties. Perhaps more significant, the foster children reported increased personal satisfaction during the two years. At least with regard to the factors measured by our self-esteem scale, they consistently seemed somewhat more satisfied than the home children. There also seemed to be much less adult-child conflict in the foster setting. Thus, foster care appeared to be meeting some of the emotional needs of the children, as well as enhancing their physical and academic development.

In reaching this conclusion, we are mindful of the fact that even though the foster children were not worse off, foster care did not alleviate some of the problems that the children evidenced when they entered care. For example, almost half the foster children exhibited emotional problems throughout the two years; although some children's school performances improved, the majority were still doing poorly academically. Moreover, the majority of the foster children still seemed to retain an emotional commitment to their biological parents; half expressed a desire to return to them. Like children of divorce, they expressed a psychological need to maintain previous ties. In addition, there were individual foster children, especially among the blacks, who experienced a general decline in overall well-being. However, for both black and white children, the chances of a child's declining in overall well-being was no greater in foster care than at home. There is every reason to believe that the children who experienced problems in foster care would have experienced problems had they been left at home, based on the findings that the home children did not do well and the biological parents of the foster children also showed little ability to change their behaviors.

In sum, although there was relatively little major change among the children in either group, there is some indication that foster care was more beneficial to the children most at risk, at least with regard to improving physical health, school attendance, and academic performance and preventing deterioration in social behavior at school. Both situations—remaining at home and placement in foster care—involved emotional stress for the children, but the stress caused by the conflict and chaos in their home environments may have had a more negative impact on the home children than the stress that separation, movement, and adjustment to new "parents" had on the foster children.

The analysis, to this point, is based only on changes we noted in the children between our initial and final data-gathering points. As we have shown, the white foster children were, on average, better off initially in terms of teachers' ratings, degree of parent-child conflict, and their own reports of personal satisfaction and peer relations. The case for favoring foster care is obviously stronger if we assume that the home and foster children were exactly comparable prior to intervention. If that were true, we would have to conclude that the initial status of the foster children represented an immediate positive impact of foster care, which did not diminish over time. However, if the two groups were noncomparable because of random factors or systematic differences in the type of children considered for home and foster care in the three counties, we can conclude only that foster care was not detrimental to the children.

As we discussed in Chapter 5, there is no way of scientifically determining the reasons for initial differences between the home and foster groups. It is possible that foster care had an initial positive impact: the children may have been responding to the greater structure provided by the foster homes. The day-to-day stability of life in a foster home, regular school attendance, freedom from fear of abuse, all may have led the children to perform better in school and to engage in less acting-out behavior in the foster homes. The greater security, material comforts, and attention to their personal needs may have increased the children's personal satisfaction (on those issues measured by our self-esteem scale) and enabled them to develop better peer relations.

We recognize that most literature reports an association of initial trauma with foster placement, and we also found evidence of such trauma. Many foster children in our study exhibited sleep and eating problems; virtually all of them initially said that they wanted to return home. Yet they might have had these experiences and still reacted positively to the foster homes, which provided them with stability and material advantages.

An equally strong case can be made that the initial differences between the home and foster groups were the result of chance, or reflective of nonrandom factors, or both. Two factors may have "caused" the group differences. One is the difference in the proportion of abused children in each group. There were more abused children at home. Abused children tended to be more troubled than neglected children in terms of emotional problems, self-esteem, and perception of peer relations. This factor only partially explains the group differences, however, since the foster children who were in placement because of neglect generally received higher ratings on our measures than neglected children in the home group.

A second possibility is that the home sample contained an atypical group of abused and neglected children. Among the home children, there was a small group of quite disturbed children who came from families with a great deal of parent-child conflict. We cannot know whether these children's emotional problems resulted from, or led to, parental abuse or neglect. However, these children clearly seemed more disturbed than the rest of the sample. Why were there no such children in foster care? Perhaps in Alameda and Santa Clara counties such children were handled in the mental health system, not the child-abuse/-neglect system. In San Mateo County the best way to provide services to a child was through abuse-and-neglect legal proceedings, since the special legislation provided the Department of Social Services with extra funds to handle such cases. No such services were available through that department in Alameda or Santa Clara counties. Therefore, in these counties difficult cases may have been routed to the mental health system, which had its own funding.

There are many other arguments that could be made to support either hypothesis. For example, some theorists argue that the poor social skills of abused and neglected children result from major inadequacies in the mother-child relationship, which are likely to have a lasting impact on the child's development (Sroufe 1983; Erickson, Sroufe, and Egeland 1985). If a child's social development is impaired by the quality of early mother-child attachment, it seems unlikely that the child's social skills and "likability" will improve significantly just as a result of three or four months of foster care.[2] On the other hand, a number of studies indicate that ongoing stress and conflict are particularly detrimental to children (Emery 1982). Removal from such stressful situations might have a significant impact on a child's behavior (Rutter 1980). It may also be that the foster children came to school looking more presentable and that teachers' ratings of the child's likability and social behavior are heavily influenced by the children's appearance.[3]

After weighing and reweighing all arguments many times, we find ourselves unable to choose between the competing hypotheses. Since there is a substantial possibility that the initial differences did not result from a positive impact of foster care, we would not base new policies on the assumption that foster care can have consequential short-term impact. We suggest incorporating into policy decisions only the findings that, over the two years, foster care was not detrimental to most children, that the home children seemed to remain at substantial risk in terms of social, emotional, and academic development, and that foster care may have been slightly more beneficial than home placement in terms of the children's health and academic performance.

POLICY IMPLICATIONS OF THE FINDINGS

Regardless of whether we conclude only that foster care was not detrimental, or that the higher level of overall well-being of the foster children reflected, at least to some degree, a positive impact of foster care, we are left with a value choice. Were the benefits of foster care of such a nature that legislators should direct child welfare agencies and courts to prefer foster care for the type of cases that were the focus of this study? As a general rule, our society does not transfer children from parents to nonparents just because the child might do "better," in some aspects of development, in a new home. In addition to concern over the impact of separation from the child's perspective, our society defers to biological ties because of the importance of children to parents and in order not to impose majoritarian notions about rearing children, and because as a society we value cultural, social, and political diversity.

In considering whether to adopt a preference for foster care, it must be recognized that the benefits of foster care may be dependent upon making foster placement permanent—that is, never returning a child to the biological parents. There is no evidence indicating that the type of benefits that seemed to come from foster care would continue if a child were returned home. In fact, by subjecting children to multiple separations from attachment figures, removal and return may be particularly difficult on children. In addition, there is little reason to expect that significant changes will occur in the behavior of the biological parents while the child is away from them, at least with regard to those behaviors that might negatively affect the child's academic, social, and emotional well-being.[4] In most instances, effecting significant changes in parental behavior such that a child's academic, social, and emotional well-being will improve probably requires working with both parent and child. There are also cost considerations in the use of foster care in cases of non-serious injury. If the majority of children in these cases are returned to their biological parents, it may be a waste of resources to remove them in the first place. Unless the child cannot be protected at home, it may be less expensive and more efficacious to leave the child at home and work with the entire family.

Although the benefits of foster care may depend on not returning the child, it seems harsh to terminate parental rights without any effort at reunification in cases in which abuse or neglect did not result in serious injury. In fact, judges and social workers generally are reluctant to terminate parental rights except in compelling cases. The more marginal the grounds for removal, the less likely that judges will terminate parental rights (Wald 1976). As a result, many children may be kept in nonpermanent foster homes and subjected to multiple placements. Without permanent placement, any benefits of foster care may disappear over time.[5]

Thus, a legislator must decide if the harm we found to be associated with leaving a child at home, or the benefit associated with foster care, justify depriving parents of custody, perhaps on a permanent basis. What would be achieved by such a policy? The reabuse or continued neglect among the home cases was not at a level that put the child in jeopardy of serious physical harm. However, many of the home parents failed to ensure their children's school attendance. In addition, half the home environments were marked by high levels of parent-child conflict, which very likely had a negative impact on the child's emotional development. In terms of social development, the greatest problems for the home children were their poor peer relations and low ratings by teachers on social skills and likability. The home children also were, on average, less satisfied with themselves, their peers, and their schools than the foster children, though by the end of the two years the home children's overall satisfaction was not substantially different from that of the foster or comparison children.

In contrast, foster care may improve school performance and physical health and prevent deterioration in social skills. Still, placement resulted in only marginal improvement in most areas—none, on average, for the black children—unless we attribute most of the initial differences between the groups to the positive impact of foster care. We certainly should be concerned with poor academic performance, since this increases the chances of the child's dropping out of school. The poor peer relations, "unlikability," and the emotional problems of the home children are also worrisome signs.[6] They might well portend more future problems for the children than would physical injuries (Roff and Wirt 1984). A legislator might consider these signs serious enough to justify a legal standard that tells judges, "When in doubt, opt for foster care."

However, there are several considerations in addition to those previously discussed, that militate against increased use of foster care. Most important, the services provided to the majority of the home families were not directed at improving the children's social skills. In fact, the children were not the primary recipients of the services. Most services were directed at the parents, since it was their behaviors that triggered the intervention. We are not certain whether special services to children can compensate for deficiencies in the home environment. There is little evidence that services provided to chronically abusing and neglecting parents have been able to improve parent-child relations or parenting skills significantly. Some good programs may not have been evaluated, however. Moreover, intervention programs have been carried out in less than an ideal fashion. Before adopting a preference for foster care, a legislator might want to require that home-based services, aimed at helping children overcome developmental deficits, be tried and evaluated. The argument for such a policy is even stronger if the benefits of foster care can be achieved only by permanently terminating the biological parents' opportunities to regain custody.

It may also be relevant that many children in our society show the same type of problems as our study children, though their parents are neither abusive nor neglectful even as these terms are currently defined in the broadest abuse and neglect laws. For example, several recent studies of children living with their mothers following divorce report that a substantial minority of the children had significant social and emotional problems, at least for some period following their parents' separation (Wallerstein and Kelly 1980; Hetherington, Cox, and Cox 1982). Children in only mildly neglectful homes—where removal would not be contemplated in any jurisdiction—also show an increased likelihood of social and emotional problems (Egeland, Sroufe, and Erickson 1983). Research by Sroufe and his colleagues (Sroufe 1983; Erickson, Sroufe, and Egeland 1985) indicates that children who are "insecurely attached" to their mothers are at increased risk of poor social development, even if they have not been abused or neglected (as these terms are legally defined). There is also some evidence that poverty alone is related to deficits in a child's development (Elmer 1977).

A legislator might conclude that removal of an abused or neglected child is unjustified if done to achieve better peer relations, better academic performance, or higher self-esteem when other children with similar problems continue to live with their parents. These other situations are distinguishable, of course. Most children in divorced families eventually "recover," and attachment relations change. Still, we believe that a legislator must address the question of whether abuse or neglect justifies differential treatment. Does the fact that the parents have abused or neglected the child weaken their claim to custody, even if the state can prevent recurrence of the specific type of harm (e.g., physical injury) that justified initial intervention?

On the other hand, it is possible that if we had followed the children for a period longer than two years, the positive aspects of foster care would have emerged more strongly. It seemed likely that most of the foster children in our sample would continue to experience stable care. The opposite seemed true for the home children. Over a longer time, differences in the quality of the two types of environments may have an increasing impact on the children's development.

As we have noted, the ultimate choice of a legislative standard requires making value judgments, balancing, among other considerations, parental interests,[7] the likely impact of alternatives on the well-being of the children, the impact of various rules on the functioning of the foster care system, the availability of good foster homes (which are in short supply), and cost considerations. The children's interests clearly should be primary when there is a substantial risk to their physical well-being (Wald 1976). To date, legislatures and courts have been less willing to sever parent-child relationships in order to promote the child's social, emotional, or academic development. A few highly respected child development experts would intervene only to protect a child's physical well-being (see Goldstein, Freud, and Solnit 1979).

Our data persuade us that abused and neglected children are at substantial risk emotionally, and that intervention programs are necessary to protect their emotional, as well as physical, development. However, because of our small sample and the problematic interpretation of the initial differences between groups, we do not conclude that foster care is preferable to home placement. Moreover, because we believe that most benefits of foster care are likely to be lost if a child is returned home, we recommend that the changes in the intervention process suggested in the next section be tried before a legal standard favoring foster care is adopted. We reach this conclusion in part because we believe that foster care followed by reunification is not likely to benefit many children. Yet we think it is inappropriate to terminate parental rights without efforts at reunification when the child is not in physical danger.[8]

Our judgment applies only to children five to ten years of age. Our findings do raise serious questions about the best policy for younger children, especially those younger than two years. Younger children probably would retain fewer ties to their biological parents. Quick removal of younger children would minimize the negative impact of the home environment, which probably has a greater impact the longer the child is in it. Many child development experts believe that the first several years of life are an especially important period in a child's development. Foster care leading to adoption also might be more beneficial for younger children than for children in the five-to-ten-year age range.

The Impact of Abuse and Neglect on Children: Implications for Intervention Programs

Although our findings do not point clearly to the best policy regarding home versus foster placement, the data do lead to some compelling conclusions about the intervention process. In many respects, we are left with a very sad picture. Our data clearly demonstrate that the great majority of the abused and neglected children were at substantial risk in terms of academic and social development even if they were not at risk of serious physical injury. Unfortunately, many of the children continued to exhibit problems in these aspects of development throughout the two years. Moreover, despite the provision of services, half the home children were reabused or neglected and nearly all were subjected to intense parent-child conflict. Many continued to fear for their physical safety. They also bore the burdens of family conflict and of being forced to cope with problems their parents should have been handling. Although the children in foster care appeared to be somewhat less at risk in social development, they still had more problems than the comparison children. Half the foster children evidenced significant emotional problems; almost all of them indicated difficulty in dealing with the loss of their parents.

The nature and extent of these children's problems raise significant questions about current means of intervention. All courts and child welfare agencies assume that the purpose of intervention in abuse and neglect cases is to protect the child. However, the focus of intervention services in the majority of cases is on the parent. Unless the child exhibits significant behavioral problems, most agencies do not evaluate the child's academic or social development. The majority of children do not receive any services aimed at promoting their social development. Social service agencies often do not work with a child's school in developing a special academic program.[9]

Moreover, in recent years, social service agencies have been encouraged to provide interventions that are extensive, but of limited duration. For the most part, an agency will intervene for only six months or, at most, a year.[10] Even during this period, the services focus primarily on parents' problems, for example, helping them to obtain jobs or cope with drug or alcohol problems, or overcome depression, or become better housekeepers. In abuse cases, they may be offered counseling or classes designed to teach them alternative ways of disciplining their children. It is rare, however, that services are provided that are designed to change the nature of the interaction between parent and child.

We doubt that the services generally being provided can alter the nature of the parent-child interaction or help the child develop social or academic skills, though they may somewhat benefit the parent. The precise reasons why abused and neglected children have peer problems has not been established by previous research. It has been argued both that the problems stem from inadequacy in the attachment relationship between abusive and neglectful parents and their children (Sroufe 1983; Erickson, Sroufe, and Egeland 1985), and that the differences result from deficiencies in the child-rearing techniques or socialization practices of the parents (Susman et al. 1985; Trickett, Susman, and Lourie 1980; Lewis and Schaeffer 1981). It also is not fully clear why abused and neglected children perform so poorly academically. Obviously the high rate of absenteeism does not help. The limited involvement of the neglecting parents in their children's school lives is another likely factor. However, these factors do not explain all our cases.

It may be that the children's deficits resulted from factors in the family other than (or in addition to) the abuse or neglect per se. As described in Chapter 6, the majority of abusive and neglecting parents experienced high levels of conflict with their spouses: a substantial proportion of their children had experienced divorce, parental separations, and family violence. A number of studies indicate that divorce and high levels of family conflict impair children's social and academic development (Wallerstein and Kelly, 1980; Hetherington, Cox, and Cox 1982; Rutter 1979), though some of these children in these families may, in fact, have been abused or neglected as well. Moreover, many of the parents were poor and had limited education. Elmer (1977) has argued that social class is as important as abuse or neglect in accounting for developmental problems.

Because family conflict, divorce, low income, and abuse or neglect are so frequently intertwined, it is not possible, on the basis of existing research, to separate out which factors "cause" which problem. Most likely each factor contributes to developmental problems. The cumulation of factors may be critical. Characteristics of individual children also may mitigate or exacerbate the impact of parental behavior or environmental deprivations. Knowing the relative importance of various factors would help in designing the precise types of interventions (especially preventive interventions) needed to help the children overcome these deficits. But agencies need not wait until the exact causes are determined. Certain changes in the process of intervention should be implemented now.

First, we recommend that full developmental assessments of the child be made in all cases serious enough to require supervision of the family or placement of the child in foster care. The assessment should include an evaluation of the children's emotional status, social skills, academic performance, and peer relationships, and their perceptions of their relationship with their parents. If the child remains at home, the social service agency should ask the schools to assess the child's academic skills and performance and to develop programs to help children who evidence deficiencies. Clearly, the social service agency should monitor the child's school attendance and, if necessary, provide the means for getting children to school.

Counseling, support services, or both must be focused on the child as well as the parents. There is extraordinarily little research indicating what services would be most appropriate. At present, the most common services for children are individual or group counseling, usually by mental health professionals, aimed at treating children with obvious psychological problems (usually evidenced by acting-out behaviors). Although such services undoubtedly are necessary for some children, they may not be the most appropriate service for the majority of children. The major problems for the children in our study related to academic performance, peer relations, and parent-child relations. Individual therapy may not be the best way of dealing with these problems. A number of clinicians are trying therapies that include "peer group" treatment—that is, treatment modalities that involve working with children in groups that often contain nonabused as well as abused children. This may be a better way of improving a child's social skills.

In many cases, family rather than individual therapy is needed, since many abusive or neglectful families experience a great deal of parent-child conflict. Although family counseling, like individual therapy for children and parents, has been only moderately successful at best (Magura 1981), a few programs have reported success (Provence and Naylor 1983; Patterson 1982). These programs are costly, but we cannot get by cheaply if we want to protect the child's emotional development. In addition, child welfare agencies must consider experimenting with new types of programs. In some cases, the best intervention may entail providing the children with as much in the way of alternative support systems as possible. After-school day-care programs, community centers for older children, and providing a "Big Sister" or "Big Brother" may help children cope with a poor home environment, even if there is not much change in the parents' behavior.

Special services also must be developed for children placed in foster care. To a large degree, the system now operates as if foster placement, in and of itself, will solve the child's problems. Foster parents are assumed to be competent in child-rearing skills; therefore the child's care primarily is left in their hands (we recognize that some foster children also receive mental health therapy). Although many foster parents are caring individuals, with excellent child-rearing skills, they often will need help in promoting the child's well-being.

We have no ready prescriptions for ensuring that foster care will help children. Unquestionably the success or failure of a placement turns on the quality of the foster home. The foster parents have the primary influence on the child's development. It seems obvious that training foster parents to be aware of the development problems the children may exhibit is a first step. Foster parents also should be taught methods for helping children improve their social skills. Particular care should be taken to ensure that the children receive proper educational help. In some instances, a child might even be placed with particular foster parents primarily because they live in a school district with an outstanding special education program.

We recognize that social work agencies face a difficult task just in finding placements. Matching child and foster parent or child and school district may be a luxury beyond the wildest dreams of a social agency. However, recognizing the need for such matching is a necessary step in convincing legislators that more funding is needed if we really intend to help abused and neglected children. Placement policies also should be affected by the goal of the placement. If the goal is reunification, it may be best to place the child as close as possible to the biological parent, to facilitate contact and promote the parent-child relationship. If a return home is not contemplated, other placement goals can be emphasized. In addition, children who evidence developmental problems should be monitored regularly, so that additional services can be provided if the child is not overcoming them. Mental health services to the children may also help prepare them to cope with foster care (Kliman, Schaeffer, and Friedman 1982).

The critical point is that at present, abused and neglected children remain at substantial risk of poor development, whether at home or in foster care. A legislator concerned with protecting abused and neglected children cannot focus only on the standard for removal. Legislatures must provide funding to permit the development of services that may overcome the problems faced by children both at home and in foster care.

Our findings are relevant to another policy issue regarding interventions to protect abused and neglected children. There is a substantial debate about whether intervention should be permitted because a child is being emotionally neglected (see Wald 1976; Wald 1980; Goldstein, Freud, and Solnit 1979). At present most intervention is based on evidence of physical abuse or neglect, or sexual abuse. Our findings indicate that potentially the most damaging aspects of the home environment may be a parent's emotional rejection of a child, or conflict between family members, not physical abuse or neglect. Inasmuch as there are substantial difficulties in using emotional abuse as a basis for intervention (Wald 1976; Wald 1980), ways of protecting children who are objects of this kind of mistreatment require further consideration.

Issues of General Child Development and the Impact of Abuse and Neglect

Throughout this book we have organized our data around the central issue of home versus foster care. As we have indicated at various points in the book, many of our findings also are relevant to some general theoretical issues of child development, and to theories about the impact of abuse and neglect on children. In this section, we briefly review some of these issues.

DETERMINING THE "CAUSES" OF DEVELOPMENTAL DEFICITS

As previously discussed, one of our more puzzling findings was the initial differences between the home and foster children we studied. Although we cannot determine whether this was due to random variation among the children or to an initial impact of foster care, either explanation raises important questions about child development.

If we assume that the differences reflected an initial positive impact of foster care, we must ask why. The impact was greatest with regard to the children's social skills. There is a substantial debate in the child development literature about why children develop poor social skills. Some theorists believe the problem stems from deficiencies in the mother-child attachment relationship; others attribute the problem to deficiencies in parental socialization practices. Finally, some experts believe that the problems are related to stress and conflict in the family.

We cannot provide any direct information about the causes of our children's problems, since we know little about the parent-child relationship prior to intervention. If we assume, however, that the higher scores of the foster children reflected an initial impact of foster care, this would raise significant doubts about the causal model based on attachment theory. Proponents of this theory argue that a poor early attachment relationship leaves the child with a mental model of "the world as comfortless and unpredictable; and they respond either by shrinking from it or doing battle with it" (Bowlby 1973, p. 208). If children's problems result from the development of a bad "mental model," it seems highly unlikely that they could change their patterns of interaction after just a few months in foster care. Certainly the foster children had not developed a new attachment relationship; in fact, few of them were in stable placements at the time we first saw them. Although the performance of the foster children lends support to the "socialization" theory, it also seems unlikely that this short exposure to new socialization techniques could significantly enhance the child's social skills. Thus, if we assume an immediate impact of foster care, our data are most supportive of the theory that the children's deficits were related to conflict in the biological family's environment or of the view that the children were responding to the greater structure and predictability of the foster homes.

As previously argued, it also is quite possible that the social skills of the foster children did not improve as a result of placement. Some children may have possessed the better skills prior to removal. If that were the case, we again must ask why some abused and neglected children were more adept socially than others. The differences were not related to whether the child had been abused or neglected. Further research is needed to determine which factors in the environment or in the parent-child relationship affect the development of abused and neglected children.

ABUSE/NEGLECT AND ACADEMIC PERFORMANCE

The poor academic performance of the children also requires further examination. Although some of the children's problems clearly related to poor school attendance, the children's continued poor performance even after foster placement (the foster children did attend school regularly) indicates that the problem goes beyond attendance. A much fuller study of the learning problems associated with abuse and neglect is needed. There are many possible factors; for example, the earlier absences may have made catching up very difficult, or learning problems may have been related to neuropsychological deficits. It is particularly important that neurological explanations be explored since environmental manipulations alone may not be adequate to help neuropsychologically deficient children.

DIFFERENTIAL IMPACT OF ABUSE AND NEGLECT

As just discussed, we were surprised that a child's social skills seemed to be unrelated to whether the child had been abused or neglected. In fact, we are puzzled by the lack of difference in most areas of development between the abused and the neglected children. We expected abuse and neglect to have different impacts on children's development. Perhaps the majority of children experienced both abuse and neglect. As we discussed in Chapter 4, the triggering incident often was a matter of happenstance. Many of the abused children had been neglected; at least some of the neglected children had been abused. Yet even when we looked at the "pure" cases, there was no clear pattern of differences between abuse and neglect cases.

There are some hints in our data that a critical factor was the emotional relationship between the mother and child. Our ability to draw conclusions is limited by the small size of the sample and the limited quantity and quality of our data regarding the preintervention parent-child relationship. Our clinical impression is that the worst-off children came from families with long histories of emotional rejection of the child. For example, the data suggest that the children who were initially doing most poorly were the result of unwanted pregnancies and were perceived as troublesome by their mothers right from the time of birth. The fact that the children were unwanted would undoubtedly lead one to predict that these mothers and children did not develop a secure attachment relationship. These mothers were the most likely to report that they did not "feel close" to their child. These data are consistent with the theories of Sroufe (1983) and Main, Kaplan, and Cassidy (1985).

We do not think enough is known about the impact of the parent-child emotional relationship on the child's development to use this relationship as a factor in placement decisions. We also lack means of assessing the relationship with sufficient reliability to justify basing decisions on it. However, social workers clearly should be sensitive to the relationship, and where there are indications of emotional rejection, special efforts should be made to improve the relationship and to monitor the child's development. We suggest that researchers interested in abused and neglected children focus studies on this issue.

ETHNIC DIFFERENCES

As we discussed in Chapter 10, there were significant differences in the social skills and emotional status of the black, Hispanic, and white children. These were not attributable to economic or family structure factors. The black children in our abused and neglected group seemed to show few developmental deficits in relation to the comparison black children, unlike the other ethnic groups. Whereas the Hispanic children tended to have social and emotional problems similar to those of the white children, their social behavior at school was exceptionally good. We have no explanations for these differences. The small number of black and Hispanic children in our study prevented us from examining family variables that might have been important. There has been virtually no research looking specifically at minority abused and neglected children. We believe such research is badly needed, since our research indicates there may be systematic and persistent differences. This research must focus on unique cultural factors that may affect the impact of abuse or neglect on minority children.

Conclusion

We began our study in order to test the impact of then-new proposals to maintain abused and neglected children in their own home. We hoped to provide data that would help policy makers decide which policies would best help the hundreds of thousands of abused and neglected children who are the focus of state interventions each year.

As tends to be the case with longitudinal research, it took a long time for us to develop and conduct our research. Not surprisingly, the world did not stand still while we labored. The experimental law we were studying in San Mateo County became the model for federal legislation (Public Law 94-272, The Adoption Assistance and Child Welfare Act of 1980). This legislation created financial inducements for states to limit the number of children placed in foster care. In California and throughout the country, state legislatures have since enacted new laws directing social service agencies to prefer keeping children at home whenever possible. This book comes at a time when major policy shifts already have taken place.

Our research raises some questions about the desirability of the current approach. The findings, although limited, indicate that children can be kept at home, but not without costs. If the only goal of public policy is to prevent severe physical harm to the children, the current policy is justifiable. If legislators are concerned, however, with children's academic, social, and emotional development, as we believe they should be, our data indicate that legislators have to do more than adopt a preference for home or foster care. Under present policies, abused and neglected children remain at serious risk in both settings. We believe that they and their caretakers must be provided with extensive services to help the children overcome the developmental problems associated with abuse and neglect. Most likely, the needed services cannot be short-term or inexpensive. In many instances, both the children and the family may require several years of assistance. Although we cannot be certain that new services will alleviate their problems, current efforts are not adequate.

We hope that this study helps illuminate the policy considerations that must be addressed in developing interventions to help abused and neglected children. As it turned out, we may have learned more about a question we did not set out to examine (the services needed by abused/neglected children) than we did about our central research issue. Sadly, we found that current options leave children in great distress. Unless we find more effective interventions and, even more important, ways of preventing abuse and neglect, many children will, as Ken Wooden has said, continue "weeping in the play time of others."

Reference Matter

The Foster Children: Parental Visitation and Family Reunification

———

IN CHAPTER 6 we described the visiting patterns of the biological parents of the white foster children in our study. Although a larger percentage of the black parents visited frequently (most of their children were living with relatives who lived close to the parents), the majority of black parents visited infrequently, as did virtually all the white parents. Why did so many parents lose contact with their children? Were they discouraged by social work agencies? Did they lack financial resources? Were they uninterested? All these factors have been offered by others as explanations for low visiting rates.

We look here at the situation of the biological parents of the foster children. We are interested in seeing how they felt about the placement, their attitudes toward getting the child back, and whether there was a change in their situation that would have made reunification possible. We include all twenty-nine parents whose children were initially placed in foster care.* Twenty-one of the children remained in care throughout the two years.†

Our information comes from interviews with these parents following placement. Of the twenty-nine children removed initially, we saw sixteen of the parents regularly throughout the two years (these parents stayed in the area and were willing to participate in the study). We

---

*This includes eleven black families, two Hispanic families, and sixteen white families.

†Nine children eventually returned to their biological parents, including four black and three white children and one Hispanic child. Three of the children were returned *after* the two-year study period.

interviewed seven others initially and at the end of the first year, but could not interview them at the end of two years, because they left the area (one case), refused to participate or could not be located (three cases), or had relinquished custody and thus no longer had any involvement with the child (three cases). Finally, we interviewed six parents only once: four parents left northern California shortly after foster placement of their children, and two other parents moved repeatedly throughout the Bay Area until contact with them was lost.

The residence of the twenty-nine foster children's biological mothers during the study period may be summarized as follows: twenty-four remained in the Bay Area (three left it for a while but then returned); four left the Bay Area within a year (and did not return); and one left the area during the second year.

Parents' Attitudes Toward Reunification

Most of the parents initially opposed the prospect of losing custody of their children, though five did support the idea of foster placement. Once a child is in a foster home, however, attitudes can change; relieved of the burden of childcare, some parents may prefer placement for their children. Therefore, we regularly asked the parents if they wanted the children to be returned to them and, if so, how soon.

Measuring the parents' attitudes turned out not to be straightforward, however. Their attitudes often fluctuated. Many expressed real ambivalence about return—either because they felt it would not be good for themselves or because the child seemed to be benefiting from foster care. Moreover, the parents often acted in ways inconsistent with their stated attitudes. For example, five parents who said that they wanted the child back as soon as possible visited irregularly and took no actions to facilitate return. Conversely, four mothers who expressed ambivalence about reunification with their children made efforts to maintain visiting and to improve the quality of their living environments in order to resume custody.

The foster care system is often criticized for discouraging parents from visiting or from resuming custody. We wanted to see if this was true with our parents. Therefore, we developed a picture of each parent's primary attitude toward reunification during the two years. We rely primarily on their stated positions, but take into account actions totally inconsistent with these positions.

Thirteen parents consistently said they wanted their children to rejoin them and maintained some contact throughout the time the child was in placement. Eleven of these thirteen said they wanted reunification as soon as possible. Two initially conditioned their responses by saying that they wanted the child returned as soon as they solved their problems (each of these parents in fact resumed custody within a year). In addition to these thirteen, one mother initially was happy to have the child live with her father (the parents were divorced); but eventually this mother wanted and got custody. We believe that all fourteen of these parents were committed to reunification.

Five other parents stated at our first interview that they hoped the child would be returned as soon as possible, but their actions raised doubts about their real wishes. Four of these five left the area within six months. None of the five made an effort to maintain regular contact with the child or the new caretakers; one had no contact at all, and the other four merely phoned once or twice a year. All five had a long history of problems with drugs, alcohol, or mental illness. Although increased efforts by the social service agencies might have preserved a relationship between one parent and her child, little could be done with the other four parents, at least after their children had been removed.

In contrast to those parents who said they wanted reunification with their children, three parents indicated little desire for this from the outset of placement. One mother moved into an expensive adults-only apartment complex and remained there with her boyfriend throughout the time of our study, though she said she was looking for other housing. Another mother, who had been the custodial parent, felt that the child fared better living with his father. The third parent, a father, was happy to have the child gone. None of these parents did anything to change the situation that led to placement. None of them ever stated that they wanted the child returned in the near future.

The remaining seven parents seemed ambivalent about reunification. Four initially said that they hoped the child would be returned as soon as possible, but at later interviews expressed uncertainty about this. Usually they told us that they still had not overcome the problems that led to placement and that perhaps "it is better for the child not to return." Although this attitude undoubtedly reflected concern for the child, in most cases our interviewers, who spoke with these parents a number of times, felt that a primary motivation for these parents was relief over not having to care for the child. The other three expressed ambivalence right from the start. They kept saying they wanted custody "as soon as I deal with my problems." None did, and their children remained in foster care.

In this ambivalent group, all but one or two parents seemed satisfied to leave the child in foster care. It is true they did not always receive help overcoming their problems. Moreover, most of them would have kept the child if the child had been returned, but none seemed eager for that to occur. Thus, the ambivalent parents were very different from those who constantly expressed the desire to have the child returned.

In sum, about half the twenty-nine parents seemed to want reunification and half were content to leave the child in placement.

Changes in Parents' Behaviors

In most cases it was not the parents' attitudes that led to removal but their behavior. Their behavior also affected their visitation patterns and their ability to resume custody. For example, we have said that five parents left the Bay Area. What happened to the other twenty-four? We believe that in six cases there was a substantial improvement in the underlying situations that originally led to separation from their children; in the other eighteen there was little change in the parents' behaviors or conditions.

Ten of these eighteen parents continued to suffer from mental illness or serious drug or alcohol problems, which clearly impaired their child-rearing capacity or led them to abuse their children. One such parent was Mrs. S, who was divorced three years before intervention and began drinking heavily at that time. Her child was removed from her care when Mrs. S was found unconscious from excessive drinking in a public parking lot. She entered a detoxification center but left after a brief stay. She continued to drink heavily, traveled frequently, and rarely visited her son, who had been placed with his maternal grandparents. Like Mrs. S, most others among these ten parents attempted rehabilitation but left the programs before completion.

Five other parents continued to live in physical surroundings that were unsafe for the child. Most also had problems with alcohol. Three appeared not to want to change their living situations, though they said that they hoped for reunion with their children. The A's were one of these families. Their daughter had been separated from them and placed with her older sister because her parents' home had become unsanitary (decaying food and undiscarded refuse was found throughout the house). Both parents drank excessively. Despite its condition, making the house safe would not have required overwhelming work. The parents, however, made no effort to accomplish this. Their daughter was the youngest of nineteen children and the A's seemed content to let her older siblings raise her. In contrast to the A's, the parent in another case, Mr. L, said he wanted his son back. However, Mr. L continued to live in a camper, drank excessively, quit several alcohol rehabilitation programs, and kept getting fired from jobs because of lateness and alcoholism. He thus never established a home to which his son could be returned.

Finally, in three cases, the home conditions were adequate, and the parents showed no pathologies but were either uninterested in retaining their children or had abused them and refused therapy the court deemed necessary before reunification could be safely ventured. These three parents seemed content to leave the child in foster care. For example, Mrs. K severely beat her daughter, bruising her face and entire body. However, she steadfastly insisted that it was her daughter who was at fault and had to change. She therefore refused counseling and did not appear at court hearings.

How did the six parents who showed improvement differ from the eighteen who did not? First, most began with fewer problems. None had a history of drug or alcohol abuse or mental illness. Five of the six were single parents who had abused the child during periods of high stress. Finding new housing, obtaining jobs, and participating in counseling helped these parents minimize stresses. It must be emphasized that five of the six parents still were experiencing problems, though less than before. Moreover, in those families to which the child was returned, the parent-child relationship was by no means trouble-free. In comparison with the other eighteen, however, these six parents did make substantial progress.

For the most part the eighteen parents who showed little change neither requested nor received much in the way of services to help them overcome the problems that led to intervention. The parents suffering from mental illness or drug or alcohol problems had a long history of such problems. Given this history, it is not surprising that their behavior changed so little in the absence of services. Unfortunately, we cannot tell whether they would have responded favorably had better services been offered, either as an alternative to removal or in the months immediately following removal.

The Relationship Between Parents' Attitudes Toward Return, Behavioral Problems, and Visitation

During the two-year period of our study, thirteen parents visited their children on average at least once a month; sixteen parents visited either sporadically or not at all.* How did the parents' attitudes toward reunification and their physical or mental conditions affect visiting? We looked at the parents' stated responses for not visiting and their behaviors during the two years in assessing the reasons for limited visiting.

In most cases, there were various reasons for infrequent visitation. The major reasons are: parents' pathological condition impaired their functioning (seven cases), lack of interest (six cases), stress related to unemployment or lack of housing (two cases), and conflict with foster parent (one case). It is frequently asserted that low visitation rates are related to factors within the foster care system itself, e.g., social workers' discouragement of visits, placement of children in families greatly distant from the parents. We did find that such factors were important in some cases. A court or social work agency restricted visiting in three or four cases—either the frequency of visits or the place of a visit, or both. Several foster parents discouraged visiting; interestingly, grandmothers who became custodians were particularly likely to show hostility about a daughter's visitation. Four children were placed in out-of-state families, but in all four cases the parent had not visited before the child left the area.

"External" factors, however, did not seem to be the major reason for infrequent visitation in the great majority of cases, fifteen of sixteen, in fact. Instead, the major problems seemed to lie in the parents themselves. Seven had little interest in visiting. Three of these parents supported placement of the child; the other four found life easier without the child. The other eight parents were unable to cope with their own problems—continued drug or alcohol abuse, mental illness, or inability to find a job or housing—and, as a result, seemed to be unable to remain involved in their children's lives. Most of these eight seemed concerned about the child; however, they were sufficiently disorga-

---

*We are again considering the twenty-nine initial placements. Since five of the six children who were reunited returned home within six months of placement, their parents did not have to maintain visitation for a substantial period. The exclusion of these and of cases involving black and Hispanic parents accounts for the difference between figures given here and those cited in Chapter 6.

nized that they could not take the actions needed to resume custody and did not seem to want to visit.

A parent's expressed desire that the child be returned correlated with frequent visits, but it did not guarantee frequent visits:

Visits	Parent consistently wanted child returned	Parent ambivalent	Parent did not want child returned
Frequent	9	4	0
Infrequent	5	8	3

Similarly, the absence of drug or alcohol problems or mental illness made it more likely that parents would visit, though some parents with these problems visited frequently and some without these problems visited rarely:

Visits	Parents with pathological condition	Parents with no pathological condition
Frequent	4	9
Infrequent	12	4

When we look at attitude and pathology together, we see that even though a combination of positive or negative factors is highly predictive of frequency of visitation, either factor by itself also has an impact:

Visits	No pathology, parent wants child returned	No pathology, parent ambivalent	Pathology, parent wants child returned	Pathology, parent ambivalent
Frequent	6	3	3	1
Infrequent	1	3	4	8

Looking at all the data, it seems that attitude, pathology, and general disorganization all contributed to infrequent visitation. Visiting a child in foster care is not easy. Visits can be emotionally draining, as well as difficult to arrange, and though some parents dealt with these difficulties despite adversity, most did not.

Factors Related to Reunification

Of the twenty-nine children initially in foster care, nine ultimately returned home (three after the study period ended). Previous studies have found that reunification is more likely if the parent has visited frequently (Fanshel 1975). However, these studies looked at visitation in

TABLE A.I

*Parental Attitudes Toward Reunification, Visitation Patterns,
and Behavioral Changes, Related to Outcomes*

Parent's attitude: positive (+), negative (−)	Parent's visits: frequent (+), infrequent (−)	Parent's situation: improved (+), not improved (−)	Child returned	Child not returned
+	+	+	5	0
+	+	−	2	2
−	+	+	1	0
+	−	−	1	4
−	+	−	0	3
−	−	−	0	11

isolation, without considering changes in the parents' situations or their attitudes toward return. We looked at the parents' attitudes toward return, their visitation patterns, and the degree to which they appeared to show behavioral change, to see if any of these factors, or a combination of them, were related to reunification. Table A.I shows how the parents ranked on the three factors.

We cannot draw any conclusions about the importance of any one factor because the parents tended to be either totally positive or totally negative on all three items. Nearly a third rated poorly in all areas. Not surprisingly, none of their children were returned. Neither is it surprising that the children of all five parents who received positive ratings in all areas were returned. Beyond this it appears that frequent visitation may have been a prerequisite to return. Only one child was returned despite infrequent visiting. This child was returned by his father to his mother, who was the original custodial parent: the social work agency went along reluctantly, only because both the father and the child supported the move. Although frequent visiting was not sufficient to ensure return, in three cases children were returned to frequently visiting mothers, even though there had not been significant behavioral change in the mother. In all three cases in which a child was returned despite an absence of change on the parent's part, the child was reabused or neglected, in one case quite severely.*

* There were four cases that we categorized as "not returned," in which the child was actually returned for a short period and then removed again. In three of these, the mothers initially wanted the child returned as soon as possible, visited regularly, and participated actively in counseling and other therapy. Because of the mothers' positive attitudes, the children were returned to their homes but, in all three cases, the situation worsened quickly and the children had to be removed again. In the fourth case, the mother had participated in counseling but had not visited her child.

Notes

Chapter 1

1. By foster care we mean both placement with a relative and placement in a nonrelative family home. We do not include placement in a group home or other residential setting. Although foster care was viewed favorably during the 1960's (Mnookin 1973), removal was never a clearly stated statutory preference and many social workers and judges undoubtedly placed children in foster care reluctantly. The number of children in foster care increased steadily from 1960 until the late 1970's; however, the majority of children referred to social service agencies were not placed in foster care.

2. This analysis focuses primarily on the child's interests. A legislative body might also limit removal in order to protect parental rights to child custody, even if this meant some risk to the child, not considering the harms suffered by these children sufficiently serious to justify depriving the parents of custody.

3. The other was Shasta, a small rural county.

4. A given juvenile court or social work agency might adopt its own policies regarding placement to be applied by individual judges or social workers. In effect, the court or agency administrator would be acting like a legislature. Our data are relevant to such policymaking.

Chapter 2

1. In thinking about the risk of reabuse or continued neglect, it is essential to recognize that under current law and practice the terms abuse and neglect cover a broad range of actual or potential injuries to a child (Wald 1975). Physical abuse ranges from extreme brutality resulting in severe injuries to cases of overdiscipline resulting in bruises on arms, legs, or other parts of the body, injuries that are unlikely to be permanent or to lead to physical impairment. Neglect is even less well-defined. It ranges from inattention resulting in physical injury—for example, inadequate supervision of young children—to inat-

tention that may prompt concern about the social and emotional development of the child, such as inadequate parenting or supervision, or lack of involvement with the child. Thus, if there are harms associated with foster care, we might, for example, want to accept the risk of reabuse if this might be bruises on the buttocks but not if there could be a possibility of severe injury.

On the other hand, it is by no means clear that the only reason to remove an abused or neglected child is to prevent physical reabuse or continued neglect. Abused and neglected children often suffer developmental problems beyond physical injury. Abused children are reported to have a number of emotional problems associated with abuse, including very poor self-esteem, severe depression or other psychopathological symptoms, abuse of animals, poor peer relations, and poor language development. Moreover, many abused children become abusing parents. Neglected children are also reported to have a variety of problems beyond just poor physical health. Removal may be necessary to alleviate one or all of these problems, even in situations where the child's physical safety can be protected at home.

2. Bowlby's work, and much of the research it inspired, applied to very young children, usually under two years of age. Recent research has applied the concept in describing parent-child relationships for children up to five years old (Sroufe 1983). Main, Kaplan, and Cassidy (1985) also have extended the conceptual framework to older children. Though our study sample was aged five to ten, we believe that the issues regarding child development raised by attachment theory are relevant at least throughout childhood, if not into adulthood.

3. In making policy it is also desirable to research the costs and benefits of all potentially desirable policy options. Unfortunately, it is often not possible to study certain options that, from a theoretical perspective, might be the most desirable. For example, when we analyze the potentially most damaging aspects of foster care, it appears that for very young children these are the instability of foster placements and a lack of strong emotional commitment between the foster parents and the child (or the breaking of such bonds when they do develop). Therefore, an ideal study would compare children left at home with children who remain in single, long-term placements or whose biological parents' rights to custody are permanently severed immediately upon removal of the child and who are adopted by other families. Such cases are relatively rare, however, and involve unusual circumstances. As a practical matter, it would be extremely difficult to do an adequate study examining the option of immediate permanent severance of parental rights. Thus, we can only study "second-best" options.

4. Except for Fanshel's, even those studies that are longitudinal and have base-line data are inadequate because the base-line data are derived from casework records, rather than direct observations. Casework records have been shown to be highly unreliable sources of information.

5. Of course, one task for child development experts interested in public policy is to educate policymakers about those aspects of development viewed as important by experts.

Chapter 3

1. Several commentators have suggested that because of the lack of criteria guiding placement decisions, such decisions are made in an essentially random manner at present (Groeneveld and Giovannoni 1977; Runyan et al. 1982). Although there is some support for this proposition, we believe that, *at least within a given jurisdiction*, there are likely to be systematic differences between children placed in foster care and those left at home. Admittedly decisions might vary somewhat depending upon which childcare worker makes the decision about a child, but courts and agencies in a given city or county are sufficiently systematic that it would be hard to identify the "marginal" cases (where the decision could have gone either way) after the decision. Perhaps comparable children could be found by drawing a sample from two different counties, one with a high level of services designed to prevent removal, another with a low level of such services; presumably, in the county with more services children would be left at home who would be removed in the second county. We originally planned to use this method of finding comparable children when designing our study, before the California legislation was adopted. This became unnecessary after the legislation.

2. Although methodologically desirable, it is infeasible to study a large group of children in the hope that some will become abused or neglected and that, among those who do become abused or neglected, some children will be placed in foster care while other, comparable children will remain at home. In the one study that has longitudinally assessed the development of a large number of children *at risk* of abuse or neglect, only a very small number of children were actually abused or neglected and a still smaller number placed in foster care (Egeland, Sroufe, and Erickson 1983).

3. Two children were two months younger than five years when we first saw them.

4. In our definition of foster care we included placement with a relative if the child had not previously lived with, or been raised by, that relative. We excluded children placed with relatives who had cared for them previously, because it is unlikely that such children experience the same separation problems as children placed with strangers or with relatives with whom they have had little contact. Undoubtedly, all relative placements have a different psychological meaning to the child than do placements with strangers. Interestingly, however, there were no systematic differences in development, or in self-reports of happiness, between children placed with relatives and those placed with strangers.

5. We included only one abused or neglected child per family in the study. If a family contained two or more children in our age range who were abused or neglected, we selected one randomly. Considerably fewer foster cases were referred to us than we had expected based on our pilot study. In fact, we extended case selection from one year to eighteen months and initially still obtained only twenty-nine children for our foster care group. Problems in acquiring adequate samples plague field research. In our case, we believe that the decline in placement of children of ages five to ten resulted from a change in California law, which occurred just as we began the study. Prior to 1977, teenagers who were considered "unmanageable," or truants, or who ran away from home, were subject to placement in juvenile detention facilities run by county probation departments. In 1977, the state legislature forbade placement of such children in secure detention facilities. As a result, responsibility for these cases often shifted from probation departments to county welfare departments, which were also responsible for abused and neglected children. We believe that these agencies, newly faced with the necessity of placing large numbers of teenagers who could not be returned home, began paying less attention to any abused or neglected children who were not in imminent danger.

6. Of the eighteen refusal cases, the largest group to analyze for possible biasing trends, twelve involved abuse, the rest neglect. Half involved children placed at home. Of the nine cases in foster care, six were placed with relatives—all of whom wanted to have as little to do with the social service system as possible. We had more refusals from black families, primarily relatives. The parents' age, marital status, and income were similar to those of parents who agreed to participate. We could not find any factors, other than relative placement, that seemed to indicate a systematic bias in the refusal group.

7. We excluded one American Indian child and one Filipino child from all analyses, since single cases cannot be placed in two categories.

8. Privacy regulations meant that schools could not give us information about specific children. We would have had to interview many families to find comparison group children with the "right" characteristics, and we did not have the resources to do this. We also lacked the resources to study a large number of comparison children spread throughout the three counties.

9. As might be expected, a comparison sample selected in this manner might yield families and children where abuse and neglect were occurring. One such instance was discovered when one of the comparison-sample families later turned up in our study sample. A sibling of the child in the comparison group had been abused.

10. In the ten years between the time we began this study and the time of writing this book, a number of researchers have developed quite good measurement scales for assessing the impact of abuse and neglect on children. We wish these had been available to us.

11. It seems likely, however, that there was some "learning" effect. For example, virtually all the children increased their IQ scores during our three tests. Likewise, repeated questioning of the parents about specific child-rearing practices probably made them aware of those aspects of parent behavior we considered important. We discuss the possibility of testing effects when we present our data.

12. We spent two months training the interviewers in the use of the questionnaires and other data-gathering techniques. This included having them role-play interviews and having the project director accompany them on actual interviews. The entire staff met weekly throughout the data-gathering stage of the project, and periodically we reviewed how the interviews were being conducted. We also periodically analyzed the data, controlling for interviewer bias, to make sure there were no systematic differences in the responses.

13. We established a weekly staff meeting to allow the interviewers to vent their personal concerns for the children and families. At these meetings they also provided clinical material about the families.

14. We used the van so that the parents would not need to transport the children to a testing site. Even though we arranged all visits in advance, parents still missed appointments.

15. As a general rule, children removed from their original home pending court proceedings were not placed directly in a "permanent" foster home. Instead, they were placed in a children's shelter or in an interim foster home, pending completion of the court proceedings. After the court hearing at which it was decided whether to return the child to her parents or to use foster care for an extended time (the dispositional hearing), the social work agency looked for a longer-term or "permanent" foster home, that is, a home in which the child could be kept until she was returned to the parent or parental rights to custody were permanently terminated. It was assumed by the child protection agency that efforts would be made to reunite the parents and child in all the cases we studied.

Thus, most of our foster children had to adjust to at least two new environments in the first few months following removal from their parents. In fact, only five children were still in their initial placement at the time of our first interview. Of the remaining eight children, six had been in one other home or in the children's shelter, and two had been in more than one other home.

16. Since we could not have seen the children until after their removal under any circumstance, this problem was unavoidable. Would we have done better if we had not waited until court proceedings were completed? Data obtained from children immediately following removal, at the height of a crisis, and when they were experiencing separation trauma, certainly would not be the same as data obtained prior to intervention. There is no reason to believe that such data would be more helpful in assessing the children's status *prior to intervention* than data obtained after a period in foster care.

17. In this section we reference only those studies published, or available to us, prior to commencement of our data gathering, since these were the studies upon which we relied in selecting our measures.

18. In our pilot study these examinations were conducted by a pediatrician. However, so few problems were uncovered that the pediatrician decided it would be a better use of resources (hers and ours) to have the interviewers do the exam.

19. Although a number of people have developed social competence scales, none seemed to fit our sample. Therefore, drawing on the work of Anderson and Messick (1974), Baumrind (1973), Garmezy (1970), Kohn (1977), and White (1959), we developed our own scale. In retrospect, we strongly recommend use of established scales, even if the fit is not perfect. Testing new scales is best done in research that is not primarily policy-oriented.

20. The teachers probably were aware that a child was in foster care, although they may not have known why; some teachers knew that a "home" child had been abused or neglected, others probably did not.

21. Main, Kaplan, and Cassidy (1985) recently have developed a method for assessing the nature of the attachment relationship between parents and older children.

22. To plan the study took one year; to conduct and analyze the data from a pilot study required one year; to collect the data required three and one-half years; and to code, record, and analyze the data required two and one-half years. Additional time was spent in writing.

23. Ideally the sample would have been larger. This number was dictated by our funding. Significantly, we had a large budget for a social science research project—nearly $1.5 million, not including the salaries of the three principal investigators, who worked on the project for ten years. It is very expensive to gather extensive field data on a regular basis over a number of years. We had a full-time staff of eight people, including four interviewers, a project director, a computer and data management specialist, and secretarial help. In addition, we needed coders, research assistants, and other personnel during various phases of the project. We urge funders to recognize the need for substantial levels of support, if they hope to obtain policy-relevant data from field research studies.

Chapter 4

1. All the children, except two, initially were living in families that included their mothers. The other two children were living with their fathers, their mothers having left the family. All interviews, except these two, were with the mothers, and therefore we use the term mothers even though it includes the two fathers. (The term parent also refers to the mothers except in these two cases.) In the case of the home children, there were nine two-parent families at

the beginning of the study, but we interviewed only mothers in these families because there were too few fathers to obtain generalizable information.

2. These two cases involved self-reports by the mothers. In each family there was a history of severe physical discipline, although the current injuries were minor.

3. The mother was the perpetrator in six cases, the father in six. In one case both parents hit the child. Two of the abusing fathers were separated from the mothers, and were visiting the child at the time of the incident.

4. A good example of this problem occurred in one of the black families we studied. The mother broke her son's arm while spanking him. However, examination of the situation revealed that the injury occurred when the child reached back to block being hit on the buttocks by a belt. There was no prior history of physical punishment and the mother and child had a close relationship. The child was being spanked for missing school. We view this as a less serious case despite the severity of the injury.

5. We recognize that parental background characteristics and family structure are only proxies. The ideal procedure for assessing the influence of the parent's skill in child-rearing would have been to oversample abused and neglected children initially, obtain measures of parenting behavior that might affect child development prior to including a case in the study, and then select subject groups matched on these measures. However, such data could not be obtained before we had included a case in our study. The process is too costly, in time and money. We had to include all cases in which an incident of mistreatment was sufficiently serious to justify removal. We therefore estimated parental skills on the basis of characteristics related to child-rearing ability— namely, socioeconomic status, family structure, and the mother's emotional state.

6. We do not present any statistical tests of these differences. The statisticians we consulted seem agreed that tests for significance with samples of this size are not informative.

7. To help courts decide on the disposition of potential placement cases, protection agencies prepare extensive court reports. Since the home cases never came to court, agency investigators did not do such extensive background evaluations of the home families.

8. We did not ask the comparison mothers these questions because we thought some of them might refuse to cooperate if we asked excessively personal questions. We had more time to build rapport with the mothers of the abused and neglected children.

9. The lower scores of the mothers whose children had been removed might be related to the removal itself. It frequently meant that they had to change residence. As a result, they might have had fewer friends and social supports.

10. We used five dimensions of the scale. The cohesion dimension is a measure of "the extent to which family members are concerned and committed to

the family" and the degree to which members are "helpful and supportive of each other." The expressiveness dimension measures "the extent to which family members are allowed and encouraged to act openly and to express their feelings directly." The conflict dimension measures "the extent to which the open expression of anger and aggression and general conflictual interactions are characteristic of the family." Cohesion, expressiveness and conflict are the relationship dimensions of the Moos Family Environment Scale. The system maintenance dimensions are organization and control. The organization dimension is designed to measure "how important order and organization are in the family in terms of structuring the family activities, financial planning and explicitness and clarity in regard to family rules and responsibilities." The control dimension "assesses the extent to which the family is organized in a hierarchical manner, the rigidity of family rules and procedures and the extent to which family members order each other around."

11. The scores, listing the home group first and the foster group second, were: cohesion 6.1, 7.5; expression: 6.3, 5.4; conflict: 3.7, 2.4; organization: 5.2, 5.2; control: 5.2, 4.3.

12. We delayed administering this scale for two reasons: (a) our initial interview with a child's parents took over three hours and we felt we could not ask for more time; (b) we felt that foster parents could respond more accurately after they had gotten to know the children.

13. We stressed to all mothers that our findings would not be shared with the agencies unless we learned of continued serious abuse or neglect. Undoubtedly some mothers did not believe that we were totally separate from the agencies.

Chapter 5

1. If a child is subsequently left at home, little information is gathered about the child's development. More extensive evaluations of children are done prior to the juvenile court's dispositional hearing. We obtained copies of these reports about the children we studied. Although social workers had little information about mistreated children, based on the incidents leading to intervention, the parents' backgrounds, and the past history of abuse or neglect in many of the families, they were justified in assuming that the mistreatment had damaged the child, because many studies report neurological or other physical problems, low IQ scores on intelligence tests, and severe emotional problems such as extreme aggressiveness or withdrawal and poor self-image among abused and neglected children. Nevertheless most studies find some children who are relatively unscathed by severe physical punishments or neglect.

2. Since our sample was too small to allow adequate statistical analysis or controls for relevant variables, we do not report any statistical tests comparing

the abused or neglected group with the comparison children. We had fifty white children in the comparison sample at our first interviews. Eight families moved before the second interviews eighteen months later. However, the comparison group scores do not change whether we use fifty or forty-two children. We present the data for the forty-two because we use those children in our analysis of change over time.

3. We performed statistical tests examining differences in average scores between the home and the foster groups, but such tests tell us relatively little. First, we would expect some statistically significant differences given the number of variables we examined. Second, as we discuss at the end of this chapter, we cannot tell whether differences reflect the impact of intervention or existed prior to intervention. Finally, as noted in the text, there were a number of potentially confounding variables that might account for the differences, which we could not analyze because of our sample size.

4. The sample size in most of our analyses is nineteen for home cases and thirteen for foster cases. Occasionally, when there was a missing case—usually because the information was not completed by the respondent—the sample size varied by one or two. Missing cases were evaluated to ensure that their loss would not appreciably affect the basic findings. Percentages were calculated for the home and foster groups, taking into account the variation in sample size. The percentages were calculated to ease comparison of the different-sized groups, and not to provide a basis for making a statement of statistical significance.

5. Each child's height and weight was converted to percentile scores for his or her age and sex, using standard pediatric growth charts. We then averaged the percentiles and checked them against the Stuart Pediatric Growth Chart. The percentile scores were also checked against the more comprehensive scores of the National Health Examination Cycle II for Children 6–11 (National Health Examination 1979). The differences between the two scales were minimal.

6. We did not have a test for one foster child.

7. Because of limited resources, we did not screen the comparison children. Instead we use data from the National Health Examination Cycle II for Children 6–11 of similar economic background. Although more extensive neurological examinations might have uncovered more problems, such problems would certainly be subtle in their manifestation.

8. We did not attempt to obtain a formal clinical assessment of each child, which would have been the best way of determining psychopathology. We felt that we could not subject the children to lengthy assessments. The additional burden on the children seemed particularly unjustified because the formal assessments done in the Fanshel and Shinn (1978) study did not produce a significant amount of information beyond that already available about the child.

We did have access to any mental health reports contained in the social workers' files and used these records in forming an overall evaluation of the children's psychological well-being.

9. In the absence of a formal clinical examination, we will not emphasize diagnostic assessment. However, for our clinically oriented readers, we did formulate a clinical diagnosis based on social workers' reports, written narratives by the testing psychologist, and written comments about the children made at the time of the interviews. On the basis of this information, more than two-thirds of the foster children and nine-tenths of the home children would be classified as having significant behavioral or psychological pathology, as contrasted with one-third of the comparison children. Conduct disorder was the most prevalent diagnosis for all three groups, with depression, developmental delay, and anxiety somewhat less usual and about equal to one another in frequency. A few children could also be described as "hyperactive."

10. Robert was clearly a child in trouble. Yet he illustrates the complexity of evaluating the impact of abuse or neglect. Robert was well liked by his teacher, who did not find him difficult in class, and whereas Robert reported problems with other kids at school, he had good neighborhood friends.

11. Our data about the initial impact of foster care on the children's emotional well-being came from the foster mothers, the biological mothers, and the children. None of these was an unbiased source. The foster parents certainly had incentive to paint a good picture, since they derived satisfaction from "helping" the children. Some of the new caretakers, especially the relatives, were quite hostile to the child's mother and anxious to show that the child was better off with them. In contrast, we expected to find a more negative picture from the biological parents, at least from those who opposed the placement. While the children's views were likely to be less biased, this was our initial contact with them and it is unlikely that they were prepared to be totally open with a stranger. However, through our multiple sources of information we believe that we can accurately identify children who had substantial adjustment problems or who were clearly unhappy with their placement.

12. We administered this questionnaire to all the mothers in our study, including those whose children were in placement, and the foster mothers; we readministered it at six-month intervals but only to the child's current caretaker at each later period.

13. Because the scale was completed by the foster parent, it is not useful in assessing comparability prior to intervention. The children had been in foster care for five to eight months; their behavior undoubtedly was affected by foster care. Second, the foster mothers may have been using different standards than the biological mothers. Third, there is little reason to believe that the children would behave the same in a foster home as in their own homes. Finally, some of the items seemed to have special relevance at the initial stages of foster care. For example, the foster children were rated low in terms of willing-

ness to share toys or food, a not unexpected behavior in a strange setting. The social situation of a foster child is sufficiently different from that of a home child that the items themselves cannot have comparable meanings.

14. The absence of a correlation between the mothers' ratings and the teachers' ratings on the social competence scale, though the instruments looked at the same type of behaviors, lends support to the premise that the scales measured relationships rather than traits. Of course, the children might have had different traits in different settings.

15. These data provide base-line scores and allow us to contrast the abused and neglected sample with the comparison group. Since the questionnaires were completed two to four months after intervention, and we have data for only eight of the thirteen foster children, they are of limited utility in estimating comparability prior to intervention.

16. If a child was missing a single item (occasionally teachers failed to answer a specific question), we substituted the group mean on that item.

17. Girls were rated significantly higher than boys in all groups. The lowest-rated group of girls, the abused/neglected home-group girls, were rated higher than the highest-rated boys—the comparison boys.

18. The data were incomplete. Two of the foster children were in preschool at the time of the initial interviews and two others, interviewed during the summer, had not yet begun school. Thus we have data for only nine of the thirteen foster children. Four other children (two home, two foster) were first seen in the summer, so their responses pertained to the previous school year.

19. Zill (1976) reports a similar finding in a study of 2,000 children. In that study the children in high-conflict, two-parent homes were the least happy group of children. Rutter (1980) reports similar findings. However, in our comparison group there was no relationship between marital status and the child's well-being.

20. Social-bonding theory suggests that difficulties in the very earliest periods after birth, or even during pregnancy, affect the mother's subsequent relationship to her child (Barnett et al. 1970; Klaus and Kennell 1976). This theory proposes that perceived or real problems affecting the mother's attitudes toward her child can influence her sensitivity to her child's needs in the earliest caretaking months. This relative insensitivity is thought to lead to an insecure attachment relationship between the infant and mother. It is then argued that persistence of an insecure or anxious attachment relationship through the child's earliest years can be expected to lead to eventual lower self-worth, poor peer relationships, and inadequate relationships with authority figures for the child in the early and middle school years (Sroufe 1983). This is particularly true for families with multiple risks, particularly low socioeconomic status (Leiderman 1983).

21. We compared the eleven white abused and neglected children who rated themselves low on self-worth and peer relationships at the beginning of the

study to the eleven who rated themselves high on the same variables. We used the same procedure with regard to the teachers' ratings of the children's social behavior, peer relationships, and likability. We excluded the parents' reports for the socioemotional status score because of the possible retrospective bias (or mere continuity of response set) over time by these mothers. The low- and high-scoring children were determined separately for the child and teacher ratings and were derived from the entire sample of abused and neglected children without respect to placement. The results yielded a clear pattern. Mothers who had reported the greater number of problems with pregnancy, delivery, and early care had children who were self-reported and teacher-reported to be in the group with the lowest socioemotional status. Further support of the findings was provided by a separate examination of the black sample, which yielded the same pattern of results.

These findings appear to support the notion that negative initial encounters of the mother with pregnancy and her infant foreshadow later socioemotional difficulties. Whether the mechanism producing these findings is one of initial bonding alone or is due to child-derived problems connected with birth, or a combination of the two, is impossible to determine in this study. However, the findings are consistent with the theory that early negative encounters may entrain subsequent negative relationships.

Chapter 6

1. In considering the impact that changes of placement may have had on the children, it is important to recognize how little they knew about what was going to happen to them. None of them had known that the initial separation from biological parents would occur. When first interviewed, most of them still had only a limited idea of how long they would remain in placement, why they were in placement, and how it would be determined if and when they would be returned to their biological mother. Ten of the twelve children who were asked this question thought they would be returned home at some point. The other two children, each with relatives, thought they would remain in their new home permanently. When asked how they knew whether they would be reunited with their parent, five said they were told something by their parent, relative, or social worker, two were told by police, one said he "just knew," and four could give no reason.

These children's views generally corresponded with those of their parents and caretakers. All thirteen biological parents viewed the placements as temporary. Ten foster parents thought the placement would last no more than a year, one was planning adoption, and two were unsure of how long the placement would last. Thus, nearly all children and adults approached foster care expecting it to be a temporary placement, albeit for an indeterminate time.

2. Although the psychological relation between the foster parents and their

foster child unquestionably differed with every new placement, the factors described in this section were quite constant. The description of the foster homes contained here would not have differed much if we focused on the last rather than the initial placement.

3. We did not observe the housing in which five children lived prior to their removal because their parents moved to other residences between the time of the original intervention and the time of our interview. In several of these cases, we learned enough about the living environment from court records and parental reports to enable us to estimate a score for the physical environment.

4. We looked only at mothers, for two reasons. First, in many of the biological families there were no fathers. Second, even though all the foster mothers were married it was clear from our contacts that most of the foster fathers were not highly involved with the children, *at least in the initial stages of placement*. It was usually the mothers who decided to take foster children into the family.

Chapter 7

1. The limited ability of service agencies to prevent further harm to the children was further evidenced in the six children who were returned home after an initial period in care. Two of these children were abused again—one had her arm broken and was raped by her mentally ill father. Two others were neglected both physically and emotionally by parents who were ambivalent about caring for them.

2. We include here the one child placed in a residential institution since, like the home children who had to be removed before two years, a full assessment of permanence requires looking at all the initial placements.

Chapter 8

1. When we began the study we planned to present data for each six-month assessment. However, after analyzing the data we decided not to include trend data (i.e., scores at interim measurement times) for several reasons. First, a variety of factors virtually inherent in field research meant that different intervals elapsed between measurements for different children. These differences were systematic between the home and foster children. Thus, it would be misleading to think of each measurement period as representing a "real" time period. Second, on some variables there are many missing data points for individual children, again because of problems related to field research, where subjects move, fail to respond, etc. On some variables we had only two data points for many children. Third, any measure of the slope of regression on individual growth curves is unreliable for samples our size. Finally, for most of the data our inspection indicated that attempts at developing precise time

trends would add nothing to what we learned by looking solely at initial and end data. The picture at one year would have been the same as at two, for the most part, except that fewer children in foster care would have been in stable placements.

2. A word about sample size is necessary. Initially, there were nineteen children at home, thirteen in foster care, and fifty comparison children. However, on some measures we were unable to compile complete data for some children—through error, failure of the parent or child to respond to a question, or because some children were not in school initially. As discussed in Chapter 5, we have complete data for forty-two comparison children. Because we are primarily interested in changes of scores, we include in our analyses only those children for whom we have both initial and end data. This number differs slightly for each measure, but enables us to present data for all measures. For a few variables it made sense to present data on all available children rather than look solely at initial and end scores. We hope that the reasons for the different sample sizes will be clear.

3. Although we performed simple statistical analyses on all the group data presented in this chapter, we have elected not to report tests of statistical significance because such tests can be misleading in studies with small samples. For example, in any small study, there is a danger of accepting a statistically significant difference as valid when the difference came about through changes in only one or two cases. Such a difference in group means, even though statistically significant, does not adequately reflect the real situation. On the other hand, the presence of small differences between groups on several variables, which point in the same direction, often deserve thought, even when none of the differences is statistically significant.

All the findings presented in this chapter were conditioned by a full reading of individual cases. We interpreted differences between groups, or over time, by taking into account our clinical knowledge of all cases. We also take into account data that might not be reflected in the reported group means because for the reasons discussed previously, we have presented means based only on those children for whom we have both initial and end scores. This occasionally meant excluding cases for which we had three or four data points but were missing the initial or end score. In drawing conclusions from the data, we have attempted to be quite conservative. If we err, it is on the side of concluding that there were no differences between groups, no changes over time, or both.

4. The totals do not include the change in schools resulting from the original intervention. The reasons for changes were very different for the two groups. Of the thirteen children who were placed in foster care and subsequently changed schools, seven did so because of a change of caretaker. In general, the living situation of the foster parents was stable; the child changed schools because of a change in foster parents. In contrast, the children who were placed at home changed schools because the parents moved.

5. The absenteeism estimates are probably low. We counted a child as absent only if there was positive evidence of this. Given the erratic quality of many of the school records, it is likely that many of the children missed school more often than an estimate would indicate. Case records containing other evidence of absenteeism support this conclusion.

6. We have pre- and postintervention data for four foster children. Three of them had substantial absenteeism rates before placement. None of the four had high rates afterward. The same pattern occurred for two children who were originally at home and later placed in foster care: one had been absent 47 percent of the time at home, and this declined to 6 percent; the other was constantly tardy before placement, but had no absences or tardiness while in foster care.

7. Our information on whether a child was ever in a special class for learning-disabled children comes from the school records, and appears to be reasonably complete. We also asked the child's teachers and parents whether the child was in a special class. Although agreement of these sources was high, it was not perfect. On a few occasions the teacher said that the child was in an EH class for educationally handicapped children; school records indicated that the child had been recommended but not placed. We have not classed these children as in an EH class. Curiously, two of the home children were in EH classes but their parents reported them in regular classes. Again, we used the school records for these.

8. Eight of the ten comparison children who were retained had average or above-average test scores and were rated above-average academically by their teachers. Their parents also were in the highest income category. Income was unrelated to retention in the study sample.

9. Since the comparison sample children were somewhat older, on average, than the study children, they also had been "at risk" of retention longer.

10. The nine home children who were retained or in special classes tended to be rated higher by their teachers than the children in regular classes. Five of these children were rated above-average after retention or placement in the special class. Three children were below-average throughout, and one, in a special program for autistic children, steadily declined.

11. We also looked separately at the relationship between IQ and teachers' rankings in the first and last years of the study. The number of children in school at each time was smaller since some children were not in school initially (we used average rank to increase our sample size). Significantly, there was no relationship between teachers' rankings and IQ among the foster children in the first year. Thus, the pattern shown in Figure 1 is a clear improvement for this group.

12. The lack of a relationship between IQ and teachers' rankings among the home children holds when we look at the first- and last-year scores separately, as well.

13. Two of the four children were absent more than 10 percent of the time; a third was absent 9 percent.

One other piece of evidence indicates academic decline among the home children: the children's performance on objective tests given by their schools. Most schools gave all children the California Test of Basic Skills at least once a year (if the child happened to be present on the day it was given). Unfortunately, the CTBS scores were unavailable for many children because they missed so much school. We have enough data to use these scores only for the home children, owing to the extent of missing data for the foster group. We looked for patterns in the test scores over time. If the child was tested twice, we always used the data from the spring testing. Each child's score was converted to a national percentile score if the school had not already done so. Scores were typically available on three subtests of the CTBS: reading, arithmetic, and language. Of the home-placed children for whom we did have CTBS scores, nine declined on at least two of the three subscales, with most of the children declining in mathematics. In contrast, 70 percent of the comparison children increased their mathematics scores in subsequent CTBS testing and a majority increased on the other two subscales as well.

14. Virtually all the scores in Table 8.5 are based on the first and last of three scores, since most children were in three grades during the study. If a child was in school for only two years, one of which was the initial year, we included data for this child. This was true in three of the twenty-five cases. We excluded all children who were not in school the first year because their initial scores, obtained a year after intervention, are not comparable to the other base-line score.

15. An interpolation procedure was used that allowed for scale discontinuity and sampling error. For each group, frequencies were converted to percentages and a cumulative plot against score interval was made and smoothed. In the comparison group, the score corresponding to the 25th percentile was identified (2.4, for example). From the home and school curves, the percentile corresponding to that score was read off. To the extent that the percentage exceeded 25, that was taken as an indication that the home or school group was more at risk than the comparison group.

16. Because the numbers were small and the group means are affected by a few outliers, we have not presented the peer data in numerical form.

17. By looking only at the children who stayed in care for two full years, we also understate the overall problem of conflict between the child and the foster parent. All three children who were returned home were seen as having many problems by their foster parents.

18. We have another indication that the CBS understates problems in the foster home. We asked the foster mothers, "How do members of your family react to having the child?" In five cases, the foster mother reported that either

her spouse or one or more of her biological children were having trouble getting along with the child or were reacting unfavorably.

19. Interestingly, throughout the two years the ratings for the abused/neglected children in both settings were similar to each other and to the comparison children on those items in the social competence scale that related to ability to take initiative and act independently in the home setting. Typical questions were: "How much does your child try to do new or different things without your help?"; "How much does your child need help or suggestions to get started in a task?"; "Does your child ask for help when he/she can't do some task, problem, or activity?" Thus at home, in contrast to school, the abused and neglected children were not seen as having poorer work skills, as acting less autonomously, or as more lacking in initiative than the comparison children. This finding is surprising. We expected the children to have poorer skills, especially given the low teacher ratings. Of course, the parents did not have a yearly sample of thirty children from which to make comparisons.

20. We also asked the children if the adults differed between their parental home and foster home, and if so, how. Seven of the children saw differences; five described the foster parents more favorably and two less favorably (both objecting to the greater strictness of foster parents). Although some of the reasons given for both liking and disliking the adults seem somewhat superficial—for example, the foster parents "do not let me swear"—two of the children said their new caretakers were nicer because they paid more attention to and did more things with them.

21. We examined the statistical relationships between the measures derived from a single respondent (e.g., all the teacher ratings) and the relationship of measures across respondents (parents, teachers, and children). We looked at both the abused and neglected and comparison groups. There was reasonably high consistency across different measures from a single respondent, but little or no consistency across respondents, at either our initial or our final interviews. These same patterns of relationships existed for all groups—home, foster, and comparison.

22. The measures were the child's self-esteem and report of peer relations; the teachers' rankings on social behavior, likability, and peer relations; and the parents' reports of extreme behaviors (fire-setting, etc.) and problem behaviors (crying, whining); and social competence.

Because of scale variation for the measures and because of differences in distribution of responses on these measures, we standardized each of them. The standardizing procedure consisted of determining the mean and standard deviation for each measure. All means were essentially set at zero and each child's score on that measure was then expressed as deviation from that mean.

For readers not familiar with statistics, the process involved the same type of transformation that takes place when one converts information into percentages in reporting about variables like weight or height for a given age of a child, or achievement test scores. A nine-year-old child standing five feet high, weighing 60 pounds, with an IQ of 90, might have percentile scores of 50, 32, and 25 respectively in terms of national averages. Pounds, inches, and IQ have all been converted to scores of one kind—the percentile rank—showing the child's relative standing in a group for each measure. Standard scores are another means of replacing raw scores by new ones that allow comparison across several measures, which are not comparable in their raw form (pounds, inches, IQ). Necessarily, the standard scores on a variable average to zero, and most of the scores (often all) lie between −2.5 and +2.5. The *order* of the children's standard scores on any variable is exactly the same as the order of the original scores. The advantage of standard scores is that, like percentile scores, they allow comparison among children and across variables.

Chapter 9

1. Most other child development experts agree with this proposition. We use the words attachment, bonding, or emotional commitment to describe the aspect of the relationship about which we are concerned. These terms are often used imprecisely, though we believe the work of John Bowlby, Mary Ainsworth, Alan Sroufe, and others has given special meaning to the terms when describing the relationship between mothers and children under five. Unfortunately, the literature is much more sparse regarding older children. As we discuss in the text, there are no measures of attachment for older children. Thus, we do not have a precise definition for these terms.

2. Although these children ended up in a permanent home, several of them were previously in supposedly permanent homes headed by foster parents who later had a change of mind or heart. The early rejections may have affected the children's willingness or ability to commit themselves to a permanent relationship. The most distressing situation involved a Chicana (whose case is not included in the data for the white children) who was placed in an adoptive home along with two siblings. After a year the family adopted her siblings but not her because of her behavioral problems. She was moved to another family.

3. This child had been living with her father at the time of removal. Following a series of placements, she ended up in the home of an aunt. Just before the end of the two years, her mother moved in with them. Because the mother was with the child for such a short period, we considered this a "regular" foster care case.

4. The question on which Table 9.1 is based was also asked of the four other white children who entered care after having been left at home initially. At the end of two years, three had been in care for at least fifteen months. Of these four children, two wanted to live with both their foster parent and their natu-

ral parent, one wanted to live with a previously noncustodial parent, and one boy, who was in an institution, wanted to return home. Interestingly, except for the institutionalized child, these other children had much less desire to return home than the group of children removed initially. All these children had been severely neglected, which might account for the differences. It may also be that our sample of thirteen foster children is not adequately representative.

5. Initially all children reported similar responses about how they were getting along with their caretakers. However, by two years the children who wanted to stay with their foster parents reported improved relations with their caretakers; this was not true for the children who wanted to return to their biological parents. Similarly, the children in each group made equal use of the foster parents as resources initially. At the end of two years, however, the children who wanted to stay made much greater use of their foster parents. This increased integration also was reflected in the caretakers' attitudes. Although there was no initial difference in how much the caretakers "liked" the children, at the end of the two years, the caretakers of the children who wanted to stay reported that they felt closer to the child and found the child more likable than did the caretakers of the other children. Interestingly, these same patterns appeared when we looked at the black children in foster care.

6. These children reflected the type of role reversal frequently reported in abuse and neglect cases. The following statements, all made by minority children who are not part of this chapter's statistics, indicate the kinds of feelings expressed by these children: "My mom needs me. I don't care if she hits me, I want to stay with her." "I want to grow up and take care of Mommy." "I love to take care of her. She didn't mean to hurt me."

Chapter 11

1. This child functioned poorly in virtually every aspect of development. His teacher's ratings were near the lowest for the black children initially and near or at the bottom in the last year. He attended a special school for retarded children but, in part because of frequent absences, received the lowest academic ratings. Throughout our study his self-esteem ranked low. He also indicated that he did not get along with his mother and did not see her as a resource. Only his assessment of his peer relations was high. He spent most of his time with an older brother and the brother's friends, engaged in criminal activities.

2. Their experiences were quite different from those of the two white children returned from foster care, both of whom showed improved development following reunification.

3. Although this was our analysis at the end of the study period, we later learned that the girl who was living with her father eventually returned to her mother, at her own request.

4. We had home children in Santa Clara for two reasons. Two children originally were selected for our foster group but were returned home shortly after the court hearings. We kept them in the study for the reason discussed in the text. In addition, we originally planned to include a small group of foster children from San Mateo County and a small group of home children from Alameda and Santa Clara counties, in order to examine whether there were, in fact, differences *within* counties, between cases chosen for home placement and those chosen for foster care. For a variety of reasons we were not able to follow this plan, but we did have a few San Mateo County foster cases and a few Alameda and Santa Clara County home cases. All but one of these children were black or Hispanic, however, so they were not relevant to the main focus of this study.

5. Aside from wanting to minimize the confusion caused by a changing sample size, we lacked all initial data for the child who remained in continuous foster care, and including the child who was passed between foster and home care would not have altered the general picture of the children's development in any significant way. Since these were single cases, we can infer nothing from their outcomes.

6. The child was extremely frightened that she might be placed in foster care by her mother. She had spent one month in a foster home, where she alleged that she had been beaten by the foster mother.

Chapter 12

1. Even if money were available, it might be impossible to study large numbers of children intensively in a methodologically sound manner. For example, it is difficult to recruit, train, and monitor the work of a large field staff. Yet if the field staff are not constantly monitored, it is likely that data will be "contaminated" by interviewer differences. Moreover, in a longitudinal study it is often desirable to have the same field researcher deal with a participant for the entire study period. Some staff turnover is inevitable in any longitudinal study; the larger the staff the more difficult it is to ensure continuity. Logistics also can be a problem. To obtain a large sample of foster children, we would have had to enroll cases from all over California, given the relatively small number of children who entered foster care meeting our study criteria. It would have been extremely difficult to supervise a staff spread throughout California. Without close supervision, it is hard to ensure that the data obtained are accurate.

2. It does seem reasonable, however, that the child's self-reported peer relations, and general satisfaction as measured by our self-esteem scale, could change rapidly as a result of placement. We believe that the children's responses on these measures were highly influenced by situational factors.

3. Another argument supportive of an initial impact of foster care relates to the background characteristics of the mothers of the children. The biological mothers of the foster children were somewhat more likely to be divorced or never married. They were poorer, less educated, had less stable living arrangements, were more likely to have a history of alcoholism or mental illness, and were more socially isolated. It seems unlikely that less adequate homes would result in children in better emotional or social conditions. We remain puzzled, however, by the similarity between the foster children and the comparison children at the time of the initial interviews, especially in terms of social behavior at school and general behavior in the home setting. In light of their past histories of deprivation and the well-documented anxieties created by the separation of children from their parents, we would expect the foster children to have shown some signs of behavioral problems. Perhaps they felt the need to be especially good in foster care.

4. The parents may benefit from a period of reduced stress, which will enable them to relate better to their child after the child is returned, but there is little evidence that many parents undergo behavioral change. (See the Appendix.) There is more justification for efforts at reunification when the reason the child was removed was to protect the child from imminent physical harm. In such cases reunification services may be appropriate if there is reason to believe that counseling or providing the parent with services while the child is in foster care will lessen the threat of reabuse or neglect.

5. It is generally assumed that multiple placements, or the failure to provide a single permanent placement, is harmful to children. On this assumption, the gains we found in foster care might dissipate if the children did not remain in a permanent home. However, the only empirical study examining multiple placements (Fanshel and Shinn 1978) found no differences in children's development over a five-year period relating to the number of placements the child experienced.

6. With regard to peer relations, our findings closely parallel, and extend, the findings of other researchers who report that abused and neglected children are at a particular risk of poor peer relations (Pavenstedt 1973; Lewis and Schaeffer 1981; Jacobson and Straker 1982). Thus, it seems highly likely that most abused and neglected children are at risk in this domain. There are few other studies that report on academic performance and the findings have been mixed; however, these studies often include foster children who were neither abused nor neglected (Fanshel and Shinn 1978; Fox and Arcuri 1980). Thus, our findings with regard to academic performance require confirmation from other research.

7. Parents develop strong ties to their children, as well as children to their parents (Leiderman and Seashore 1975). Although there is evidence that abusing parents may be less bonded to their children (DeLozier 1982; Main, Kaplan, and

Cassidy 1985), it seems clear even abusing and neglecting parents feel a profound loss when their children are removed from them and placed in foster care (see Sinanoglu and Maluccio 1981, Part VII).

8. This conclusion does not, of course, necessarily follow from our data; it involves the value judgments of the individual authors of this study. The reasons for judgments are developed in articles by the first author (Wald 1976; Wald 1980). Although the findings from this study call into question some of Wald's previous conclusions, they do not nullify the basic propositions spelled out in the earlier articles. Leiderman's views on this issue are, in part, based on his reluctance to conclude solely from the findings in this study that foster care is in fact beneficial to children. Contrary to his previous views, he is now skeptical that home-based services can be developed that will truly allow the optimal development of abused and neglected children once they have reached five years of age. He believes, however, that such services should be tested and that more research is needed on the impact of foster care. If the findings of our study are replicated with larger and more diverse samples, Leiderman might favor greater use of foster care even if that required not reuniting children with their biological parents.

9. There are no studies that provide a complete picture of the type of services generally received by parents or children following state intervention. Some children receive services from other sources. For example, many abused and neglected children are in special education classes. However, in many instances the school may not explore the relationship between the home environment and the child's problems. As a result, the school program may not be able to help the child fully.

10. The legislation creating the special project in San Mateo County limited intervention in most cases to six months, though for cases under court supervision the court could order that services be continued. As indicated in the Preface, one author of this study (Wald) drafted that legislation. He now believes the six-month limitation was a mistake.

References

Aber, J. L., III. 1980. The involuntary child placement decision: Solomon's dilemma revisited. In G. Gerber, C. Ross, and E. Zigler, eds., *Child abuse: An agenda for action*. New York.

American Bar Association. 1977. Juvenile Justice Standards Project: Standards relating to abuse and neglect. Cambridge, Mass.

American Humane Association. 1984. Trends in child abuse and neglect: A national perspective. Denver.

Anderson, S., and S. Messick. 1974. Social competency in young children. *Developmental Psychology*, *10*, 282–93.

Barnett, C., P. H. Leiderman, R. Grobstein, and M. Klaus. 1970. Neonatal separation: The maternal side of interactional deprivation. *Pediatrics*, *45*, 197–205.

Baumrind, D. 1973. The development of instrumental competence through socialization. In A. D. Pick, ed., *Minnesota Symposium on Child Psychology*, vol. 7. Minneapolis.

Baylor, E. M. H., and E. D. Monachesi. 1939. The rehabilitation of children: The theory and practice. New York.

Bohman, M., and S. Sigvardsson. 1980. Negative social heritage. *Adoption and Fostering*, *3*, 25–34.

Bolton, F. G., Jr., R. H. Laner, and D. S. Gia. 1981. For better or worse? Foster parents and foster children in an officially reported child maltreatment population. *Children and Youth Services Review*, *3*, 37–53.

Bowlby, J. 1944. Forty-four juvenile thieves: Their characters and homelife. *International Journal of Psychoanalysis*, *25*, 19–52, 107–27.

———. 1951. Maternal care and mental health. Geneva.

———. 1965. Childcare and the growth of love. London.

———. 1973. Attachment and loss. Vol. 2: Separation. New York.

———. 1982. Attachment and loss: Retrospect and prospect. *American Journal of Orthopsychiatry*, *52*, 664–78.

Bryce, M. E., and R. C. Ehlert. 1971. 144 foster children. *Child Welfare*, 50, 499–503.

Burgess, R. L., and R. D. Conger. 1978. Family interaction in abusive, neglectful and normal families. *Child Development*, 49, 1163–73.

Bush, M. 1980. Institutions for dependent and neglected children: Therapeutic option of choice or last resort? *American Journal of Orthopsychiatry*, 50, 239–55.

California State Legislature. 1977. *California Family Protection Act SB30*. California Legislature West Cal Code SS 300ff.

Canning, R. 1974. School experiences of foster children. *Child Welfare*, 53, 582–87.

Cohn, A. H., and F. C. Collignon. 1979. *NCHSR Research Report Series*. Vols. 1 and 2: *Evaluation of child abuse and neglect demonstration projects, 1974–1977*. DHEW Publication Number PHS 79-3217.1.

Cowen, E. L., A. Pederson, H. Babijian, L. D. Izzo, and M. A. Trost. 1973. Long-term follow-up of early detected vulnerable children. *Journal of Consulting and Clinical Psychology*, 41, 438–46.

Cronbach, L. J. 1982. Designing evaluations of educational and social programs. San Francisco.

Cronbach, L. J., and Associates. 1980. Toward reform of program evaluation: Aims, methods and institutional arrangements. San Francisco.

DeLozier, P. 1982. Attachment theory and child abuse. In C. M. Parkes and J. Stevenson-Hinde, eds., *The place of attachment in human behavior*. New York.

Egeland, B., and L. A. Sroufe. 1981. Attachment and early maltreatment. *Child Development*, 52, 44–52.

Egeland, B., L. A. Sroufe, and M. Erickson. 1983. The development consequence of different patterns of maltreatment. *Child Abuse and Neglect, The International Journal*, 7, 459–69.

Elmer, E. 1977. Fragile families, troubled children: The aftermath of infant trauma. Pittsburgh.

Emery, R. E. 1982. Interparental conflict and the children of discord and divorce. *Psychological Bulletin*, 92, 310–30.

Erickson, M., L. A. Sroufe, and B. Egeland. 1985. The relationship between quality of attachment and behavior problems in preschool in a high-risk sample. In I. Bretherton and E. Waters, eds., *Growing points of attachment theory and research*. Monographs of the Society for Research in Child Development.

Fanshel, D. 1966. Foster parenthood: A role analysis. Minneapolis.

———. 1975. Parental visiting in foster care: Key to discharge. *Social Service Review*, 49, 493–514.

Fanshel, D., and E. Shinn. 1978. Children in foster care. New York.

Ferguson, T. 1966. Children in care—and after. London.

Festinger, T. 1983. No one ever asked us: A postscript to foster care. New York.

Fox, M., and K. Arcuri. 1980. Mental functioning in foster children. *Child Welfare*, 59, 491–96.

Frank, G. 1980. Treatment needs of children in foster care. *American Journal of Orthopsychiatry*, 50, 256–63.

Garmezy, N. 1970. Vulnerable children: Implications derived from studies of an internalizing-externalizing symptom dimension. In J. Zubin and A. M. Freeman, eds., *Psychopathology of adolescence*. New York.

———. 1981. Children under stress: Perspectives on antecedents of vulnerability and resistance to psychopathology. In I. A. Rabin, J. Arnoff, A. M. Barclay, and R. A. Zucker, eds., *Further explorations in personality*. New York.

Geiser, R. L. 1973. The illusion of caring. Boston.

George, C., and M. Main. 1979. Social interactions of young abused children: Approach, avoidance, and aggression. *Child Development*, 50, 306–18.

Giovannoni, J., and R. M. Becerra. 1979. Defining child abuse. New York.

Goldstein, J., A. Freud, and A. J. Solnit. 1973. Beyond the best interests of the child. New York.

———. 1979. Before the best interests of the child. New York.

Groeneveld, L. G., and J. Giovannoni. 1977. The deposition of child abuse and neglect cases. *Social Work Research and Abstracts*, 13, 36–47.

Gruber, A. R. 1978. Children in foster care. New York.

Hartup, W. W. 1983. Two social worlds: Family relations and peer relations. In M. Rutter, ed., *Scientific foundations of development psychiatry*. London.

Herrenkohl, R. C., E. Herrenkohl, M. Seech, and B. Egolf. 1980. The repetition of child abuse: How frequently does it occur? *Child Abuse and Neglect, The International Journal*, 3, 67–72.

Hetherington, E. M., M. Cox, and R. Cox. 1982. Effects of divorce on parents and children. In M. Lamb, ed., *Parenting and child development*. Hillsdale, New Jersey.

Hobbs, N. 1980. Knowledge transfer and the policy process. In G. Gerbner, C. J. Ross, and E. Zigler, eds., *Child abuse: An agenda for action*. New York.

Hubbell, R. 1981. Foster care and families: Conflicting values and policies. Philadelphia.

Jacobson, R. S., and G. Straker. 1982. Peer group interaction of physically abused children. *Child Abuse and Neglect, The International Journal*, 6, 321–27.

Jones, F. H. 1976. The Rochester Adaptive Behavior Inventory: A parallel series of instruments for assessing social competence during early and middle childhood and adolescence. In J. S. Strauss, H. M. Babigian, and M. Roff, eds., *The origins and course of psychopathology*. New York.

Kent, J. T. 1976. A follow-up study of abused children. *Journal of Pediatric Psychology*, 1(2), 25–31.

Kinard, E. M. 1982. Experiencing child abuse: Effects on emotional adjustment. *American Journal of Orthopsychiatry*, 52, 82–91.

Klaus, M. H., and J. H. Kennell. 1976. Maternal-infant bonding. St. Louis.

Kliman, G., M. H. Schaeffer, and M. Friedman. 1982. Preventive mental health services for children entering foster home care. New York.

Knitzer, J., and M. L. Allen. Children without homes. Washington, D.C.

Kohn, M. 1977. Social competence, symptoms, and underachievement in childhood: A longitudinal perspective. Washington, D.C.

Lamb, M. E., T. J. Gaensbauer, C. M. Malkin, and L. A. Schultz. 1985. The effects of abuse and neglect on security of infant adult attachment. *Infant Behavior and Development*, *8*, 35–45.

Leiderman, P. H. 1983. Social ecology and childbirth: The newborn nursery as environmental stressor. In N. Garmezy and M. Rutter, eds., *Stress, coping, & development in children*. New York.

Leiderman, P. H., and M. J. Seashore. 1975. Mother-infant separation: Some delayed consequences. In M. A. Hofer, ed., *Parent-infant interaction*. Amsterdam.

Leitenberg, H., J. D. Burchard, D. Healy, and E. J. Fuller. 1981. Nondelinquent children in state custody: Does type of placement matter? *American Journal of Community Psychology*, *9*, 347–59.

Lemmon, J. A. 1975. Self concept and the foster adolescent. *Dissertation Abstract International*, *36*, 313A. Ph.D. diss, University of Illinois, 1975.

Lewis, M., and S. Schaeffer. 1981. Peer behavior and mother-infant interaction in maltreated children. In M. Lewis and L. A. Rosenblum, eds., *The uncommon child*. New York.

Littner, N. 1956. Some traumatic effects of separation and placement. New York.

———. 1974. The challenge to make fuller use of our knowledge about children. *Child Welfare*, *53*, 287–94.

Maccoby, E. E. 1980. Social development. New York.

Magura, S. 1981. Are services to prevent foster care effective? *Children and Youth Services Review*, *3*, 193–212.

Main, M., N. Kaplan, and J. Cassidy. 1985. Security in infancy, childhood and adulthood: A move to the level of representation. In I. Bretherton and E. Waters, eds., *Growing points in attachment theory and research*. Monographs of the Society for Research in Child Development.

Martin H. 1976. The abused child. Cambridge, Massachusetts.

———. 1980. The consequences of being abused and neglected: How the child fares. In C. H. Kempe and R. E. Helfer, eds., *The battered child*. Chicago.

Meier, E. 1965. Current circumstances of former foster children. *Child Welfare*, *44*, 196–206.

Mnookin, R. H. 1973. Foster care—In whose best interest? *Harvard Educational Review*, *43*, 599–638.

Moos, R. H., and B. S. Moos. 1981. Family Environment Scale manual. Palo Alto, California.

National Commission on Children in Need of Parents. 1979. Who knows? Who cares? Forgotten children in foster care. New York.

National Health Examination. 1979 (May). *Integrated data tape file from the National Health Examination of Children 6–11 years: Cycle II 1963–1965* (Tech. Rep.). Washington, D.C.: U. S. Department of Health, Education, and Welfare, Public Health Services, Division of Health Examination Statistics.

Palmer, S. E. 1979. Predicting outcome in long term foster care. *Journal of Social Service Research, 3*, 201–14.

Patterson, G. 1982. Coercive family process. Eugene, Oregon.

Pavenstedt, E. 1973. An intervention program for infants from high risk homes. *American Journal of Public Health, 63*, 393–95.

Polansky, N. A., M. A. Chalmers, E. Buttenwieser, and D. P. Williams. 1981. Damaged parents: Anatomy of child neglect. Chicago.

Provence, S., and A. Naylor. 1983. Working with disadvantaged parents and their children. New Haven.

Robertson, J., and J. Robertson. 1971. Young children in brief separation: A fresh look. *Psychoanalytic Study of the Child, 26*, 264–315.

Roff, J. D., and R. D. Wirt. 1984. Childhood social adjustment, adolescent status, and young adult mental health. *American Journal of Orthopsychiatry, 54*, 595–602.

Roff, M., S. B. Sells, and M. M. Golden. 1972. Social adjustment and personality development in children. Minneapolis.

Runyan, D. 1985. Foster care for child maltreatment: Impact on delinquency. *Pediatrics, 75*, 562–68.

Runyan, D., C. Gould, D. Trost, and A. Loda. 1982. Determinants of foster care placement for the maltreated child. *Child Abuse and Neglect, The International Journal, 6*, 343–50.

Rutter, M. 1972. Maternal deprivation reassessed. Baltimore.

——. 1976. Parent-child separation: The psychological effects on the child. In A. M. Clark and A. D. B. Clark, eds., *Early experience: Myth and evidence*. New York.

——. 1979. Maternal deprivation, 1972–1978: New findings, new concepts, new approaches. *Child Development, 50*, 283–305.

——. 1980. Protective factors in children's responses to stress and disadvantage. In M. W. Kent and J. E. Rolf, eds., *Primary prevention of psychopathology: III. Promoting social competence and coping in children*. Hanover, New Hampshire.

Schneider-Rosen, K., K. G. Braunwald, V. Carlson, and D. Cicchetti. 1985. Current perspectives in attachment theory: Illustration from the study of maltreated infants. In I. Bretherton and M. E. Waters, eds., *Growing points of attachment theory and research*. Monographs of the Society for Research in Child Development.

Schneider-Rosen, K., and D. Cicchetti. 1984. The relationship between affect and cognition in maltreated infants: Quality of attachment and the development of visual self-recognition. *Child Development, 55,* 648–58.

Seligman, L. 1979. Understanding the black foster child through assessment. *Journal of Non-White Concerns in Personnel and Guidance, 7,* 183–91.

Sinanoglu, P., and A. Maluccio. 1981. Parents of children in placement: Perspectives and programs. New York.

Sroufe, L. A. 1983. Infant-caregiver attachment and patterns of adaptation in preschool: The roots of maladaptation and competence. In M. Perlmutter, ed., *Minnesota Symposium on Child Psychology,* Vol. 16. Hillsdale, New Jersey.

Susman, E., P. Trickett, R. Iannotti, B. Hollenbeck, and C. Zahn-Waxler. 1985. Child-rearing patterns in depressed, abusive, and normal mothers. *American Journal of Orthopsychiatry, 55,* 237–51.

Swire, M. R., and F. Kavaler. 1977. The health status of foster children. *Child Welfare, 56,* 635–50.

Theis, S. V. S. 1924. How foster children turn out. New York.

Toro, P. A. 1982. Developmental effects of child abuse: A review. *Child Abuse and Neglect, The International Journal, 6,* 423–31.

Trickett, P., E. Susman, and I. Lourie. 1980. The impact of the childrearing environment on the social and emotional development of the physically abused child. NIMH Research Protocol. Clinical Project Number 80-CM-112.

Van Der Waals, P. 1960. Former foster children reflect on their childhood. *Children, 7,* 29–33.

Wald, M. S. 1975. State intervention on behalf of neglected children: A search for realistic standards. *Stanford Law Review, 27,* 985–1040.

———. 1976. State intervention on behalf of neglected children: Standards for removal of children from their homes, monitoring the status of children in foster care, and termination of parental rights. *Stanford Law Review, 28,* 625–706.

———. 1980. Thinking about public policy toward abuse and neglect of children: A review of "Before the best interests of the child." *Michigan Law Review, 78,* 645–93.

Wald, M. S., J. M. Carlsmith, P. H. Leiderman, and C. Smith. 1983. Intervention to protect abused and neglected children. In M. Perlmutter, ed., *Minnesota Symposium on Child Psychology,* Vol. 16. Hillsdale, New Jersey.

Wallerstein, J. 1985. The overburdened child: Some long-term consequences of divorce. *Columbia Journal of Law and Social Problems, 19,* 165–82.

Wallerstein, J., and J. Kelly. 1980. Surviving the breakup: How children and parents cope with divorce. New York.

Waters, E., and K. Deane. 1985. Defining and assessing individual differences in attachment relationships: Q-Methodology and the organization of behavior in infancy and early childhood. In I. Bretherton and E. Waters, eds.,

Growing points in attachment theory and research. Monographs of the Society for Research in Child Development.

Waters, E., J. Wippman, and L. A. Sroufe. 1979. Attachment, positive affect, and competence in the peer group: Two studies in construct validation. *Child Development*, *50*, 821–29.

Weinstein, E. A. 1960. The self-image of the foster child. New York.

White, R. W. 1959. Motivation reconsidered: The concept of competence. *Psychological Review*, *66*, 297–333.

Zigler, E. 1980. Controlling child abuse: Do we have the knowledge and/or the will? In G. Gerbner, C. Ross, and E. Zigler, eds., *Child abuse: An agenda for action.* New York.

Zill, N. 1976. National Survey of Children. New York.

Zimmerman, R. B. 1982. Foster care in retrospect. New Orleans.

Index

___

In this index an "f" after a number indicates a separate reference on the next page, and an "ff" indicates separate references on the next two pages. A continuous discussion over two or more pages is indicated by a span of page numbers, e.g., "pp. 57–58." *Passim* is used for a cluster of references in close but not consecutive sequence.

Library of Congress Cataloging-in-Publication Data

Wald, Michael S., 1941–
  Protecting abused and neglected children.

  Bibliography: p.
  Includes index.
  1. Child abuse—Services—United States. 2. Abused
children—Protection—United States. 3. Abused children—
Protection—California. 4. Social work with children—
United States. 5. Child development. I. Carlsmith,
J. Merrill, 1936–84. II. Leiderman, P. Herbert III. Title.
HV741.W24 1988   362.7′044   87-10208
ISBN 0-8047-1420-7 (alk. paper)